THE GOSPEL OF JOHN

THE
GOSPEL OF JOHN

JOHN CARTER

THE CHRISTADELPHIAN
404 SHAFTMOOR LANE
HALL GREEN
BIRMINGHAM B28 8SZ

First Edition: 1943
Reprinted: 1953
: 1972
: 1980
Reset: 2006

ISBN 0 85189 059 8

Printed and bound by

THE CROMWELL PRESS
TROWBRIDGE
WILTSHIRE
ENGLAND
BA14 0XB

CONTENTS

In the Gospel of John he is portrayed who, when asked by Philip to shew them the Father, answered, "He that hath seen me hath seen the Father." May these reflections help readers to "know that the Son of God is come, and hath given us an understanding," and "hath declared the Father."

The background of ideas, Gentile and Jewish, of the opening verses of John's gospel, and some of the associations of the words he uses – The Old Testament shewn to be most essential to the understanding of his words – The term logos considered

John's style – The Word as light in creation and in the "new creation" – Human history in relation to God epitomised – The Light in God's Son, The Lord manifested – Significance of the names of the Baptist and his parents – "Every" and "all" – Parable of the householder – Children of God – divine parentage

The word made flesh – significance of John's words; "flesh"; "dwelt"; "glory"; "full"; "grace and truth"

The witness of the Baptist

"fulness" bestowed on others – the fulness of Christ bestowed on others

The deputation to John – his witness to Jesus – the Baptism of John – the failure of the rulers to apply God's law testing the claims of a prophet

vi

vii

his words – the teaching of the Spirit – parting "Peace" – responsibility of the world

PREFACE

THE writings of John, "the beloved disciple", contain some of the simplest language and some of the profoundest thoughts. Where else can we read a statement expressed in monosyllables which yet calls for such continued application of thought to understand it, as that contained in the opening verses of the fourth gospel? And the beloved disciple also loved, and he caught the accents of his Master. There are in the other gospels a few recorded words of Jesus which match in style the addresses recorded in John, which are expressed in the same simple language with the same depth of thought. For example: "At that time Jesus answered and said, I thank thee, O Father, Lord of heaven and earth, because thou hast hid these things from the wise and prudent, and hast revealed them unto babes" (Matthew 11:25) and "For my yoke is easy, and my burden is light" (verse 30).

But there are other features of John's record to be kept in mind. The casual reader thinks of the Letter to the Hebrews as the New Testament exposition of Old Testament typology. But nearly all of the addresses of the Lord in John's gospel are based on the types of the Law of Moses. For example: "And as Moses lifted up the serpent in the wilderness, even so must the Son of man be lifted up: that whosoever believeth in him should not perish, but have eternal life (John 3:14,15). See also chapter 6.

Another feature is John's ironic undertone as he records words used by the enemies of Jesus which had a larger significance than they who uttered them realized, and which partook of the character of unconscious prophecies. Examples are: "If we let him thus alone, all men will believe on him: and the Romans shall come and take away both our place and nation. And one of them, named Caiaphas, being the high priest that same year, said unto them, Ye know nothing at all, nor consider that it is expedient for us, that one man should die for the people, and that the whole nation perish not. And this spake he not of himself: but being high priest that year, he prophesied that Jesus should die for that nation; and not for that nation only, but that also he should gather together in one the children of God that were scattered abroad" (11:48–52). Or again: "The Pharisees therefore said among themselves, Perceive ye how ye prevail nothing? behold, the world is gone after him" (12:19). John also finds a significance in events, the outward circumstances of which were symbols of an inner meaning; for example: "He then having received the sop went immediately out: and it was night" (13:30) and: "When Jesus had spoken these words, he went forth with his disciples over the brook Cedron, where was a garden, into the which he entered, and his disciples" (18:1).

In this study these features are noted, and may suggest still further investigation to readers. Repeated meditation on the writings of John leave the student with a feeling that their depth cannot be fully reached, nor their meaning exhausted.

"The Gospel of John" was the theme of a Study Class in Birmingham in the winter of 1934. The addresses were attended by about one hundred and fifty brethren and sisters; and were later written for *The Christadelphian* where they appeared from January 1937, to March 1941. They are now reproduced, slightly revised, at the request of many, in the hope that thus a further service may be rendered towards understanding that which was written "that ye might believe that Jesus is the Christ, the Son of God; and that believing ye might have life through his name" (John 20:31).

JOHN CARTER
September 1943

JOHN CARTER
(1889 – 1962)
Late Editor of *The Christadelphian*

SECTION 1

INTRODUCTION

THERE are four books in the New Testament which record the words and works of Jesus Christ. They are not strictly lives of Christ, but they give selections of incidents, the first three having many matters in common, though with individual differences. The last of the four differs most from the others.

WHY FOUR GOSPELS?

THERE are four because God has given four, is perhaps the final answer. Many were written and circulated during the early years of the labours of the apostles, but by whom written we do not know. Luke speaks of these in the opening words of his Gospel.

"Forasmuch as many have taken in hand to set forth in order a declaration of those things which are most surely believed among us, even as they delivered them unto us, which from the beginning were eyewitnesses, and ministers of the word; it seemed good to me also, having had perfect understanding of all things from the very first, to write unto thee in order, most excellent Theophilus, that thou mightest know the certainty of those things, wherein thou hast been instructed." (Luke 1:1–4)

The word translated "from the very first" means also "from above", and this rendering is preferred by many while rejected by others. It yields excellent sense, for Luke is claiming that there was that about *his* understanding, or *his* accurate tracing of events, that enabled the noble Theophilus to know that the things which he had been taught were certain. Luke does not impugn the veracity of these other writers, or question the sources of their information. Yet it is well known that, with the best of intentions, and with every endeavour to be accurate, it is difficult for anyone to describe events in detail truthfully. A humanly produced "Life of Christ" could not be accepted with confidence. There would be no security concerning its accuracy. But Luke being guided "from above"

1

has written that which gives assurance of the truth of the things believed. Even if the translation "from above" is not accepted, the fact of Luke's inspiration is not affected; and it is the inspiration of the writers that makes their writing authoritative.

In recent times small fragments of papyrus have been unearthed in Egypt, two Englishmen, Grenfell and Hunt, being prominent in the work. On some of the fragments are certain "sayings of Jesus". Can anyone say that they are genuine? No one can. In fact they do not bear comparison with the gospel writings. But it is possible that they afford illustrations of some of the writings which were current in the first century.

What happened to these many writings to which Luke refers? They were destroyed as insufficient and inadequate when the inspired "gospels" were given to the ecclesias. And these four gospels were recognized as the authoritative records; authoritative because written under the guidance of that "spirit of truth" which the Lord said should be given to the apostles after his departure, and which he said would guide them into all truth, and bring to their remembrance all things which he had said.

The decision as to what was and what was not inspired was not dependent upon erring human judgment. The "spirit gifts" enabled the brethren possessing them to "discern the spirits". It was a period of active thought and interchange of opinion, and only authoritative guidance would have given the four gospels the undisputed position which they have occupied from the earliest days. They were accepted because of the witness given to them in an age of free discussion and criticism. In the words of Nolloth:

"The history of the Canon of the New Testament shows that criticism was not only being freely exercised in the Church during that period, but that its decisions were of so sound and satisfying a character as to secure the almost unanimous approval of Christendom down to recent times. It is to the keen criticism and enlightened judgment of those early days that we owe the selection and preservation of our present Gospels from among the mass of similar literature which then abounded everywhere. If ever there were a time in the long course of Christian history when the right of criticism was claimed and exercised to the full, it was when the New Testament Canon was receiving its authoritative shape. Moreover, we are fortunately in a position to form our own estimate of the value of the critical judgments which were then being passed; we possess fragments of Gospel writings which, in their day, were read and circulated and compared with the Gospels that found their way into the Canon. In every case, comparison upholds the decisions which the Church has formed; decisions which are the more significant because they were come to in communities far separated from one another by distance and by difficulty of travelling; yet decisions which the whole body of the Church came to confirm and to make its own."

If by the *"enlightened* judgment" mentioned in this extract we understand that enlightenment which came from the possession of the Spirit, then we can understand why in widely separated communities the same decision was reached, and why everywhere the humanly-produced writings quietly passed out of use.

But are there any reasons why there are *four* gospels? A remark of John's leads along a line of approach which gives a satisfactory answer. He says that the blindness of the rulers fulfilled the words of Isaiah that God had blinded their eyes (12:40); and adds, "These things said Isaiah, when he saw his glory, and spake of him."

Four Cherubim

WHAT Isaiah saw was a vision of the manifestation of God in the house of God, when the Son of God will be enthroned in the earth. He saw the Lord with attendant Seraphim. The whole represents Jesus and the saints forming that unity which is the aim of the work of Christ. "(I pray) that they all may be one; as thou, Father, art in me, and I in thee, that they also may be one in us ... that they may behold my glory, which thou hast given me" (John 17:21,24).

This plurality in unity is indicated in the enquiry, "Whom shall *I* send, and who will go for *us?*" The prophet, who later recognized that he and his children were for "signs" (as Paul also indicates by his quotation of Isaiah's words, in Hebrews 2:13, that the prophet and his children represented Jesus and the "children" given to him), stepped forward and said, "Send me". There was then given to him the message which the Lord Jesus gave to Israel as already quoted from John; a message which each of the four gospels quotes as fulfilled in Christ. It was even fulfilled in a sense in the Christ-body, for Paul quotes the words again at the close of the age, as recorded in the last chapter in Acts.

The Seraphim of Isaiah are identical with the Cherubim of Ezekiel, chapter 1. These latter have four faces; of a lion, an ox, a man, and an eagle. There is in the manifestation of God in the children of the resurrection that which corresponds to this representation of the four faces. The same might be expected in the one who has been "sent for them". Now there is a correspondence between the four gospels and the four faces of the cherubim.

Matthew

The genealogy in this gospel goes back to Abraham and David, suggesting that we have here a list giving the connection with the promises made to the fathers of Israel. In the genealogy we find the name Jechoniah (otherwise known as Coniah). This man was the subject of a very solemn curse. The word of the LORD through Jeremiah, in a threefold call to the earth to hear, decrees the man childless as to the succession to the throne.

"O earth, earth, earth, hear the word of the LORD. Thus saith the LORD, Write ye this man childless, a man that shall not prosper in his days: for no man of his seed shall prosper, sitting upon the throne of David, and ruling any more in Judah." (Jeremiah 22:29,30)

That he had seed is evident, for none had to prosper. It is not a matter of childlessness but of heirship to the throne. This shows that Matthew's genealogy is not that of Mary. The Coniah line was "abased" in the overthrow of Zedekiah, and the promise was made of the exaltation of another line.

Consistently with the idea that Matthew gives us Joseph's line, we find he records the announcement that was made to Joseph (who being a righteous man was about to put away Mary), that the child to be born was the Son of God. Joseph's anxiety concerning the matter was set at rest. In his projected action he was repudiating paternity of the child; but the angelic visitor in his dream announced the divine paternity. An adopted father of the royal line was thus found for the Son of God during his growing years, an arrangement necessary for the convenience of Mary and the well-being of the child.

Matthew treats of the King—the lion phase. His parables are parables of the kingdom. His gospel, coming first in the New Testament, links the New with the Old Testament, and shows that prophecy was fulfilled in what happened to Jesus.

4

Mark

This gospel has no genealogy; it tells of service and sacrifice, and corresponds to the ox phase.

Luke

Here we find the genealogy of Mary; the words introducing it—"as was supposed"—meaning "as it was the custom to reckon". (See *Companion Bible*, and Lexicons). This explains why Joseph's name is recorded as the son of Heli, when really Mary was Heli's daughter. In this gospel the announcement of the birth is made to Mary; and in keeping with the idea that we have in this genealogy the tracing of the flesh descent, we are in it taken back to Adam, the son of God. Two sons of God, one at each end of the chain; but with a difference. The first was son by creation of the dust; the second was raised up of the human race, Son of God and son of man, though not son of a man. Luke's gospel gives us the man phase.

John

The author of this gospel tells us his object: "These things are written that ye might believe that Jesus is the Christ, the Son of God; and that believing ye might have life through his name" (20:31). The Christ, the Son of God, and life through his name—then John must show that Jesus was the one contemplated by the Father from the beginning, that he died that men might have life, and that he gave such evidence as marked him out as the descendant of David prepared by God to be the King of Israel. In keeping with this purpose the Prologue can be called the divine genealogy of Jesus, thereby completing the view of the man who was the manifestation of God—God manifest in flesh. John gives us the eagle phase. That John achieves his purpose we shall find abundant evidence as we proceed with the study.

The Author of the Gospel

JOHN is not mentioned by name in the gospel, but he is spoken of as "the disciple whom Jesus loved". The identity of the loved disciple and the son of Zebedee has been disputed, but there are many little touches which support the traditional view. In the first three gospels John figures prominently with Peter and James; but John and James are effaced in the fourth gospel, and their mother is referred to not by name but as the sister of Mary. The loved disciple was at the supper, at the cross, at the grave, and at the Sea of Galilee. If the loved

5

disciple is not the apostle John there is no place for him in the first three gospels, as there is no place for John in the fourth gospel if he is not the loved disciple.

It is generally agreed that the gospel shows the writer was a Jew of Palestine, and an eyewitness of what he wrote. He claims to be this (1 John 1:1–3); and such a claim should not be set aside without good cause. Sanday, a generation ago, entered a well-merited protest against the doubts about accepting such a statement when he said: "The critics who assert that this gospel is not the work of an eyewitness, and even those who say that the last chapter was not written by the author of the whole, wantonly accuse these last words of untruth. That is another of the methods of modern criticism that seems to me sorely in need of reforming. I hope that a time may come when it will be considered as wrong to libel the dead as it is to libel the living."

CANONICITY

IT is usual to start the consideration of this by citing external evidence that it was accepted during the second century, and then working backwards. We prefer to start further back. God did not leave the selection of the books which together make up the Word of God to unaided human choice. Properly speaking, man did not select at all. When the gospels were written there were brethren with Spirit gifts, and among them were prophets whose function it was to act as God's mouthpieces. Prophetic endorsement determined the inclusion of a writing in the Scriptures. To this fact we would refer the words of 21:24. First the writer identifies himself as the one about whom the mistaken story that he should not die had been spread; then we have the words: "and we know that his testimony is true". Who are the "we" in this place? We suggest that it comes from those who were fitted to give such an endorsement, from the Spirit-gifted eldership of Ephesus, whom Christ commends for having tried those who said that they were apostles and were not, and had found them liars. The rejection of the spurious implies the acceptance of the true.

But external evidence is not lacking. It has been well examined in the last half-century in the contentions about the authorship of this gospel. Two quotations summarizing the conclusions of investigations might be given. Sanday says:

6

"I would invite attention to the distribution of the evidence in this period: Irenaeus and the Letter of the Christians of Vienne and Lyons in Gaul, Heracleon in Italy, Tertullian at Carthage, Polycrates at Ephesus, Theophilus at Antioch, Tatian at Rome and in Syria, Clement at Alexandria. The strategical positions are occupied, one might say, all over the Empire. In the great majority of cases there is not a hint of dissent. On the contrary the four-fold gospel is regarded for the most part as one and indivisible."

J. Drummond says:

"The external evidence is all on one side, and for my part I cannot easily repel its force. A considerable mass of internal evidence is in harmony with the external. ... On weighing the arguments for and against to the best of my power, I must give my own judgment in favour of the Johannine authorship."

But it was not settled by Councils. They at best could only weigh the evidence and examine the witness that had been given to any particular book. In the words of Nolloth:

"There is another consideration, which may fairly be taken into account. He who inspired the men who wrote the Scriptures did not fail those whose judgment determined the selection. The conclusions which were everywhere being formed, silently and on no arranged system, were guided by the Holy Spirit. The value of the books which passed the process of sifting and discrimination bears witness to this fact."

We believe that in an even more definite sense than this writer indicates, as we have before shown, the Spirit determined the selection.

STYLE

SOME objection has been made to the fourth gospel on the point of style of writing. It has been argued that the fourth gospel is an interpretation and not a history. But if we compare Matthew 11:25–27 with the writings of John, and the reported discourses of Jesus in John's gospel, we find the style characteristic of John is not exclusive to him. That forms of expression used by John resemble the reported words of Jesus is admitted. But did not the disciple whom Jesus loved reciprocate that love? John was the cousin of Jesus, their mothers being sisters. With such a double bond of kinship and mutual love, is it to be wondered at that John's words echo the words of the Lord, and that John's style resembles that of him whom he acknowledges as Master?

John's words are at once simple and profound. Their depth becomes more evident the longer they are studied. This befits the subject matter, for it concerns the highest claims ever made by any man. "As the living Father hath sent me, and I live by the Father: so he that eateth me shall live by me." "I speak that which I have seen with my Father. ... If God were your Father ye would love me: for I proceeded forth and came from God; neither came I of myself, but he sent me." There is no word which a child could not understand, but it is only when "the eyes of the understanding are enlightened ... that we know ... what is the exceeding greatness of his power to usward who believe, according to the working of his mighty power, which he wrought in Christ when he raised him from the dead". Christ is then seen as a manifestation of Almighty Power, set forth for men's salvation; and his words are perceived to have reference to that great mystery, God manifest in the flesh.

It has been truly said:

"It is sometimes said that to produce an untrue narrative possessing such verisimilitude as the Gospel (of John) would have been quite beyond the capacity of any writer of the second century. In making this allegation people seem to forget that the book is in any case unique. Whether it be true history, or the offspring of spiritual imagination, or a mixture of both, no one, so far as we know, could have written it in the second or any other century, except the man who did write it; and to assert that an unexampled, unknown, and unmeasured literary genius could not have done this or that seems to me extremely hazardous."

Here is the book; it is unique. And if it can be said that so far as is known only the writer of it could produce it, we can also say that only if Jesus had lived, and had done his mighty acts, and had spoken his wonderful words, could even this writer have done it; and then only as "guided into all truth" by "the Spirit of truth" (John 16:13).

SECTION 2

THE PROLOGUE
CONTEMPORARY THINKING (1:1–18)

THE introduction to the Gospel of John gives the divine genealogy of Jesus. It is presented in forms that require a little knowledge of contemporary thought as a guide to its understanding. But, and much more important, a good understanding of the Old Testament is necessary to comprehend its meaning.

In the first century ease of travel led to the constant movement of teachers of different schools of thought. The West, tired of its philosophies, turned to the East for guidance; and the meeting of East and West quickened thought and speculation. Everywhere in the civilized world men met, talked, discussed. Into such a world the Lord's ambassadors came with the gospel of the kingdom.

It does not occasion surprise therefore that early attempts were made to combine some features of the gospel with the current philosophies; and the apostles continually exhorted the believers to keep in its purity the gospel preached unto them. The apostles speak of it in all their epistles; and Paul warned the Ephesians of the danger night and day with tears.

Discussion brings certain words into prominence, often with changed or modified meanings, sometimes with slightly different meanings when used by different groups. The second century saw the full development of Gnosticism—a fusion of religious beliefs which, it was claimed, were based on revelation communicated to the initiated in the form of symbols which were kept secret. There were elements of thought borrowed from the Christians in this developed Gnosticism, and many of its key-words, already being used in the first century in the discussions on religion, are found in Paul's letters, particularly those to Ephesus and Colosse, and also in the introduction to the Gospel of John.

This philosophy was dualistic; it sought to explain the existence of good and evil, light and darkness, a divine world and a material world. The Persians had speculated largely on these matters, and in Zoroastrianism offered the explanation of two deities, one the god of good and light, the other the god of evil and darkness. Corrupt Christianity, borrowing from pagan thought, had its counterpart of these in God and the Devil. The material world was regarded as essentially evil, while God was good and could not be the source of evil. An explanation of the existence of evil and of the material world was sought in the suggestion that there had been a series of emanations from God, each one less divine, until at last came an "*aeon*" so far removed from God that the creation of an evil world resulted. In this way they disposed of the difficulty that God was the author of evil.

This speculation was anticipated in Isaiah's prophecy of the overthrow of Babylon by the Persians under Cyrus.

"I am the LORD, and there is none else. I form the light, and create darkness: I make peace, and create evil: I the LORD do all these things." (45:6,7)

This statement is a remarkable anticipation of the Persian theory which it so definitely denies; and the assertion that God was one, and that evil and good were both in His hands, would effectively guard His people who were contemporary with the fulfilment of the prophecy, against the snares of the false views held by their deliverers.

In the theories of the early heretics who in the apostles' days were combining incipient Gnosticism with Paul's teaching, the truth concerning Jesus as Son of God was perverted by representing him as one of the successive emanations from God, thus failing to "hold fast the Head" but relegating him, in the worship of angels, to an inferior place. This idea had harmful influence at Colosse, and was before the mind of Paul when he wrote the letter to the ecclesia in that town. Such a being as set forth by the Gnostics could not be the redeemer. A development of this doctrine is opposed in the opening section of the fourth gospel.

The doctrine had a twofold moral effect upon the lives of those who accepted it. It led either to asceticism, the fault of the Colossians, or to libertinism, in which those in Ephesus who were influenced by it were disposed to indulge.

The terms used by John are found in the writings of Philo as well as in Gentile philosophies. Philo was a Jew, contemporary with Paul, who endeavoured to explain the Old Testament in the terms current in the Gentile schools of his day. His ideas are very confused, and it is generally recognized that there is little connection between John and Philo.

10

The Targums, or Jewish commentaries, used the term "word" in their paraphrases of the Old Testament, in a way that prepared to some extent for John's use of it. They personified the attributes of God, and

"where Scripture speaks of a direct communication from God to man, the Targums substituted the *Memra*, or 'Word of God'. Thus in Genesis 3:8,9, instead of 'they heard the voice of the LORD God', the Targums read, 'they heard the voice of the Word of the LORD God'; and instead of 'God called unto Adam', they put, 'the Word of the LORD called unto Adam', and so on. It is said that this phrase 'the Word of the LORD' occurs 150 times in a single Targum of the Pentateuch".

The Old Testament provides the true background to John's gospel. It is there we find the ideas which best explain John's thoughts, in language also which is used by him.

An important element of Old Testament teaching is the marked insistence upon the unity of God. "Hear, O Israel: the LORD our God is one LORD"; "I am God alone, and beside me there is no God" (Deuteronomy 6:4; Isaiah 44:8; 45:5,6,18, etc.). By His spirit God has created all things, garnishing the heavens, renewing the face of the earth; all things living move and have their being in Him, and all would perish if He withdrew His spirit and His breath.

In His creative work God commanded, and it was done. "By the word of the LORD were the heavens made; and all the host of them by the breath of his mouth" (Psalm 33:6). Enumerating the wondrous works of God, performed in His goodness to the children of men, the Psalmist says: "He sent *his word* and healed them, and delivered them from their destructions" (107:20). It is written of the peace of Jerusalem: "He sendeth forth his commandment upon earth; *his word* runneth very swiftly" (147:15). The elements are subject to God's control, snow and ice vanishing at His command: "He sendeth out *his word*, and melteth them; he causeth his wind to blow, and the waters to flow" (verse 18). For the purpose of thought, all these statements give to the word of God an objective existence, and a quasi-personification.

A similar usage is found in other books besides the Psalms. Thus Isaiah referring to the rain and snow which come from heaven to water the earth according to God's purpose, adds: "So shall my word be that goeth forth out of my mouth: it shall not return unto me void, but it shall accomplish that which I please, and it shall prosper in the thing whereto I sent it" (55:11).

11

There is a similar personification of wisdom in the Proverbs in a passage very helpful to the understanding of John.

"I wisdom dwell with prudence, and find out knowledge of witty inventions ... The LORD possessed me in the beginning of his way, before his works of old. I was set up from everlasting, from the beginning, or ever the earth was. When there were no depths, I was brought forth ... when he prepared the heavens I was there ... when he appointed the foundations of the earth; then I was by him as one brought up with him; and I was daily his delight, rejoicing always before him; rejoicing in the habitable part of his earth; and my delights were with the sons of men."

(8:12–31)

The thought of the word of God as the expression of His will, effective for its execution, passes easily to the thought of the person who is the manifestation of God, and who perfectly did His will, as seen in Hebrews 4:12,13.

"For the word of God is living, and powerful, and sharper than any two-edged sword, piercing even to the dividing asunder of soul and spirit, and of the joints and marrow, and is a discerner of the thoughts and intents of the heart. Neither is there any creature that is not manifest in his sight: but all things are naked and opened unto the eyes of him with whom we have to do."

In these verses we start with the word which is the revelation of God, which was spoken in the days of Moses, and again in the days of David, and which was "living" in Paul's day, acting upon the minds of those who heard it, instructing concerning God's rest, urging to labour to enter that rest; and we glide from the word which searches men's hearts, making known the hidden mazes there, to the one who is God's High Priest, the Word made flesh, who will scrutinize the offerings of his people and give judgment upon them, saying which are acceptable. The outcome of the operation of God's word will then be manifest through him who was the Word embodied in flesh.

It is also probable that Luke uses "the Word" as descriptive of the Lord Jesus in the opening words of his gospel, when he says that the apostles were "eyewitnesses, and ministers of the word" from the beginning (1:2).

With these illustrations of the Scripture usage of words in mind we can approach the detailed examination of John's prologue. The term "Word" at once calls for investigation. It is a translation of *logos*, from which is derived the word logic. The relative Greek adjective is defined in the *Century Dictionary*: "of, or pertaining to, speech or reason or reasoning, rational, reasonable". Under "Logos" we find: "that which is said or spoken, a word, saying, speech, also the power of the mind manifested in speech, reason"; and then the definition passes on to theological uses in connection with the second person in the Trinity, which has nothing at all to do with New Testament doctrine.

Turning to the *Greek Lexicons*, the last edition of Liddell and Scott has five and a half columns of closely printed type on the word, under ten headings. It is a verbal noun of *legō*, which is given the primary meaning of "pick up", from which the noun gets the meanings of computation, reckoning, proportion; and when applied to thought, the meanings of explanation, inward debate, as reasoning, and from that, reason as a faculty; then verbal expression, and utterance, the subject matter of the things spoken of, speech. Lastly, under "X", we find: "the word or wisdom of God personified as the agent in creation and world government: in NT identified with the person of Christ". It is evident the word was used by Greek writers in the same sense as we have found it in the citations from the Old Testament already considered.

Grimm-Thayer's *NT Greek Lexicon* defines the word: "a collecting, collection—and that, as well of those things which are put together in thought, as of those which having been thought, i.e., having been gathered together in the mind, are expressed in words. Accordingly a twofold use of the term is to be distinguished: one which relates to speaking, and one which relates to thinking". Then, under "III" we read:

"In several passages in the writings of John, *logos* denotes the essential Word of God, i.e., the personal wisdom and power in union with God, His minister in the creation and government of the universe, the cause of all the world's life both physical and ethical, which for the procurement of man's salvation put on human nature in the person of Jesus the Messiah, and shone forth conspicuously from his words and deeds".

This is not free from theological bias; but with that discounted, we learn that bound up with *logos* is the thought of wisdom and power in action; there is thought and expression; there is design and execution. As Plummer says:

"It means not only the spoken word, but the thought expressed by the spoken word; it is the spoken word as expressive of thought".

13

A word reveals thought: and the word of God is the revelation of His purpose. With Him is power to perform, and therefore there is involved the exercise of the energy by God for the fulfilling of His will.

John's opening words invite comparison with Genesis. "In the beginning God created"; so doing, "God said, Let there be light, and there was light". On each of the six days "God said", and it was so. He spake and it was done. By His word all things came into being. When man was made "God said unto them" that which made known His purpose with them and for them. Here in the case of the creatures made in the image of God that which "God said" takes the form of a revelation unfolding the divine objects in man's creation. That first revelation is taken up as a prophecy in Psalm 8, and expounded in the New Testament in its fulfilment in Christ (Hebrews 2:6–10; Ephesians 1:19–23; 1 Corinthians 15:25–28).

In the facts of Genesis 1 we have the basis of the exposition of the opening verses of John 1. "In the beginning *was* the Word"; the Word *was*, it did not come to be; and it was divine, for "the Word was with God, and the Word was God". As against the Gnostic, it was not an emanation. The Word was *with* God—the closeness of identity: as when John says "the life was *with* the Father" (1 John 1:2)—"with him" as a part of Him, having its source in Him, and expressing Him. It would be as reasonable to treat "life" as well as the "word" as a separate personality; but the use of "with" in connection with "life" in the epistle illustrates its meaning when used in connection with "word" in the gospel. And "with God" contradicts the Gnostic notion of God and the Word being separated by distance.

Verses 2–13 are a parenthesis—a literary feature of this gospel. Passing over the parenthesis, we read, "And the Word was made flesh, and dwelt among us (and we beheld his glory, the glory as of the only begotten of the Father), full of grace and truth" (verse 14). In other words, the Divine purpose unfolded at the beginning is being fulfilled in the manifestation of God in Jesus Christ. But the significance of verse 14 can only be fully appreciated when the thoughts developed in the parenthesis have been examined. These intervening verses are so important that we must look at them in some detail.

14

A PARENTHESIS (1:2–13)

THE opening verses of John's gospel show certain literary features of his style. There is the use of parenthesis; the comment upon some recorded utterance; the recapitulation of a thought with a view to carrying it further; the repetition of an idea expressed by the negation of the opposite.

In verse 2, we have a repetition of verse 1—"The same was in the beginning with God"; but the case is restated to lead on to verses 3–5.

"All things were made by him; and without him was not anything made. That which hath been made was life in him (in him was life); and the life was the light of men. And the light shineth in darkness; and the darkness comprehended it not."

"All things" is a phrase so emphasized in Paul's epistles as to suggest there is some association of ideas with the words used here. A chain of references has already been quoted. The first link is Genesis 1:26; other links being provided by Psalm 8:6, and the references to this Psalm in the epistles. "All things" in these connections are seen to be the whole range of things in heaven and earth to be subject to Christ; nothing is excepted but God who put all things under him.

"To us there is but one God, the Father, of whom are *all things*, and we in him; and one Lord Jesus Christ, through whom are *all things*, and we through him."

(1 Corinthians 8:6, RV)

God had a plan at the beginning in connection with which everything has been made. God said, and "it was so"—*it came to be*—the same word describing the result of God's fiat in both Genesis and John: all things came to be through the Word. And in a way distinctive of John among New Testament writers, by the use of what is called antithetic parallelism, he repeats the thought by the use of negatives of both elements of the statement: "without him was not anything made".

The RV, following most modern versions, alters the punctuation in verse 3, putting a full stop after "made", and joining the remaining words to the following verse. But the punctuation preferred by the early versions makes the clause in question read: "That which hath been made in him was life; and the life was the light of men". Theories of evolution are unable to explain the beginning of life—it remains an unsolved problem. The Bible proclaims that all life has its

15

source in God, and that is as far as the human mind can go. Life comes from life, and the doctrine of "spontaneous generation" has had to be abandoned as contrary to all tests and experiments, even those interested in the finding of proof to support their theories admitting that there is no evidence at all for it. But, recognizing the existence of God, a recognition consistent with the highest exercise of reason, a sufficient cause is known. God is the source of all: the physical universe; vegetable, animal and human life. "Moving creature that hath life" (Genesis 1:20); "living cattle" (verse 24); and man (2:7); all have "the breath of life" from God. "In him we live, and move, and have our being."

The life in human relationships adds the moral quality to the merely physical manifestation of lower forms of life. To man, God is a *"fountain* of *living* waters"* (Jeremiah 2:13), the source of life and light. The Psalmist brings the two together: "With thee is the fountain of life: in thy light shall we see light" (36:9). John phrases it: "the life was the light of men". Historically, we see it at the beginning, when "God said" to man the words which reveal His purpose. No such communication was made to other moving creatures having life; "the life was the light *of men".*

"God is light", perfect and absolute, for "in him is no darkness at all". Man, made in God's image, instructed by God, reflects God's light. He turns from God's commandments and he passes from light to shadow, and at last for the most part to darkness, in which he walks alienated from the life of God. But the light still shines, though "hid to them that are lost, in whom the God of this world hath blinded the minds of them which believe not, lest the light of the gospel of the glory of Christ, who is the image of God, should shine unto them" (2 Corinthians 4:3,4). Christ was light, reflecting the Father in fulness of beauty and splendour, and the gospel of his glory sheds his light abroad. He was the Son of God, but made of a woman, and not of the dust as was the first man. Of both Adams are used the words "the image of God"; in one case of form and endowment of moral powers; in the other of moral character. And Paul continues, drawing a parallel between the physical light which God caused to shine in primeval darkness, and the light of truth which is radiated in the darkness of human life. "God that said, Let light shine out of darkness, hath shined in our hearts, to give the light of the knowledge of the glory of God in the face of Jesus Christ" (verse 6).

With the proclamation of such a gospel John could say, "the darkness is passing away, and the true light already shineth". The light is not merely a form of doctrine; it is "a way" in which to walk; or, in a slightly changed figure, it is a light to the path. A man who hates his brother is in darkness and walketh in darkness, and knoweth not whither he goeth, because the darkness hath blinded his eyes (1 John 2:8–11). But a man becomes a "son of light" who believes in the light, and "walks while he has the light, lest darkness overtake him" (John 12:35).

This saying of Jesus concerns the experience of his friends who walked with him literally, and to whom he said, "Yet a little while is the light with you", adding then the words quoted. But they give particular application to the general truth expressed by John: "The life was the light of men; and the light shineth in darkness; and the darkness overcame it not" (verse 5). This is the margin of the RV, which also by a reference suggests the comparison with the saying quoted from 12:35. The RV text gives "apprehended it not". This also is true; for the most part, all through history, the promises of God have not been apprehended. Yet it would appear that John is indicating that there has been conflict between truth and error, and the truth has not been vanquished. This requires a divine knowledge of history. Elijah gave way to despair, and concluded that he was left alone, the one faithful in a whole nation. God told him that there were seven thousand men that had not bowed the knee to the image of Baal; and Paul, commenting on this, says, "even so at this present time there is a remnant according to the election of grace" (Romans 11:5).

In this election there is the guarantee of the final triumph of light. Translated into moral terms, in this epitome of history (in verse 5) John says that the knowledge of God and His ways was made known by revelation; that its object was to dissipate the ignorance in men's minds, but there was considerable failure on their part to respond. Yet God's plan did not fail; the energy of righteousness has the power to overcome sin; the "Word" is effective to do that for which it is sent.

The revelation of God, unfolded age by age in divers portions and divers manners, concerned a Son of God to be born. In him is the highest manifestation of God that is possible. In view of this, the testimony of the prophets is so framed as to suggest the unveiling of the Father Himself—a form of speech which has confused minds not established in the Bible doctrine of God-manifestation. Isaiah foretells the commissioning of a Voice, to cry "in the wilderness, Prepare ye *the way of the LORD*, make straight in the desert a *highway for, our God* ... and the *glory of the LORD* shall be revealed". It was fitting that the way should be prepared for the Lord. If human monarchs and the world's great men once had their forerunners, calling for the removing of the stones from the way, the levelling of the depressions, the smoothing of the rough places, how much more when the Majesty of the Heavens deigned to visit His people.

A restricted view of such language would leave a confused view of the nature of the revelation. How could God move among His people without some veiling? It were death to them, otherwise. And a manifestation in angelic form would not effect the purposes of salvation. It must be in one lower than the angels, the aim being to save some of the perishing ones of the human race. The background of thought in the message of the Voice is that all flesh is grass, fleeting without permanence; while the word of God stands for ever. How can the Word stand for ever, when flesh fails to reach the end the Creator designed? Only by the salvation of those who rise above the flesh by belief of the Word, and faith in the God-provided redeemer. This redeemer—a next of kin—must be son of God and son of man—God with us, manifest in flesh.

The prophet Isaiah then spans the interval between two advents and calls upon those who announce good tidings to Zion to say unto her:

"Behold, your God! Behold, the Lord GOD will come as a mighty one, and his arm shall rule for him: behold, his reward is with him, and his work before him."

(Isaiah 40:9,10, RV)

A Mighty One! The Arm of the Lord! Thus will come the Lord God.

When the Word made flesh was about to be introduced to Israel, some thirty years after the birth of the Son of God, a prophet was sent as herald. For four centuries night had fallen on the prophets and there had been no vision: darkness overtook them, and they did not divine (Micah 3:6). This blackness was to be pierced by a rising star—the morning star that heralds the dawn. In eastern lands, in the absence of good artificial light, and the mechanical contrivances for marking the passing of time so common in these last days, men were better able to discern the face of the sky. The rising of Venus in certain periods marked the coming of the day and the rising of the Sun. Under this figure, it has been suggested, John introduces the Baptist. He was "the lamp that burneth and shineth" (John 5:35); but he was not "the Light".

There was a man sent from God; "there came a man" (RV). The Word *was*: John *came*. Yet he was divinely given and named; the name being prophetic of God's work then proceeding. The forerunner of "the grace of God that bringeth salvation" was called "grace of God". And the names of his parents were also significant of elements of that work. Zacharias means "remembered of God"; Elisabeth means "God of the oath". There is a pleasing play upon the three names in the inspired utterance of the father at the circumcision of the child. "Blessed be the Lord God of Israel; for he hath visited and redeemed his people ... to perform the *mercy* (John) promised to our fathers, and to *remember* (Zacharias) his holy covenant; the *oath* (Elisabeth) which he sware to our father Abraham" (Luke 1:68–73). And God was now to confirm the truth to Jacob and the mercy to Abraham, in the manifestation of that Son whose death would ratify the covenants of promise.

The Baptist was a witness—not the light, but the witness, John repeats. He was a witness rejected; and the counsel of God was rejected in him. No wonder that the Light itself was also refused.

Verse 9 introduces us to another problem in punctuation, as illustrated in text and margin of the RV. "There was the true light, which lighteth every man, coming into the world." Does the last phrase qualify "light", or "every man"? The usage of the phrase by John points to the former. In seven passages (3:19; 6:14; 9:39; 11:27; 12:46; 16:28; 18:37) "coming" relates to Jesus, and therefore probably so in this case. The two passages, 12:46 and 16:28, in particular, might be compared.

Two things should be observed: the true light has come into the world; and his coming "lighteth every man". "True", in English, does duty for two ideas (one of which was formerly represented by "very") but which are distinguished in the Greek. There is true in contrast to the false, to a lie; and true in contrast to type. The latter is before us here; the word occurring in John's writings in all 22 times, but only five times elsewhere; the occurrences being: in the Gospel, eight times; in the first Epistle, four times; in the Apocalypse, ten times. The word has been defined as expressing the real as against the phenomenal; the perfect as against the imperfect;

the substance in contrast to the shadow; the antitype in contrast to the type.

"Every man" must not be understood as denoting every member of the race. Like the word "all" it can be used to mean, in Bullinger's words, all without exception, or all without distinction. The latter is the meaning here. For nearly two thousand years before the advent of Jesus, salvation was bound up with the nation of Israel. But the time came for the extension of the offer of salvation by the active promulgation of the gospel among the Gentiles—a change which the Lord indicated in his conversation with the woman of Samaria. With that development, every man, whether Jew or Gentile, who came within the sound of the gospel, was enlightened.

Verse 10 is a more general statement, of which verse 11 is a particular illustration. John has spoken of the true light *coming* into the world (verse 9). He then says (verse 10), "He (the light as the unfolding of the word) was in the world"; and at verse 11 he reverts to the coming—"He came". The meaning is to be found in regarding the light as the revelation of God, which at last was embodied in the Christ, the true light. The light was in the world in the testimony of faith from the days of Abel, Enoch, Noah, Abraham, and throughout the ministry of the prophets in Israel. The revelation exhibited the divine purpose in creation, and in a sense the light was synonymous with the Word. Of both the same fact is affirmed; of the word—"all things were made through him"; of the light—"the world was made through him". We might put it this way; the light expresses the word in its unfolding of the knowledge of God. John adds, "the world knew him (the light) not". This has been generally true, from Cain's rejection of God's appointments as a means of approach, onward to the universal corruption of God's way in the days of Noah; then history repeated itself in the history of Israel who turned aside from God and refused to believe His promises.

In the closing days of that history in the land of Palestine the climax of God's revelation was made, and in Israel's rejection of it we see the outstanding illustration of human perversity and rejection of God's mercy. "He came unto his own (inheritance), and his own (people) received him not."

The parable of the householder tells in story form what John compresses into so few words. The householder planted a vineyard and made all preparations for its fruit-bearing, and left it in charge of husbandmen. At the time of fruit servants were sent, but they were ill-treated in various ways.

At last the husbandman sent his son, saying, "They will reverence my son". But the husbandmen, seeing the son, plotted his death, saying, "This is the heir, come, let us kill him, and let us seize on the inheritance". Thus was fulfilled the prophecy of the builders who rejected the stone which God made the head of the corner; and the kingdom was taken from Israel, and given to a nation bringing forth the fruits thereof (Matthew 21:33–46).

In his words of comment following this parable, Jesus shows that while the chosen nation which had been the light-bearer refused to have the light, others not of Israel would receive it, and share the reward which God had provided. On another occasion Jesus said of Gentiles:

"They shall come from the east, and from the west, and from the north, and from the south, and shall sit down in the kingdom of God."   (Luke 13:28)

In John's prologue, after the rejection of the light by his own people (verse 11), there is revealed the progress and success of the divine plan among an elect remnant of the nation of Israel and then of the Gentiles.

Israel as a nation first rejected the counsel of God declared to them by John, and then "received not" the Lord, who was the "true light". But the purpose of God did not fail; some responded, first of the Jews and then of the Gentiles.

"As many as received him, to them gave he power to become the sons of God, even to them that believe on his name: which were born, not of blood, nor of the will of the flesh, nor of the will of man, but of God."   (verses 12,13)

There are two words translated "received" in verses 11 and 12; the former has been translated "accepted", and the thought is of the rejection of the light by an action of the will. In the latter case it denotes acceptance as a possession, an acceptance which is individual, and not national, as further shown by the phrase "as many as". "Power" (AV), "right" (RV), means "liberty, authority, right to do anything". Those who believe receive a title to become children of God. The difference between "sons" (AV) and "children" (RV) is that the former has to do with status, the latter with descent. In a real, though spiritual sense, those who receive Christ are God's children.

The full manifestation of this relationship of sons is a future development, when a new family, every member equal to the angels by change of nature, is revealed in the day of the Lord's return. Meanwhile the reception of the light has given

21

the title to that destiny. It is predicated upon "belief on his name", as John adds in further definition of what he means by "receive". "On his name" differs from believing "on him" only in this, that the name emphasizes the doctrinal facts connected with Christ, and connects him with the teaching of the "name" of God that runs through the Old Testament.

God is the Father of this family, which is the outcome of human history, with its story of sin and toil and discipline, with the generally self-willed pursuit of men's own devices, but which has yet yielded sufficient individuals of contrite heart and willing obedience to God's Word for the Father's purpose. This divine paternity of those who believe on His name is emphasized by a three-fold denial of natural birth. "Which were begotten (1) not of blood, (2) nor of the will of the flesh, (3) nor of the will of man." Fleshly life, physical impulse, human paternity, contribute nothing to the begettal of this family. It is of God. "The Father of our Lord Jesus Christ" is also the God and Father (but not in the same sense) of all His family.

The phrase "but of God" touches the nerve of Jewish claims of preference by physical descent. That counts nothing as a title to this relationship. While the human response is expressed in the words "as many as receive" and "believe on his name", the phrase "begotten of God" tells of the divine initiative and will, operative in the cases of all begotten by "the word of truth" (James 1:18). Human boasting and pride of descent are excluded, and humble acceptance of him who was the light, the Word made flesh, is the condition of favour.

There is an interesting reading in verse 13, which, though defended by able scholars, is not of sufficient authority to claim acceptance, but which warrants a remark. This reading is "who was born" and refers back to "him" who was the light. It would be an emphatic testimony to the virgin birth if the reading was authentic. But at any rate it provokes the thought, since in this birth of the children of God human begettal is so emphatically repudiated, because in redemption all is of God, that by analogy the Redeemer must be in the fullest sense what is affirmed of the believer in a spiritual sense, "not begotten of bloods, nor of the will of the flesh, nor of the will of man, but of God".

Having traced the story of the Word to this point, John reverts to the first verse, connecting the purpose at the beginning with its highest manifestation in time—the birth of the Son of God.

THE WORD MADE FLESH (1:14)

"IN the beginning was the Word, and the Word was with God, and the Word was God ... and the Word was made flesh, and dwelt among us (and we beheld his glory, the glory as of the only begotten of the Father), full of grace and truth."

Nearly every word in verse 14 is important. The Word *"became flesh"*. Every child is *born*, and Jesus was no exception. But the nature of his begettal was exceptional, and John and Paul both, by using the word "became", point to the higher origin of Jesus. Paul says, "God sent forth his son, *made* of a woman" (Galatians 4:4), "which was *made* of the seed of David according to the flesh" (Romans 1:3). In both these cases the RV changes the word "made" to "born"; yet when Paul speaks in the same chapter in Galatians of the birth of Ishmael he uses the usual term for "born", the Revisers by the change removing the marks of discrimination. Why should he speak of Christ "becoming" of a woman, unless he wishes to signify something different from the natural birth, even divine parentage?

"The word became *flesh*"—the child born was a member of the human race. The word "flesh" acquired an emphasis from the controversies in which John had to engage in defence of the Truth. Some denied that the nature which Christ bore was like ours, saying that he only "seemed" to suffer, a doctrine which earned for themselves the descriptive name of *Docetæ*, or "Seemers". But John opposed these teachers, and refused to be associated with them in any way. Although the false teachers claimed inspiration, John instructed the brethren to try them by the doctrine which they brought (1 John 4:1–3). "Many deceivers are entered into the world, who confess not that Jesus Christ is come in the flesh. This is a deceiver and an antichrist ... If there come any unto you, and bring not this doctrine, receive him not into your house, neither bid him God speed" (2 John 7,10).

The subject of the nature of Christ has always been the cause of contention. Because of this some would avoid the subject altogether. But that is not the way to hold fast the truth. "Contend earnestly for the faith" is apostolic counsel; for certain men crept in whose teaching was contrary to sound doctrine. Almost all the epistles were written to correct error, and while disputation is often an unpleasant experience, it is the means of preventing the truth from being submerged in human speculation.

"Flesh", then, as used by John in this expression, must be understood in the light of his epistles to affirm strongly that the nature of the Son of God was like that of all mankind. "God (was) manifest in *flesh*."

This Word made flesh *"dwelt"* among us; or "tabernacled" as the margin of the RV rightly indicates. "Let them make me a tabernacle, that I may dwell among them", God commanded Moses. This was done, and the glory of God filled the tabernacle (Exodus 25:8,9). But God forsook the tabernacle that He had pitched among men (Psalm 78:60) because of the wickedness of the people. Ezekiel saw in the vision the glory of God leave the house and ascend from the Mount of Olives. But the tabernacle in the wilderness was only typical of "the true tabernacle which the Lord pitched and not man"; the one was a "worldly sanctuary", made of wood and gold, draped with curtains; the other was a man who trembled at God's word, who was "a body prepared", and who spake of the temple of his body when he gave Israel's rulers a sign of his authority to cleanse God's house—"Destroy *this* temple, and in three days I will raise it up".

He was the Father's dwelling-place among men. "In him dwells all the fulness of the Godhead bodily." So much was this the case that when Philip said, "Show us the Father, and it sufficeth us", Jesus answered, "Have I been so long with you, Philip, and thou sayest, Shew us the Father? He that hath seen me hath seen the Father". Emmanuel was "for a sanctuary" (Isaiah 8:14). The glory of God's character was visible in him, and John says, "We beheld his glory, the glory as of the only begotten of the Father". The glory of God, as revealed to Moses, consisted of a declaration of His character and purpose (Exodus 34:4–8). Such a glory was discernible in Jesus, since he manifested the character of God, and accomplished His purpose. He did always those things which pleased the Father.

Those who "beheld" this glory in Jesus were few in number, even of the chosen nation. But "the glory of the LORD shall be revealed, and all flesh shall see it together; for the mouth of the LORD hath spoken it" (Isaiah 40:5). These words are part of the message of the forerunner of the Lord, John the Baptist. He prepared the way, and the Lord was revealed, but all flesh did not then see his glory. That will come later; but the past revelation is an earnest of the fuller one to come.

It required spiritual discernment to appreciate the glory of the Lord in Jesus. This was lacking in the princes of this world, through a want of understanding of the purpose

of God. None of the princes of this world knew him, and
therefore they crucified the Lord of Glory.

There will be no mistaking the revelation of God's glory in
the days when all flesh shall see it together. It will be manifested in connection with both a spiritual house and a house
of prayer for all nations. The spiritual house is composed of
the redeemed, Jesus himself being the chief corner-stone, the
rest "living stones" built upon him to make "a habitation of
God through the Spirit". These redeemed with their Head are
the channel of the manifestation of the glory in the restored
temple. In the days of Moses, and again in the days of
Solomon, at the erection of God's house, His glory descended
and abode upon it. But when iniquity increased and there
was no remedy, the glory departed from the house in the days
of Ezekiel. After the exile, the prophet Haggai encouraged the
workers engaged in rebuilding God's house, and when it was
completed it was revealed that further calamities would come
upon it. But it was to be only "once more", and then another
rebuilding on a much vaster scale, to be no more "shaken",
and "the latter glory of this house shall be greater than the
former" which they had known before the exile (Haggai 2:9).

The character of this surpassing glory was made known to
Ezekiel in the vision of the restored temple of the age to
come. He witnessed the return of the glory, and thus
described it:

"Behold, the glory of the God of Israel came from the
way of the east: and his voice was like a noise of many
waters: and the earth shined with his glory. And it was
according to the appearance of the vision which I saw, even
according to the vision that I saw when I came to destroy
the city: and the visions were like the vision that I saw by
the river Chebar."   (43:2,3)

The identification of this glory with the saints glorified with
their Lord is established by the description of the noise being
like the sound of many waters, indicating a multitude, and by
the Chebar vision, described in chapters 1 and 10, where the
throne of the age to come is revealed in a number of interesting symbols.

The Word made flesh was "full of grace and truth". These
are divine attributes: "The LORD God, merciful and gracious,
long-suffering, and abundant in goodness and truth".

Grace is favour; shown by God in greatest fulness in His
Son. His words were "gracious", as his hearers remarked.
And "grace reigns through righteousness unto eternal life".

God's "purpose and grace", made "manifest by the appearing of Jesus Christ" (2 Timothy 1:10), was naturally accompanied by grace in him.

Truth is the reality foreshadowed by all revelations of Old Testament times. It covers not only the word spoken, but the integrity of the speaker. It assures the fulfilment of God's purpose, and is charged with moral as well as intellectual force. It is not limited to knowledge, although it includes knowledge. It covers all the moral attributes; hence Paul can say "Truth is in Jesus" (Ephesians 4:21). Truth in life was illustrated in Jesus. To the Hebrews looking for the fulfilment of the promises of God to their race, the truth of God stood for the assurance that God would perform the truth to Jacob and the mercy to Israel. God could not fail of His Word; hence the high moral meaning of the word "truth". God's truth shone forth in Jesus.

Of "grace and truth" Jesus was *"full"*. He was "the brightness of God's glory, and the express image of his person" (Hebrews 1:3). He was "the mystery of godliness, God manifested in the flesh". This fulness is in Jesus for others to share, but before John moves forward to show that men partake of the divine nature in Jesus, he introduces in parenthesis the witness of the Baptist to the fact that Jesus was all he had set forth.

THE WITNESS OF JOHN (1:15)

JOHN has already said that the Baptist was sent of God to bear witness of the light (verses 6,7). Having now recorded the manifestation of the Word in flesh, he records the Baptist's testimony: "This was he of whom I spake, He that cometh after me is preferred before me".

Jesus was after John in time, but he "became before him" in status, as in "foreordination" (1 Peter 1:20)—the cause of such priority being that Jesus "was first in regard of me" (RV). As a man, Jesus was John's junior by six months, but viewed as the manifestation of the Word the relationship is reversed. The "Word" is first by unmentioned ages. A similar paradoxical relativity is connected with David. Jesus is the *root* and *offspring* of David; the branch of Jesse and the root of Jesse. Branch and offspring inasmuch as he was of the seed of David according to the flesh; but the root because he was the Son of God, the manifestation of the Eternal who is the source of all things. This is one of the many hard sayings which are to be found in this gospel, which occasion stumbling to those who judge after the flesh. They see in Jesus either a mere man of human parentage, or a pre-existent member of the Godhead clothed in flesh. Both extremes are contrary to the truth.

FULNESS BESTOWED (1:16–18)

VERSE 15 could with advantage be put in parenthesis to make clear that verses 16–18 resume the record of the beloved disciple.

The word made flesh was *full* of grace and truth; "and of his *fulness* have we all received, and grace for grace". John repeats the language used by Paul in his letters to Ephesus and Colosse; for both apostles were opposing the same error but in different stages of development. Paul would have his readers "filled with the knowledge of his will in all wisdom and spiritual understanding", that they might be prepared for the kingdom of God's Son, "in whom we have redemption through his blood, the forgiveness of sins"; "who is the image of the invisible God, the firstborn of every creature ... and he is before all things, and by him all things consist. And he is the head of the body, the church: who is the beginning, the firstborn from the dead; that in all things he might have the pre-eminence. For it pleased the Father that in him should *all fulness* dwell" (Colossians 1:9–19). Again he says: "In him dwelleth all the *fulness* of the Godhead bodily, and in him ye are made full, who is the head of all principality and power ... buried with him in baptism, wherein also ye are risen with him through the faith of the operation of God, who raised him from the dead" (Colossians 2: 9–12).

The "fulness" of Christ is therefore extended to those who are in him by baptism, buried with him and risen with him, a blessedness to be reached in completeness when the life which is hid with Christ in God is bestowed at his appearing. "When Christ, who is our life, shall appear, then shall ye also appear with him in glory" (3:3,4).

To the Ephesians Paul says that the church, which is Christ's "body" is the "fulness" of Christ, "who filleth all in all" (1:23). God gave the Lord Jesus to the church, and every member of it shares his fulness, and is complete in him, as the body and the head make one whole.

John defines the fulness as "grace for grace", an expression which he elucidates by saying "for the law was given by

Moses, but grace and truth came by Jesus Christ". There was a grace connected with Moses, but it is surpassed by the grace in Christ Jesus. Mark the precision of John's words: the law was *given*: grace *came*. Moses was the mediator of a covenant in which the favour of God made Israel His own nation, but he was only the channel of this grace which bestowed this privilege on Israel. Moses died; and the law given through him was abolished. Jesus is also the mediator of a covenant, but of better things, and the grace of this covenant *was*—it *came to be*—it resided in Jesus and remained in him. One was but the channel; the other the embodiment of all embraced in the covenant established in him. The further excellence of Jesus is shown by the addition of "and truth"; it was grace, even true grace; true as the anti-type, the fulfilment of the revelation given through Moses.

With these words of John, a comparison with Paul's teaching in 2 Corinthians 3 might be made. These two covenants are contrasted: and the basis of the contrast is the temporary glory of Moses, the mediator of the one covenant, and the abiding glory of Jesus, the mediator of the Abrahamic covenant. One was transitory, passing away; the other was abiding, and the source of abiding glory to those who catch its radiance. "We all, with unveiled face beholding as in a mirror the glory of the Lord, are transformed into the same image, as by the Spirit of the Lord."

It must be recognized that there was a glory and a grace given through Moses. Israel's position was one of prestige and of favour, the extent of which may be measured by comparing their position with that of the nations around; but the same language which is used of Israel is charged with higher significance in its application to those in Christ. Were Israel God's people, His purchased possession, His kingdom, His priests, and His holy nation? All these things are affirmed in quoted language of those in Christ (e.g., in 1 Peter 2). But who does not recognize the higher values of the terms when used of Israel after the spirit?

John advances further evidence of the excellence of the "true grace" in Christ over the grace given through Moses. "No man hath seen God at any time: the only begotten Son, which is in the bosom of the Father, he hath declared him." *No man*—not even Moses, with whom God spake face to face, as a man does to his friend, and who dared to prefer the request, "Show me thy glory", and to whom God made answer, "Thou canst not see my face; for man shall not see me and live" (Exodus 33:20). The evident allusion to this incident

28

marks out the meaning of John's words, showing the inferiority of Moses to Jesus. Of the latter he says that he declared God, and is now in the bosom of the Father. God cannot be seen; but here is one in whom He is seen, is revealed, declared, or interpreted (*exegesis*).

The comprehensiveness of the declaration is shown in the definition of relationships: a man (Moses), and God, are the parties connected with the giving of the law; the only begotten Son, and the Father, in the revelation of true grace. Only one can "interpret" God, and that is the Son. The final mark of the excellence of the purpose accomplished in him, is his place in the bosom of the Father; there is no withholding of anything, no words "Thou canst not", such as were spoken to Moses; but in everything the closest intimacy and fellowship. As we receive of "his fulness" so we share the fellowship of the Father and the Son.

THE GOSPEL OF JOHN

SECTION 3

THE BEGINNINGS OF JESUS' MINISTRY
THE WITNESS OF THE BAPTIST (1:19–34)

WHEN the Word of God came unto John in the wilderness he came into all the country round about Jordan, preaching the baptism of repentance for the remission of sins. Multitudes from all over the land came to hear the preacher. It was a time of expectation, when men were looking for the fulfilment of the prophecies of the coming of Israel's Messiah. Excitement was soon aroused, and this would not long escape the notice of the ever-watchful rulers of Israel. They hated Rome, but feared that a popular movement might further restrict their national independence, and jeopardize their own position and wealth.

John describes the rulers as "the Jews". The word is used by him over fifty times, but it only occurs four or five times in the other gospels. It is not used of the people as a whole, but of the authorities as representing the nation. The authorities sent a deputation to John: "And this is the record of John, when the Jews sent priests and Levites from Jerusalem to ask him, Who art thou?" (verse 19).

The priests and Levites were the teachers of the Law. In the words of the Chronicler, "The Levites taught all Israel" (2 Chronicles 35:3). And Malachi says, "The priest's lips should keep knowledge, and they should seek the law at his mouth; for he is the messenger of the LORD of hosts" (2:7).

Israel were unlike any other nation in their relation to God. They were God's people; He was their Ruler. Their land was His; He gave them laws. And in the foundation laws of their Constitution given through Moses arrangements were made for the administration of God's laws. A careful observance of the several duties assigned to those in authority is essential.

The section Deuteronomy 16:18—18:22 contains regulations for local officers, a high court of appeal, the king's duties, and also defines the position of the prophet. Local matters were settled by the judges and officers, who were appointed in all the towns, and who were to "judge the people with just judgment". Difficult cases were taken to "the priests, the Levites, and unto the judge that shall be in those days", whose duty was "to show the sentence of judgment", while the appellant's duty was to "do according to all that they inform thee; according to the sentence of the law which they shall teach thee". Thus the priests and Levites were the teachers of the law, and its interpreters in the high court, and the standard copy of the law was in their keeping. The king was required to write for himself a copy of the law, and to meditate therein, that he might learn to fear God and to keep His laws. But to none of these was entrusted the duty of adding to the law; another class of men was appointed to declare the Word of God, and hand the written messages into the custody of the priests.

Forbidding recourse to the various mediums and sooth-sayers of the nations around, God said He would raise up prophets among His people. The promise culminates in Jesus, as the New Testament application of the words of Moses demonstrates (Deuteronomy 18:18; Acts 3:22; 7:37). But that there was a succession of prophets also covered by the promise, is evident from the test by which they should determine the truth of a prophet's claims:

"When a prophet speaketh in the name of the LORD, if the thing follow not, nor come to pass, that is the thing which the LORD hath not spoken, but the prophet hath spoken it presumptuously: thou shalt not be afraid of him."
(18:22)

The true prophet was known by the fulfilment of his words, and the true prophets were ready to invite the test (Jeremiah 28:9). But the prophet's message did not consist entirely of prediction. He was God's mouthpiece, and an element of his message concerned events to come to pass, some apparently within the lifetime of the prophet. The larger part of the prophet's message must have concerned immediate matters, and by Divine guidance is not included in the scriptures. When any man claimed to be a prophet the duty of the priests and Levites at the Sanctuary was to investigate the claim. There was always a possibility of an addition to those Oracles of God entrusted to them, and their responsibility to test all claimants was onerous.

When the voice of John was heard speaking with the authority of a messenger of God, there had been four centuries of silence except for certain incidents of some thirty years before when the members of an obscure family (one of them a priest), with others, had given utterance to language in prophetic strain. The child in connection with whose birth some of the phenomena had taken place, had now grown to manhood, and fulfilling the words spoken by his father, was announcing that he was preparing the way of the Lord (Luke 1:76).

The situation called for investigation; and in discharge of the duty imposed by the law a deputation of priests and Levites go to John and ask, "Who art thou?" There was evidently a further enquiry as to whether he was the Christ. But "he confessed and denied not; but confessed, I am not the Christ". "Art thou Elias? I am not. Art thou the prophet? No".

Who is "the prophet"? It is the One spoken of in Deuteronomy 18; for while a succession of prophets had in part fulfilled the prophecy, One greater had yet to come to be like unto Moses. The very writing which defined their duty was evidently before their minds in the enquiry that they were making. Since their questions had only produced negative answers, they now asked for positive information. Whereupon John said he was the one of whom Isaiah spake: "The Voice crying in the wilderness, Make straight the way of the LORD".

The delegation included some who were sent by the Pharisees. The Sadducees were the ruling body; the Pharisees, the popular party, were leaders who kept before the people the Messianic hope, insisting on separateness, and the observance of the law of God. "And certain had been sent from among the Pharisees" suggests a joint conference of the two parties, so generally in opposition, to meet this new situation.

The leaders of the deputation having elicited from John a statement concerning his claims, the Pharisees ask a question. Characteristically, it concerned the rite which John commanded rather than the man. The traditions of the elders might be disturbed by innovations. They ask him, "Why baptizest thou then, if thou be not that Christ, nor Elias, nor that prophet?"

The Jews required of their proselytes submission to the rite of baptism. They also looked for a time of purification, based on Ezekiel 36:35 and Zechariah 13:1, before Messiah's manifestation. Two difficulties arose in connection with John's performance of the rite. Had he been the Christ, Elijah, or the prophet, there would have been sufficient personal authority. And how could he demand the rite of fellow Jews? Had he demanded it of Gentiles, it would not have perplexed them; but to demand that Israelites should be baptized—that excused the peremptoriness of their demand, "Why baptizest thou?"

John's answer was to the effect that his baptism was not only part of the preparation for the Lord, but was also the Divinely appointed means for the manifestation of the Messiah to Israel. We do not know what greater perplexity this caused, but John adds to the problem (to them) of a baptized Messiah, his witness to the high status of the One of whom he was but the forerunner. "I baptize with water: but there standeth One among you, whom ye know not; he it is, who coming after me is preferred before me, whose shoe's latchet I am not worthy to unloose."

It is interesting to investigate the results of this interview with John. That the deputation reported to the authorities goes without saying; that the report was duly considered is to be presumed. But from later references it is evident that nothing further was done; no decision was taken. The new problems raised by John's answers probably in their judgment made postponement advisable; and the death of John made further delay practicable.

Towards the close of his ministry Jesus was challenged upon the authority by which he taught in the temple. Jesus in return asked a question. This question had a very strict bearing upon the one they had put to him. "I also will ask you one thing, which if ye will tell me, I likewise will tell you by what authority I do these things. The baptism of John, whence was it? from heaven, or of men?" They were placed in a dilemma. If they answered "From heaven", then they should have obeyed John, and accepted his witness to Jesus; if they acknowledged that John's mission was of God, their question to Jesus was superfluous. They dare not answer that it was of men, because of the unpopularity involved, since the people believed John to be a prophet.

In esteeming John to be a prophet, the people were strictly logical according to the terms of the test required by the law. "John did no miracle; but all things which John spake of this man were true." John was proved to be a true prophet by the fulfilment of his words about Jesus.

Jesus approved the people's decision when he uttered the splendid eulogy of John which concludes with the words,

"Among those that are born of women there is not a greater prophet than John the Baptist ... And all the people that heard, and the publicans, justified God, being baptized with the baptism of John. But the Pharisees and lawyers rejected the counsel of God against themselves, being not baptized of him." (Luke 7:24–30)

Jesus himself made a further appeal to the law of Deuteronomy 18. At his trial they asked him, "Art thou the Christ?" He answered "If I tell you, ye will not believe; and if I ask you, ye will not answer me, nor let me go" (Luke 22:67). The law of Deuteronomy at once acted as safeguard to the people against the false prophet, and also as a vindication of the true prophet. An enquiry had been started in John's case, but they had faltered at a decision. While it was their duty to expose the false, it was also their duty to welcome the true. This they had failed to do in John's case, and when Jesus had appealed for a decision they had declined to give one. What could *he* expect from them? If he told them, they would not believe; if he asked for a decision on his claims, they would not answer.

He had answered the question before, and he reminded them of this when he was again questioned (John 8:25). Now at the crisis, when he knew that the question was not prompted by a desire to investigate his claims but to condemn him, he again witnesses to the truth. Having rebuked them for failure to apply the law, he affirmed that he was the one of whom David spake in Psalm 110, David's lord, who would be king in Zion.

The full significance of the discussion concerning John's baptism, and also the answer of the Lord when a prisoner before the Jewish authorities, can only be recognized against the background of the law given to Israel for determining which were the true prophets and which were false. Both John and Jesus gave abundant evidence that they were sent of God. The people recognized that John's predictions concerning Jesus had been fulfilled. There was much more evidence of the truth of the claims of Jesus, for the record of his words shows how often he had foretold what would come to pass, and they found that it was as he had said unto them. Self-interest blinded the rulers, and they crucified their Messiah.

JOHN'S WITNESS TO THE PEOPLE (1:29–34)

"ON the morrow" (verse 29) is a mark of time which shows that the baptism of Jesus must have preceded the visit of the embassage to John by the forty days spent by Jesus in the wilderness. On the morrow of John's witness to the rulers the opportunity came for his witness to the people. Seeing Jesus approaching him, he said, "Behold the Lamb of God, that taketh away the sin of the world".

Behind these words used by John were centuries of national history during which there had been offered thousands of lambs in the daily and other offerings. All his hearers were familiar with the services in the Temple, and with the language which he used, but the application of the words to a man was new to them. On the other hand, modern readers of the Bible may be so familiar with the phrase "the Lamb of God" as applied to Jesus that the metaphor has been practically lost, and through ignorance of the Old Testament the meaning is not apprehended.

The offering of sacrifice goes back to the garden of Eden, and follows the introduction of sin into the world. The first human clothing was devised by Adam and Eve to cover the nakedness of which they had become conscious by transgression. Sin and nakedness are so related that the terms are interchangeable in Revelation 16:16. God would not allow their fig-leaf covering for sin, and provided instead coats of skin. In this arrangement there is a hint of the way whereby sins should be covered and transgressions hid.

Abel manifested faith in the promises of God, and brought an offering at the appointed time, and offered it in the prescribed way. His offering was more acceptable than the firstfruits of the ground offered by Cain. Faith and obedience were shown by one, and were lacking in the other. Later, Abraham was called upon to offer his son, and the words he used in answer to Isaac—"God will provide himself a lamb"—supply a clear verbal link with the words of John about Jesus. Then at the Passover every man had to take a lamb, an annual memorial of the Exodus, that was required of the whole congregation by the Law of Moses.

Prophecy unfolded the meaning of these appointments and showed that they prefigured the offering of a sinless man. The Psalmist said:

"Sacrifice and offering thou didst not desire; mine ears hast thou opened: burnt offering and sin offering hast thou not required. Then said I, Lo, I come: in the volume of the book it is written of me, I delight to do thy will, O my God."

(Psalm 40:6-8)

In this the thought is directed from the physically unblemished animals to the morally perfect man, who, because the sacrifices of animals could not take away sin, came to do the will of God and offer himself. Of the same servant of God Isaiah spoke when telling of the rejection of the arm of the Lord, who would be led as a sheep to the slaughter, cut off out of the land of the living, stricken for the transgression of the people; whose soul would be made an offering for sin; by whose knowledge many would be justified in sins being forgiven: "for he shall bear their iniquities".

"Ye were redeemed from your vain manner of life with the precious blood of Christ, as of a lamb without blemish and without spot", says Peter (1 Peter 1:19); and John, who heard the Baptist make his announcement, wrote at the end of his life that Jesus was manifested to take away our sins.

In the Apocalypse the Lamb is brought to our notice in a very striking way. John wept that none was able to open the seals which revealed things which must come to pass. He was told not to weep: "Behold, the Lion of the tribe of Judah, the Root of David, has prevailed to open the book". Thus encouraged John looked as commanded, but it was not a Lion that met his eyes, but "a Lamb as it had been slain". The Lion phase is based upon the Lamb phase; the foundation of all future power and glory being laid in the death of the Lamb. The metaphor wears so thin that the Lamb becomes a title of the Lord Jesus in several places of the Apocalypse (14:4; 15:3; 17:14; 19:7–9; 21:9,22,23).

After pointing to Jesus as the Lamb of God, the Baptist next identified him as the one of whom he had been speaking: "This is he of whom I said, After me cometh a man which is preferred before me. And I knew him not: but that he should be made manifest to Israel, therefore am I come baptizing with water". And John bare record saying,

"I saw the Spirit descending from heaven like a dove, and it abode upon him. And I knew him not: but he that sent me to baptize with water, the same said unto me, Upon whom thou shalt see the Spirit descending, and remaining on him, the same is he which baptizeth with the Holy Spirit. And I saw, and bare record that this is the son of God."   (verses 30–34)

"I knew him not." John's words have been thought to contradict what he said when Jesus came forward to be baptized (Matthew 3:14). This is not so. John was related to Jesus, but living some distance apart, it is probable they had seen little of each other, particularly in view of John's wilderness life. How then did John know that Jesus was so holy that he had need to be baptized of him rather than that he should baptize Jesus? The answer is probably to be found in the method which was adopted by John. He did not administer the rite to all who came to him, but considered their fitness to be baptized. He denounced many who came as serpent's off-spring, and commanded them to bring forth fruits meet for repentance. Of those he received, it is written, "And they were baptized of him in Jordan, *confessing their sins*". Imagine the crowds of people gathered together, and one after another they come forward to John with a confession of sins upon their lips; and then we see Jesus step forward. What sins has he to confess? As John looks and waits, what can Jesus say but that he has lived in all good conscience before God, keeping all His commandments? Such a state-ment from any other lips would at once have condemned the speaker as presumptuous, and insensible to right and wrong. But they were true in the case of Jesus, and John recognized that they were true. He faltered; here is the one greater than himself, "before him", as he said. Their position should be reversed, and John the one to be baptized rather than the baptizer. The answer of Jesus satisfied him—baptism was necessary to fulfil all righteousness, although he had no sins to confess.

John had been proclaiming the mortality of man—"all flesh is grass, and the glory of man as the flower of the field". Jesus was mortal, righteously so by descent through his mother. His mission required the declaration of the right-eousness of God by his voluntary submission to death as a condition of the bestowal of favour in the forgiveness of sins upon all who believe. So Paul explains (Romans 3:25). God had appointed this submission to a symbolic act, signifying the same truth, at the beginning of his mission.

These circumstances also provided the conditions for the public manifestation (*phanerosis*) of Jesus to Israel—"that he might be made manifest to Israel". The Baptist had been given a sign—the Spirit would descend upon him whom he had to announce to Israel. As Jesus came up out of the water the sign was given. These things had happened some weeks before the witness of John; he here recalls the event, and repeats his witness.

The descent of the spirit, and its abiding upon Jesus, was a fulfilment of the words of the prophet:

"Behold my servant, whom I uphold ... I have put my spirit upon him"; "The spirit of the Lord GOD is upon me."
(Isaiah 42:1; 61:1)

"Being manifest to Israel" is not a revealing to the whole nation of who and what Jesus was. Many who witnessed

John's ministry saw no manifestation of God in Jesus; they refused the testimony of both John and Jesus, as well as the divine attestation that accompanied their work. Israel is used in a broader and a narrower sense; broader of the whole nation: narrower of the faithful in the nation. In the narrowest sense of all, Jesus is Israel, the prince of God; but the Christ-body are "Israelites indeed", as Jesus described Nathanael (verse 47). To *this* Israel Jesus was manifested by the baptism of John. We see it in process in this incident and the succeeding one. John has received the sign identifying Jesus as the Lord whose way he had to prepare. He now points to Jesus as "the Lamb of God"; he further says, "I have seen, and have borne witness, This is the Son of God".

In these words, John directs attention to the voice from heaven which said, "Thou art my beloved Son, in whom I am well pleased" (Mark 1:11). Two Old Testament predictions are here combined (Psalm 2:7; Isaiah 42:1); one referring to his birth, the other to his anointing of the Spirit.

JOHN'S WITNESS TO HIS DISCIPLES (1:35–42)

THE events of four consecutive days are narrated in John 1. "On the morrow" (verses 29,35,43) marks the sequence of the days. On the first he proclaims that the Messiah is in their midst; on the second the Messiah is pointed out; and now on the third John directs the attention of his disciples to Jesus, and the process of "decrease" for John and "increase" for Jesus begins. On the fourth day Jesus gains other disciples and goes to Galilee.

It is evident that when John on the third day said to the two disciples, "Behold the Lamb of God", he intended they should follow Jesus. This they did; upon which Jesus turned, and asked them, What seek ye? They answered, Teacher, where dwellest thou? It was not a matter of knowing where his abode was; they wanted to know where they might find him for further talk than was possible there and then. "Come and see", said Jesus. "Now" was the time; and they spent the day with him.

These two disciples were John and Andrew. Each had a brother, and each one went in search of his brother. The effect of the stay with Jesus is seen in this desire to pass on their knowledge of him, and also in their conviction that he was the Messiah. Of what did they talk during that day? Surely we must find the answer from the words they used, "We have found the Messiah".

Andrew was the first to find his brother; and he brings Peter to Jesus. Peter receives a "new name". Jesus looked on him, and knowing what was in man, saw his fitness for work with himself. "Thou art Simon, the son of Jona: thou shalt be called Cephas which is by interpretation, A stone." Peter at first belied the name, but later it was faithfully illustrated in his life. Simon becomes in name and fact, Simon Peter, or Peter without addition.

NATHANAEL AND PHILIP (1:43–51)

ON the way to Galilee Jesus finds Philip, and calls him to follow him. Philip and Andrew and Peter all belonged to Bethsaida (Fish-town). Their enthusiasm for Jesus was contagious, and as John and Andrew had sought their brothers, so Philip seeks out his friend, whose interest in the prophets was known to him. Often had they talked of the Deliverer promised by God; now Philip had met him, and he exclaims to Nathanael, "We have found him, of whom Moses in the law, and the prophets, did write, Jesus of Nazareth, the son of Joseph".

Nathanael is generally, and with great probability, identified with Bartholomew. The latter is a patronymic, meaning son of Talmai. Nathanael is not mentioned in the first three gospels, Bartholomew is not mentioned in the fourth. In the lists of the apostles, the former put Bartholomew next to Philip; and John mentions Nathanael in 21:2, where all others named are apostles.

Nathanael was not easily carried away. He did not look for a Messiah from Nazareth. There may be no disparagement in his remark, Can there any good thing come out of Nazareth? He looked for the Messiah from Bethlehem. Philip's answer was simple, "Come and see". When good things are to be had, and there is capacity for appreciation of them, there is no better method. Philip's confidence is shown by his desire that his friend should make a practical test.

As Nathanael approaches, Jesus makes a remark which shows he had knowledge of his thoughts; and Nathanael asks in surprise, "Whence knowest thou me?" Jesus answered that before Philip called him, while he was under the fig tree, he had seen him. Such powers convinced Nathanael that Philip's judgment was right; here was the one of whom the prophets had spoken; and he exclaims, "Rabbi, thou art the son of God; thou art the King of Israel".

There are two clues to Nathanael's thoughts—the words of Jesus when he came to him, and the promise Jesus made after his confession: "Behold an Israelite indeed, in whom is no guile"; "Because I said unto thee, I saw thee under the fig tree, believest thou? Thou shalt see greater things than these. Verily, verily, I say unto you, Hereafter ye shall see heaven open, and the angels of God ascending and descending on the Son of man."

Jacob means supplanter, but Jacob's name was changed to Israel, a prince with God. Jacob was not free from guile, but, as Israel, prevailed to the obtaining of the blessing. He was encouraged in the conflict with self by the vision of the ladder, and the promise that God would be with him. Nathanael, meditating on the lives of the fathers, the promises to them, and their victories, and desiring to share with them the heirship of God's promises, and God's friendship, is arrested by the stranger breaking in on his thoughts and telling him that *he* was an Israelite free from guile; the association of ideas is carried on, and the subject of Nathanael's meditation further exhibited by the promise that he and the disciples would see Jacob's vision of the ladder fulfilled in Jesus, in the angels of God ascending and descending upon the Son of Man.

Jacob had the vision at Bethel—the house of God. Here was the house of God, the temple which the Lord pitched; and here was to be seen communication established with God, and an ever-opened heaven. It was by faith this was seen, faith based upon the words and works of Jesus.

Nathanael humbly accepted the truth of Christ's description of him as an Israelite indeed, without guile; it recognized his endeavours; he asked how Jesus knew him, and Jesus referred to a recent incident in his life to show that he had power to know what was in man. The excitement caused by John's preaching had led Nathanael to retire for quiet reflection on all the stirring events that were happening. The knowledge of Jesus showed he possessed those powers predicted of the Messiah (Isaiah 11); the evidence of such supernatural sight caused him at once to acknowledge that Jesus was Son of God, and King of Israel. How far the full significance of his words was appreciated we do not know; many difficult experiences lay ahead of them, before the meaning of many utterances made by themselves and by Jesus, as well as the prophecies of the sufferings of Christ in relation to Jesus, was perceived.

Jesus adds a third title to the two that had fallen from the lips of Nathanael. "The Son of man" is best explained in the light of the Old Testament. There has been much speculation upon the import of the title, but it is based upon Old Testament predictions.

We find it in Psalm 8, which is prophetic of Christ, both Paul and Jesus being witness (Hebrews 2:6; Matthew 21:16). We meet it again in Psalm 80, where the branch of the broken vine of Israel, made strong for God's use, is described as "the man of thy right hand, the son of man whom thou madest strong for thyself", through whom Israel will be restored. The king of Israel is the Son of man. Is not this the source of the association of ideas in the words, "When the Son of man shall sit upon the throne of his glory ... judging the twelve tribes of Israel"? And the branch of that vine is also the branch of David of many prophetic allusions.

For the first time (verse 51) we meet the words, "Verily, verily". This doubly emphatic "Amen, amen", is found only in John, and always from the lips of the Lord. It attests with great solemnity the truth of what Jesus is saying, and connects the speaker with the title "The Amen" which he takes to himself in the Apocalypse, "I am the Amen, the faithful and true witness"; and also with the prophecy of the "God of the Amen", in whom only is blessing to be found (Isaiah 65:16). "He shall speak all the words that I command him", God had said of Jesus; he spake God's words, and God will requite failure to hearken to them. So He says (Deuteronomy 18:19). Well might Jesus say, "My words shall not pass away". He draws attention to their divine import by the impressive Amen, amen, by which he prefaces his sayings.

SECTION 4

THE SIGNS & PUBLIC DISCOURSES OF CHRIST
THE FIRST SIGN: WATER INTO WINE (2:1–11)

JOHN records eight miracles, although he never so describes them. He calls them signs. The word meaning "power" used frequently in the other gospels to describe the miracles is not used by John. Only once is the word translated "wonder" found, and then with the word "signs" (4:48). But the word translated "signs" occurs seventeen times. John's method of description invites a continued enumeration: he calls the first miracle "the beginning of signs"; the next one he calls "the second sign" (4:54). The seventh sign was the resurrection of Lazarus, while the eighth and last sign was performed after Christ's resurrection.

"On the third day" after the last event, completing one week, there was a marriage in Cana of Galilee. With this John fills out the events of the first week of the Lord's manifestation to Israel; he also notes the last week of the Lord's life (12:1).

Cana was the home of Nathanael (21:2). A wedding feast lasted several days, sometimes seven, and sometimes as many as fourteen. One or both of the marriage parties must have been friends, or possibly relatives, of the family of Jesus, for his mother "was there", that is, was staying there. Her freedom in suggesting to the servants that they do whatever Jesus commanded is confirmatory of this. Jesus was invited; and John's expression, "Jesus was called, and his disciples", suggests that the disciples were invited because of their connection with Jesus.

The wine failed—a calamity full of disgrace on such an occasion in those days. The extra number present may have helped to create the difficulty; they would certainly make the shortage more noticeable.

Mary had learned to turn to her son when in need. She had doubtless experience of his resourcefulness during the years at Nazareth; but the recent events, with the knowledge which she had of the paternity of her son, may have led her to look now for something greater, some manifestation of power. The answer of Jesus, "Mine hour is not yet come", indicates this.

The answer of Jesus to Mary has occasioned much discussion. "Woman, what have I to do with thee?" is a reply that seems to lack that filial respect we should expect from Jesus. Doctrinal considerations have influenced the discussion, particularly the Roman Catholic teaching concerning Mary. But there was no disrespect; "Woman" implies no rebuke; it was used by Augustus addressing Cleopatra. It contains no harshness, for Jesus used it under circumstances when any harshness is unthinkable (19:26; 20:13,15). At the same time, "Woman" is not "Mother". It puts aside that relationship, as much as to say that family ties took second place to his duty. And the further words, "What have I to do with thee?" certainly express idiomatically that he could not allow interference, nor be directed by another in what he should do. The phrase "rejects interference and declines association on the matter spoken of". Hitherto Jesus had been subject to his parents, but now that his ministry had begun higher considerations put aside his responsibilities to his mother.

"Mine hour is not yet come"; by this a crisis is indicated, and one near at hand. The first miracle was the beginning of the use of that power which marked him out as the Son of God, witnessing that the Father was with him.

Mary clearly did not treat the reply of Jesus as a complete refusal, for she instructed the servants: "Whatsoever he saith unto you, do it". Accordingly when he told them to *fill* the six water-pots, containing in all about 120 gallons, they at once obeyed and filled them to the brim. Jesus then told them to draw, and bear to the ruler of the feast.

The ruler was the master of ceremonies, sometimes an upper servant; but sometimes a guest appointed to preside at the feast. On tasting the water now changed into wine, the ruler remarked on its excellence, with the further comment that the best was usually drunk first, but in this case the best had been reserved. *

John's comment on the miracle guides us to its significance. "This beginning of signs did Jesus, and manifested forth his glory." Moses was given the signs of the serpent-rod

---

* How far modernism will go in its treatment of miracles is illustrated in a recent book by one of the most popular ministers of this country. He suggests that no change was made in the water, but Jesus instructed the servants to fill the jars with water as a joke, and the ruler of the feast caught up the joke.

and the leprous hand to show that God was with him; and the giving of the manna was a manifestation of the glory of the Lord. In the case of Jesus the signs that he did revealed his glory, witnessed to his work, and to what he was. As John said at the end of his gospel, "Many other signs did Jesus in the presence of his disciples, which are not written in this book: but these are written, that ye might believe that Jesus is the Christ, the Son of God; and that believing ye might have life through his name". Jesus said that the raising of Lazarus was for the glory of the Lord, that the Son of God might be glorified thereby. Again, John says that Isaiah saw the glory of Christ in the vision of the throne of the Lord when the commission to send Christ on behalf of the redeemed was foretold. His mission, his sonship, his work, are all parts of his glory. Each of John's signs exhibits some aspect of his work in relation to the Father.

In this miracle Jesus performed instantly that which was done year by year by God's power in the growth of the vine, in which by nature's chemistry the plant transforms the moisture and the nutriment in the soil into the blood of the grape. Such creative power belongs to God, who must have bestowed it on the one who exhibited it in witness to his claims. It was *his* glory which was shown forth as well as the Father's—the glory as of the only begotten of the Father. "All things were made by him", John had said of the "Word"; and in this first sign we see the "Word made flesh" exercising power creatively, which proclaims that he was the Son of God.

Jesus was greater than the prophets, and the miracles which he wrought were greater in variety and in power than those performed by them. They had also a different significance. For while miracles attested the truth of the prophet's message, the glory of Jesus himself was exhibited in the works that he did. They were servants; he was the only begotten Son.

But we might go further even than this. As we shall see in other "signs", they have a very direct bearing upon the work of Jesus. John points out that the waterpots were connected with the rites of purification practised by the Jews. This provides the first hint of an inner significance in the sign. The water stands for the legalism of the Jews, in which they so pathetically trusted. Jesus had to change this, and provide something different, something better. Jesus himself compares his teaching to "new wine", and in order that it might be preserved he provided "new bottles", even specially prepared and trained men who for three years were his pupils (Mark 2:22). The law as given by Moses was "wine"— it contained the form of the truth in Jesus: but it was insufficient. It failed as the wine failed at the feast: it was old wine, kept by the "old" men who clung to the tradition and rejected the teaching of Jesus. This was in some ways a characteristic of human nature—a conservative holding to that which once had authority before it was overlaid with the distressing "burdens" of centuries of commentators. Jesus recognized this trait of mankind, when he said, "No man having drunk old wine desireth new: for he saith, The old is better" (Luke 5:39). It was a natural human attitude, but not therefore a correct one. The steward of the feast reversed the matter; the new wine was the better: "Thou hast kept the good wine until now". So had God kept the best until then, when He sent His Son into the world to bring the "wine" of saving health, through the offering of himself. To speak of himself as "the true vine" is to maintain a connection of thought not at first evident. When Jesus bade the servants *Draw out* now", he used a term which commonly means to draw water from a well with a vessel and rope. Was he thinking of the Messianic prophecy of Isaiah: "With joy shall ye draw water from the wells of salvation" (12:3)?

CLEANSING THE TEMPLE (2:12–25)

WITH this section we pass to the public work of Jesus. After a short stay in Capernaum with his mother and brethren and disciples, Jesus went to Jerusalem for the Passover feast. This was the first feast of his ministry, and the first public appearance in the capital since it began.

The court of the temple where the Gentiles were allowed to enter and worship had been gradually appropriated for the stalls set up by the high priests for the sale of animals and birds for sacrifices, and for tables for the money-changers. These were ostensibly for the convenience of worshippers who came from distant lands. They could secure on the spot blemish-free cattle for offerings which would be sure of the approval of the priests; and also the temple coinage for the payment of the temple dues. But it was done at a price. It was a vested interest which exploited the situation shamelessly. It is told that a grandson of the great Hillel on one occasion interfered, and reduced the price of a pair of doves from over fifteen shillings to fourpence. For changing foreign money to the half-shekel, valued at about one shilling and fivepence, the extortionate rate of twopence was charged. These oppressions made the temple service a great hardship. Not only so, they intruded into worship which was adapted for the development of all the spiritual qualities in man, a spirit of trafficking altogether foreign to the objects in view. This tendency to take advantage of the privileges of priesthood must have been so general throughout their history, that it is a mark of the excellence of the arrangements of the worship of the age to come that there will be then no traffickers in the Temple.

In another aspect the thing was an evil. The Temple was for Israel's approaches to the God of Israel; but the Gentile was also provided for. A court was reserved for them. They must not indeed pass beyond the middle wall of partition on pain of death; but the court of the Gentiles was provided for them. The desecration of this court into "the shambles of Annas" left the Gentiles without a place at all.

It was an indignant man that made a scourge of small ropes and drove the cattle and their keepers out; that pushed over the tables of the money-changers, sending the piles of coins rolling over the floor of the court; and that ordered the sellers of doves to take them away. It was a controlled indignation; he did not recklessly liberate the doves, entailing a loss of property. But his bared arm, muscular with the years at carpentry, and the indignant look on his noble face, must have filled those present with fear and awe. His words were no less challenging. "Make not my Father's house a house of merchandise." "My Father's house"—God's house; what is he claiming to be? The Son of God?

The disciples remembered the words of the Psalm, full of details of suffering which they then little comprehended, which said, "The zeal of thine house hath eaten me up". The authorities, recovering from the first surprise, angry at this attack upon their authority and their actions, and ready to assert their power, gathered round Jesus and demanded his authority. "What sign showest thou unto us, seeing thou doest these things?" The answer was misunderstood, could not indeed have been understood by them. It is evident that an answer satisfying them immediately was not intended; perhaps no authority should have been asked for the attack upon such a flagrant abuse, recognized as such by all, even Josephus accusing them of "open plunder and atrocities", by which they increased the temple revenues.

"Destroy this temple, and in three days I will raise it up", said Jesus. They took his word literally, understanding it as a reference to the Temple just cleansed of the herds of cattle and the more brutish extortioners employed by the priests. It had been forty and six years in building; did they raze it to the ground, could he rear it up in three days? It was absurd. But they did not forget his words, and three years later an attempt was made to found on them some ground of accusation against him at his trial, and even when they had secured his crucifixion the words still haunted them, but with a clearer apprehension of their possible meaning. Therefore they asked Pilate that the grave might be made secure against any happening which might give an appearance that he had been raised from the dead.

It was a vain effort. They fulfilled their part—"Destroy this temple"; for he spake of the temple of his body; and by wicked hands they took him and slew him. But he had said, "And I will raise it up in three days". Guards and seals were powerless to prevent the resurrection of the Son of God. If it be said that it was the Father's work, for a dead man cannot restore himself to life, this must be admitted; but in his case his obedient life had given him a title to resurrection, and it was not possible that he should be holden of death; hence he could speak of his resurrection being his own act.

How highly they prized the Temple; and how fearful they were that the agitation in connection with Jesus should cause the Romans further to curtail their liberties, and remove their Temple. While they valued the shadow, they lightly esteemed the true tabernacle which the Lord had pitched in their midst. Here was the dwelling-place of God—a man to whom the Lord would look, when all material things of His creation were not accounted suitable for His House; "to this man will I look, even to him that is poor and of a contrite spirit, and who trembles at my word". The princes of this world knew him not, or they would not have crucified the Lord of glory. But it was written that the Lord of hosts should be for a sanctuary, but for a stone of stumbling and a rock of offence to both houses of Israel (Isaiah 8:14). So it came to pass: Jesus was the sanctuary of the Lord of hosts, the Lord's temple in the midst of His people manifesting the glory which was the mark of the divine presence; but "Israel stumbled and fell, broken, snared and taken", because they believed not; they stumbled at that stumblingstone.

Many sayings, the import of which was missed at the time they were spoken, were recalled after his resurrection. This was one; John records that it was remembered when he was risen from the dead, and they believed the scripture and the word which Jesus spake unto them.

The particular scripture of this allusion is not indicated; perhaps it was the sixteenth Psalm. But John's words are not without value as evidence of the truth of the apostles' witness to the resurrection. They did not expect it; neither had they understood the scripture predictions concerning it. Anticipation played no part in the formulation of the apostles' witness that Jesus was raised from the dead. The fact itself threw light on both the teaching of the Lord, and on the prophecies of the Old Testament.

On the day of Pentecost, Peter spoke of the many wonders and signs which God had done by Jesus in their midst, of which they had full knowledge. While John only records eight of the signs, he knew quite well of the others. At this Passover many miracles were wrought, "for many believed on his name when they saw the signs which he did".

VISIT OF NICODEMUS (3:1–15)

THE attitude of Jesus to the crowd is unlike that of an impostor, or even a social agitator. He never encouraged any enthusiasm because of his mighty works. The ebullition of feeling which they produced was as quickly changed to that of murderous hate. Therefore "he did not commit himself unto them, because he knew all men, and needed not that any man should testify of man". The people had not a full belief in all that Jesus was. It was an enthusiasm which had a Messianic basis, so incomplete as to be erroneous. John uses the same word to describe the attitude of the crowd to Jesus, and Jesus to the crowd. "Many *believed* on him ... but Jesus did not *trust* himself to them."

He was able to search the hearts; he did not judge after the sight of his eyes. He knew how little trust could be placed in their quickly-lit zeal. He knew that he would be despised and rejected by these same Jews. "What is in man" is not highly esteemed by God, and Jesus always looked at things as God did. It is only when there has been a great change in a man by contact with the word of God that any fitness for "fellowship with the Son" is apparent. God is working to prepare some to be conformed to the image of His Son, but for the most part, as God judges, "trust" cannot be placed in man. This presents a different view of Jesus and of man than is put

49

forward by many to-day; they do not understand and see the necessity for any reserve such as is here indicated.

The visit of Nicodemus to Jesus is one of the incidents connected with the first Passover of the ministry, which he spent at Jerusalem. The AV somewhat obscures this; first the chapter division cuts it off from the narrative of chapter 2; then the AV omits a connecting word in the translation. "Now there was a man of the Pharisees" (RV). But the connecting word can be used for contrast as well as addition, and to translate *"But* there was a man of the Pharisees", as many do, brings out a contrast with the concluding verse of chapter 2. "Jesus did not commit himself unto them ... for he knew what was in man."

While he did not trust the crowd, he gave an interview to Nicodemus, and explained to him his teaching. There were reasons for this. As for Nicodemus himself, Jesus knew what was in him; he knew the difficulties of his position in Israel; he knew his weaknesses and the possibilities of strong faith. This was manifested gradually; first in protest against the illegal methods of the Sanhedrin in their opposition to Jesus; and then in joining privately with Joseph of Arimathea in giving the body of Jesus an honoured if hurried burial. Additionally, it is probable that Nicodemus came as a delegate from the authorities. We have seen that a delegation was sent to John to investigate his claims, as the Law required; and while no decision was reached in John's case, the witness of John to Jesus, together with the signs which Jesus had done, made an enquiry essential in his case also. Nicodemus is described as a man *"out of* the Pharisees" and as a "ruler of the Jews", which suggests that he was commissioned by the authorities, whom John in this gospel describes as "the Jews", to visit Jesus.

It was by night—not a public questioning as in John's case. Greater care and caution were displayed; and since it was by night, it must have been by appointment—how otherwise in the crowded state of the city and its environs at the feast could this ruler of Israel have found the new preacher? The deputy chosen by the Sanhedrin was an illustrious member of the body, and one not unsympathetic towards Jesus. But he spoke for himself and his colleagues: *"We* know that thou art a teacher come from God".

The cleansing of the temple, the many miracles which Jesus had done, the state of expectancy of Messiah's appearing, the message of the forerunner, all combined to make a careful and respectful advance necessary. As yet the miracles are not disputed by the authorities; so far as we know they never at a later time were disputed by the ruler who interviewed Jesus. He therefore mentions their knowledge of the miracles, and the evidential value of these works to Jesus as a divinely sent teacher, as a reason for further enquiries. "Rabbi", he began, giving to Jesus the title accorded to teachers, "we know that thou art a teacher come from God; for no man can do these miracles which thou doest except God be with him." Since the Messiah was called The Coming One, there is perhaps a half-suggestion in saying that he had come from God, that he was that coming one, and the signs were the tokens of the Messiah. On the lowest estimate, the form of address of Nicodemus shows a recognition that Jesus was a commissioned teacher of exceptional character and power.

If we treat the words of Nicodemus as a hesitant acknowledgment that Jesus was the Messiah, we have the thought link to the answer of Jesus, which otherwise seems abrupt, and requires that we assume another question by the ruler.

In the statement of Nicodemus there is a certain faltering—courage fails him to state frankly the implied fact. "No man can do these miracles which thou doest except ..."—except what? Should it not be "except he be the Messiah"? While there is hesitation, there is implied, 'Your miracles suggest that you are the Coming One; what is your programme? How are you going to establish the Kingdom? What steps do you propose to take? and when?'

The answer was unexpected, for neither Nicodemus nor his fellow-councillors envisaged such a procedure as Jesus outlined. They looked for a conquering warrior—not altogether wrongly; and they confidently expected to be recognized by the Coming One, and to co-operate with him. Their own position they never doubted. Was it not a fundamental element of their teaching that all Israel would have a place in the world to come? How much more, then, they who were the rulers? The answer of Jesus at once cut away all such expectations.

Jesus answered, prefacing his words with the emphatic double "verily", "I say unto thee, Except a man be born again (anew, or from above, RV), he cannot see the kingdom of God". It brushed away any supposed privilege of birth; entrance to the kingdom was not dependent upon natural birth, but upon birth from above. The language was not unfamiliar to the Jewish ruler. Their teachers said, "If any man become a proselyte, he is like a child new-born". Again, "The Gentile that is made a proselyte, and the servant that is made free, behold he is like a child new-born". That Israel, the chosen of God, had need of any such change was preposterous. Yet John had said, "Think not to say within yourselves, We have Abraham to our father: for I say unto you, that God is able of these stones to raise up children unto Abraham" (Matthew 3:9). The prophets had called for circumcision of heart as well as of flesh. The Jews claimed to be children of God: "We have one Father, even God"; but Jesus disproved this by pointing to their opposition to himself, who had proceeded from God. The statement of Jesus to Nicodemus is comprehensive: "Except a man—any man—be born from above ...". There are no exceptions and no racial distinctions and preferences.

The answer amazed Nicodemus; it swept away his cherished views of privilege; it reduced him to the level of the Gentile. And the quietly expressed but emphatic "from above" left him perplexed. His bewilderment is seen in his response, "How can a man be born when he is old? Can he enter the second time into his mother's womb and be born?" The absurdity of it is the measure of his lack of comprehension. The answer was inexplicable; he answers foolishly in his effort to make foolish the words of Jesus.

Jesus answered him by enlarging upon the words "born from above". "Except a man be born of water and the Spirit, he cannot enter into the kingdom of God. That which is born of the flesh is flesh; that which is born of the Spirit is spirit." This language ought in great measure to have been intelligible to Nicodemus. That Jesus expected him to understand is clear from his reproof, "Art thou the teacher of Israel, and understandest not these things?"; and also from the further remark, "If I told you earthly things, and ye believed not, how shall ye believe if I tell you heavenly things?"

"Birth of water", like the related "born again", had a place in Jewish religious language. They baptized their proselytes, whom they described as new-born. They had also witnessed the baptism administered by John; and while the rulers had not responded to John's demands, Luke records that all the people who heard him, and the publicans, justified God, being baptized with the baptism of John (7:29). The rite, commanded by God through John, was continued by Jesus, who with his disciples "came into the land of Judea; and there he tarried with them and baptized". Jesus and John were both baptizing at the same time; "and John was baptizing in Ænon". The response to the teaching of Jesus was greater than that to John, and the greater influence of Jesus was duly reported to the rulers. "The Lord knew how the Pharisees had heard that Jesus made and baptized more disciples than John, though Jesus himself baptized not, but his disciples."

Baptism, then was a general practice followed by the Pharisees, and by John and Jesus. It was a practice consistent with Jewish expectations based upon the testimony of the prophets. Ezekiel had prophesied of the restoration:

"I will sprinkle clean water upon you, and ye shall be clean; from all your filthiness, and from all your idols, will I cleanse you. A new heart also will I give you, and a new spirit will I put within you ... and I will put my spirit within you."   (36:25–27)

This sprinkling of clean water is based upon the type of the water of separation, in which we meet one of the "divers baptisms" of the law. Persons defiled by contact with death had to be cleansed by a ceremony typical of the work of Christ. (See *The Law of Moses*, chapter xxviii). The reformation of Israel, associated with this symbolic cleansing, is also referred to by Jeremiah: "I will make a new covenant with the house of Israel ... after those days I will put my law in their inward parts, and write it in their hearts" (31:31,33). And Zechariah foretold that "in that day there shall be a fountain opened ... for sin and for uncleanness" (13:1). A student of the prophets ought to have recognized that a moral reformation had to take place in the nation before their entrance into the restored Kingdom of God.

Paul explains the language of these testimonies in 2 Corinthians 3. The new covenant is the Abrahamic, confirmed in the blood of Christ. Of this new covenant, Paul was a minister, and the Spirit through Paul had written the terms of the covenant on the fleshy tables of the believer's heart, and not on tables of stone. After contrasting the transient glory of the mediator of the old covenant with the abiding glory of Jesus, Paul affirms that Jesus is the spirit— the antitype—of the law's foreshadowings. With this exposition by Paul, John's words in 1:17,18 might be compared.

Paul's application of the new covenant promises to the saints now, and to Israel in the age to come, gives continuity to the rite of baptism and attaches the words of Jesus to ideas which Nicodemus should have comprehended. "Birth by water" is a washing of regeneration, following an understanding of the purpose of God, and the confession of sin.

What is the birth of the Spirit? There is a baptism of the Holy Spirit which is the work of Jesus in contrast with the water-baptism of John (1:33). This is a future work, and the consummation of the process begun with the birth of water. The doctrine of Christ is one that purifies and sanctifies when its principles are heartily espoused, and the mind is renewed by the gradual assimilation of divine ideas, leading to a transformation of the individual—a changing from glory to glory. The old man is put off, and the new man is put on, and the character so formed is prepared for an abiding place in the Kingdom of God. The moral man thus being developed is still restricted by the impulses of the flesh which war against his desires; but the day of deliverance is kept in mind, and the hope cherished of freedom from this body of death, not by discarding the body, but by the body of humiliation being changed and fashioned after the body of the glory of the Son of God. This is the work of a moment, in the twinkling of an eye, when death will be swallowed up in victory. The energy whereby Christ is able to subdue all things will be used to transform the bodies of his people from corruptible to incorruptible, and the Spirit of God will energize every part.

This birth of the Spirit follows the formative influence of the word of God, which has been given by His Spirit, and which brings about a moral change preparatory to the bestowal of a bodily nature which endures.

The language should not be restricted to the present or the future; there is a present moral aspect, and a future physical aspect, as becomes evident from the further remark of Jesus: "that which is born of the flesh is flesh, and that which is born of the Spirit is spirit". The flesh produces its own kind, with its limitations and weaknesses and defects; its mortality unfits it for the Kingdom of God. The source of fitness is ultimately of God: and the obvious parallel suggests that as in the birth of the flesh, flesh is put for human parents, so in the birth of the Spirit, Spirit is put for God. God's agency in begettal is His word, as James declares (1:18); and the resultant new creature is called by Paul "the spirit" in contrast with "the flesh" in a series of parallels in Romans 7 and 8. We have had fathers of our flesh, and we gave them reverence; shall we not much rather be in subjection unto the Father of our spirits, and live? as Paul asks the Hebrews (12:9).

The whole process is covered by Jesus in his next remark: "Marvel not that I said unto thee, Ye must be born again. The Spirit breathes where He pleases, and thou (Nicodemus) hearest His voice, but thou perceivest not how he is come, and in what he goes away". With this translation Dr. Thomas, the RV and others may be compared.

The Spirit, according to His will, was then speaking in Jesus. The words of Jesus were the Spirit's words, powerful with life-giving energy when received into honest hearts. But Nicodemus had not then attained to an understanding of the work of the Spirit in connection with Jesus. There was a coming and a going away of the Spirit. How had the Spirit come? The answer is to be found in the record of the birth of Jesus. "The Holy Spirit shall overshadow thee", said the angel to Mary. It is to be found again in what happened when Jesus was baptized, when the Spirit descended upon him. Jesus was such a manifestation of God as Israel had not before witnessed. He was related to the Eternal as no prophet had been. The whole operation was of God, and at the time Jesus was speaking the operation was not complete. For after his resurrection, the same Spirit, energizing with immortal life the body of Jesus, went away to the Father. How could Nicodemus "tell" this? If the previous words of Jesus had caused him surprise, it was not to be expected that he would be equal to such discernment.

But to understand the divine process qualifying men for the Kingdom, the work of God in Jesus must be perceived. For "so is every one that is born of the Spirit". In every case there is a divine begettal; in Jesus, physical, resulting in a body prepared to do the will of God; in others, mental and moral (Ephesians 4:24); but in all cases a change of nature by that transforming spirit which makes one a partaker of the divine nature.

More than ever at a loss, Nicodemus says, "How can these things be?" Should he have known? Undoubtedly, in the light of the reply of Jesus. There is reproachful surprise in the reply: "Art thou the teacher of Israel, and knowest not these things?" If the teacher had not attained to this knowledge, what was the state of his pupils?

But if Nicodemus did not know, there was not that want of knowledge in Jesus. He therefore solemnly affirms that "We speak that we do know, and testify that we have seen; and ye receive not our witness. If I have told you earthly things, and ye believe not, how shall ye believe, if I tell you heavenly things?" (verses 11,12).

"That *we* do know"—there is first of all a contrast with the claims to knowledge which Nicodemus had made at the opening of the interview: "We know that thou art a teacher come from God". Did they know that? Here then the acknowledged teacher affirms his knowledge of higher things, of experimental knowledge beyond that of Nicodemus. Who are the others included in the "we" used by Jesus? John the forerunner, without doubt (see verse 22). Then, if any of the disciples were present, they may be included also. The "we" covers the Christ-body, the rulers of the Age to Come, who had attained to a fuller knowledge than the rulers of that day, and who would supersede them.

There is a change in the pronoun to be noticed: *"ye* receive not our witness". Nicodemus may be included in the "ye"; but at any rate Jesus does not single him out by saying "thou"; he was the representative of the body which rejected the witness of Jesus, although he himself came gradually to a full acceptance of it.

"Earthly things" had been disclosed in the previous announcements of Jesus, which the rulers had not believed. It was too much to expect them to receive the heavenly things connected with the Sonship of the Messiah, the manifestation of the Father in him, and the ultimate manifestation of sons of God by adoption in him. Such communications were within his power; and, before completing his record of the interview, John interposes a parenthetic statement to prove this. Verse 13 calls for fuller consideration because of the difficulty some have found in it, and also because of its own importance.

A HARD SAYING (3:13)

SEVERAL matters in connection with this verse call for remark. There is a question of text—whether part of the verse should be omitted. Then, Are the words spoken by Jesus, or are they a comment by John? Lastly, What is the meaning of the language used?

The last clause "which is in heaven" is "omitted by many ancient authorities"; so the margin of the RV tells us. What are these "ancient authorities"? Had the Revisers good reasons for suggesting a doubt about the words? What are the facts?

The clause is found in every MS except five; it is recognized by all the Latin and all the Syriac versions and other versions except the Ethiopic; it is quoted by about forty Fathers. Why then have the Revisers cast doubt upon all these? The answer is to be found in the obsession Westcott and Hort had for the Vatican MS, particularly when supported by "Aleph" (the Sinaitic). Both these MSS are characterized by faulty omissions, and most of the marginal notes of the RV are due to the singular weakness of Hort for MS "B" (Vatican). As McClellan remarks: It is "another fatal error of Aleph, B, and of Westcott and Hort following". Against an overwhelming mass of evidence in favour of the words, they have allowed four uncials, one cursive, one MS of Memphitic version, and one version, to throw this unwarranted doubt upon the text. It is a sad defect of the Revised Version, and it is being increasingly recognized that Hort's judgment with regard to the value and accuracy of the two MSS, "B" and "Aleph", was in error. Even Tischendorf (who had an understandable weakness for the Sinaitic), with Lachman and Tregelles, acknowledges the phrase. Burgon calls this marginal note "a shameful mis-statement"; we agree with him. As A. C. Clark has shown, the words in all probability represent a line dropped by some careless scribe, and the transcribers of these two MSS were grievous offenders in this respect. It may indeed be in part only one offender, since it has been thought that one hand wrote some of both. Scrivener says:

"We have a consensus of versions and ecclesiastical writers from every part of the Christian world, joining Codex A and the later manuscripts in convicting Aleph, B, L, or the common sources from which they were derived, of the deliberate suppression of one of the most mysterious, yet one of the most glorious, glimpses afforded to us in the scripture of the nature of the Saviour."

(*Introduction to Textual Criticism*, ii,361)

For ourselves, we gravely suspect the marginal notes of the RV which begin, "Some ancient authorities read ..."; while acknowledging help received from a comparison of the two versions, the AV and RV, as translations.

The words "which is in heaven" being thus part of the text, we can pass to the next question: Were the words of verse 13 spoken by Jesus, or are they an inspired comment by John? The clause, "which is in heaven", could hardly be spoken by Jesus to Nicodemus, unless we give to them, as some have done, a very fanciful and figurative meaning. But if we treat the verse as a parenthetic remark of the gospel writer, the difficulty is removed. The AV of 1611, as printed in *Scrivener's Parallel New Testament, Greek and English,* and in the *Two Version Bible,* puts paragraph marks at verses 14 and 16; but the *Companion Bible* advances good reasons for making the break at verse 13. We therefore conclude that the verse is by John, written to show that Jesus was fully qualified to discourse to Nicodemus about "heavenly things", however lacking in understanding Nicodemus might have been.

We come then to the meaning of the words. Since we find expressions which recur in other chapters in John's gospel, a fairly exhaustive examination of their usage in the scriptures at this point will serve for later references also.

The language of the New Testament has its roots in the Old Testament. One ignorant of the Old Testament is disqualified to interpret the New Testament. To the Old Testament we must go, and trace out these ideas of "ascent" and "descent".

Twice we read of the Lord's *coming down* to judgment; when the speech of man was confounded (Genesis 11:5), and when Sodom was destroyed (18:21), both events typical of divine judgment. But we also read, and this is more important in the present investigation, of God's coming down for the deliverance of His people. Joseph looked for it when he said, "God will surely visit you, and bring you out of this land". When the time came, God appeared to Moses at the bush, and said, "I have surely seen the affliction of my people which are in Egypt, and have heard their cry by reason of their taskmasters; for I know their sorrows; and I am come down to deliver them out of the hand of the Egyptians, and to bring them up out of that land unto a good land and a large, unto a land flowing with milk and honey" (Exodus 3:7,8). The language is repeated at the revelation at Sinai: "The third day the LORD will come down ... the LORD descended ... and the LORD came down upon Mount Sinai" (Exodus 19:11,18,20). Once again, when God revealed his name to Moses, we are told, "And the LORD descended in a cloud, and stood with him there, and proclaimed the name of the LORD" (Exodus 34:5). "Thou camest down" is the mode of description employed in the song of praise of the Levites, when they recounted the events of the Exodus on their return from exile (Nehemiah 9:13). Stephen quotes the language of Exodus, as recorded in Acts 7:34. In these passages we have easily understood references to the manifestation of God, which is described as a descent of God.

This descent of God for Israel's redemption is the historical basis of the prophecy of the work of Christ in Psalm 68. In Rotherham's translation we read:

> Thou hast ascended on high,
> hast captured a body of captives,

hast accepted gifts consisting of men,
yea, even the stubborn;
that thou mayest dwell there,
O Yah Elohim.

When it is said that God has ascended on high, a prior descent and intervention on behalf of His people is implied. The work of redemption was done, the host of captives were delivered. From them God took as gifts the Levites, and gave them to Aaron (Numbers 17:6; 3:9–12; 8:15,19) for the ministry of the sanctuary.

These events of the Exodus were a parable of the redemption which is in Christ Jesus. Therefore Paul takes the language of the Psalm and applies it to Jesus and to the gifts of apostles and evangelists, given to the church for the equipment of the Body of Christ. He comments particularly upon the words "he ascended", and reasons that they show that he first descended into the lower parts of the earth (Ephesians 4:9,10). To ascend requires a previous descent; not indeed of the man Jesus, but of that spirit which had descended at his birth, and which ascended embodied in the resurrected and immortalized body of Jesus. The Dayspring from on high visited His people; and when the redemption was accomplished returned to heaven.

Long before David's day, Moses had used similar language. He tells of another covenant besides the one Israel had entered into at Sinai (Deuteronomy 29:1), when they would have returned to God, with circumcised heart, and returned to the land from which they had been driven out (Deuteronomy 30:2,4,6). Then the commandment would be nigh to them: "It is not in heaven, that thou shouldest say, Who shall go up for us to heaven, and bring it unto us, that we may hear it, and do it? Neither is it beyond the sea, that thou shouldest say, Who shall go over the sea for us, and bring it unto us, that we may hear it, and do it? But the word is very nigh unto thee, in thy mouth, and in thy heart, that thou mayest do it" (verses 11–14). This "word", Paul says, is the word of faith which he preached; the doctrine of the forgiveness of sins in a crucified obedient Son of God, raised from the dead for the justification of all who believe in him. And Paul explains the question, "Who shall go up for us into heaven?" as meaning, Who shall bring the Messiah down from above? that is, Who can bring into being the Son of God who is necessary for our salvation? The descent into the deep Paul explains as meaning, Who shall bring up Christ from the dead? (Romans 10:6,7). It is interesting to find that the

59

Jewish Rabbis made a similar application to that of Paul of these words of Moses, even connecting the reference to the deep with the experience of Jonah and his resurrection from "the belly of sheol".

The prophecy of Moses, then, in the light of Paul's application of the words, foretells that at Israel's restoration, when they see Jesus, the questions of the birth and resurrection of the Saviour will not be problems for human solution. Both will have been accomplished by God, and human achievement will be excluded. The facts connected with Jesus will be nigh to them, for the confession of their mouth and the belief of their heart.

A similar form of speech occurs in the Proverbs. Agur asks: "Who hath ascended up into heaven, or descended? Who hath gathered the winds in his fists? Who hath bound the waters in a garment? Who hath established all the ends of the earth? What is his name, and what is his son's name, if thou canst tell?" (30:4). The same association of ideas is here—an ascent, and a descent, and a son of God. We can now tell the son's name, for the account of the angelically bestowed name is recorded for us in the four gospels, and also its meaning. When he had fulfilled the prophecy of his name—He shall save his people from their sins—it was then put forward in the preaching of the apostles as the only name given among men whereby they could be saved. God has descended, and ascended; a Son has been born, has died, and been raised; and has ascended to his Father. The question of Agur, What is His Son's name? is one that clearly reveals the coming of a Son of God.

This style of language throws much light upon the prophecy of Immanuel (Isaiah 7). The critics have floundered badly here; they cannot see how a son of a virgin, born some seven hundred years after Isaiah's day, could be a sign to Ahaz, and misunderstanding the import of the sign dismiss the miraculous altogether, and treat the prophecy as having reference to a child shortly to be born of a young woman. But that will not do, in view of the New Testament application of the prophecy to Jesus. We must therefore look at it again.

The history of the time provides the first clue. Syria and Israel feared a joint attack by Assyria and Judah, a scissors action in which they would be caught between the blades. To prevent this they proposed to dethrone Ahaz, and put in his place a nominee of their own. Had Ahaz been a man of faith, he would have reasoned that God had promised that a descendant of David, who would also be the Son of God, should occupy his throne for ever. God's interest in the throne was the best security possible, and to trust in God was the best of policies as well as a duty. He might have recognized, and if he had any faith in the promises of God he would have recognized, that being in the succession he might have the honour of being the ancestor of the Son of God. But Ahaz was not a man of faith, and proposed the very alliance which the two northern confederates feared. The prophet foretold the overthrow of Syria and Ephraim, but added, "if ye will not believe, surely ye shall not be established".

Ahaz was invited to ask a sign. We must mark well the terms used describing the form of the sign, especially in the light of the usage already reviewed. "Ask thee a sign of the LORD thy God; ask it either in the depth, or in the height above." In other words, Ask a sign of the birth of the Son of God, or of his resurrection; ask a sign of the seed of David, in whose hands this throne, the safety of which you now fear, will be established for ever.

Ahaz had no faith; he did not doubt the giving of the sign, but he lacked the courage to act on the sign if given. His heart was set upon Assyria, and not on God. He therefore with hypocrisy distasteful alike to God and the prophet, said he would not tempt the Lord his God. To decline a sign on such a plea is an affront to the Holy One of Israel. No sign was to be given to the king; but the house of David is asked to give heed to the sign God would give. "A virgin *shall* conceive, and bear a son, and shall call his name Immanuel." It was the central point and the proof of God's intention to fulfil the Davidic covenant concerning the throne of Israel. Granted that, all else would follow. So God reaffirms this essential feature that a son would be born, and the throne of David would last for ever under his rule.

The language of ascent and descent is once more associated with the virgin birth.

In another chapter (64) Isaiah speaks of God's rending the heavens and coming down, and of the Messiah's vision of what God had prepared for them that love him.

"He bowed the heavens also, and came down ... and he rode upon a cherub" (Psalm 18:9,10). Thus it came to pass. "The bread of God is he that came down from heaven", who said, "I came down from heaven", and "I am the living bread which came down from heaven". He also said to the followers stumbling at these hard sayings, "What and if ye shall see the Son of Man ascend up where he was before?" At the close of his ministry he said, "I came forth from the Father, and am

61

come into the world: again I leave the world, and go to the Father".

Do we find these things "hard sayings"? Or are we prepared to study the style of scripture language, and see, in the words of Jesus, echoes of the Old Testament statements of God's manifestation in the deliverance of Israel from the bondage of Egypt, and the Old Testament prophecies of that manifestation of God in a Son which is the climax of all revelation, for the deliverance of man from the bondage of sin and death?

We go back to the meeting of Jesus and Nicodemus. We hear the teacher sent from God ask again, "If I told you earthly things, and ye believe not, how shall ye believe, if I tell you heavenly things?" Can he tell us heavenly things? Of higher truths than those pertaining to Israel's restoration, and the restoration of the kingdom to them? Of a revelation of God in a family of sons redeemed by the work of a firstborn; of the revelation of God as Father because the Son of God has come? While he phrases the words "My Father", he also teaches all who are in him to say, because they have received the spirit of adoption, "Our Father". Can he tell of these things, and of the manifestation yet to be, in sons of God all made equal unto the angels, sanctified in him whom God has made to them wisdom, and righteousness, and sanctification, and redemption? He can tell of these things; he is the chief witness of this last and completest phase of God's revelation. That he could do this, says John, is proved by fact that he has ascended to God, who first came from God, and who is now with God.

"Lifted Up" (3:14,15)

WE return to the conversation of Jesus and Nicodemus; and so doing meet again the problem of separating the discourse of Jesus and the reflections of John in what is written. There are differences of judgment; and, in some cases perhaps, certainty of where the words of Jesus end may be beyond reach. The teaching, however, remains, whether the words were spoken by Jesus or are the testimony of the gospel-writer. We give the analysis which in our judgment best accords with the facts and the language used.

Verses 14,15 continue, and probably conclude the report of the words of Jesus to Nicodemus. We are not told of their effect upon the ruler, nor of any further response on his part.

The suggestion that a "lifting up" after the type of the uplifted serpent in the wilderness was necessary for the Son of man, probably completed his bewilderment at the time. How far light began to break upon him when he saw Jesus on the cross, who can say? But with the resurrection of Jesus, the truth concerning the sacrificial work of the Messiah would become more and more clear, and life in a crucified Christ would be seen to be a necessary step to the eternal inheritance of the Kingdom of God.

It deserves note that many of the miracles of the Old Testament which are rejected by the Modernist are confirmed by Jesus, and are regarded by him as types of his own work. The events of the Exodus particularly were a source of instruction to him concerning himself. He quoted the book of Deuteronomy in his own trial in the wilderness; and the manna, the smitten rock, and the pillar of fire, were for him authoritative foreshadowings of his own origin, sufferings, and God's purpose with him. We cannot accept Christ and doubt Moses; we cannot believe what is written in the gospels and reject the record of what is written of the Exodus. The two go together—the one a divinely arranged typical history, the other a divinely guided fulfilment. If the lifting up of the serpent had all the force of a command to Jesus, telling him that he "must" be lifted up, how can the writings of Moses be regarded by the follower of Jesus as any other than the word of God, and the events recorded as true history?

Near the end of the forty years the lessons of the wandering had so far failed to teach the children of Israel trust in God, that they were again discouraged when compassing the land of Edom, and their murmuring brought the punishment of a plague of serpents, which wrought much destruction among them. The people repented and acknowledged their sin.

"And the LORD said unto Moses, Make thee a fiery serpent, and set it upon a pole: and it shall come to pass, that everyone that is bitten, when he looketh upon it, shall live. And Moses made a serpent of brass, and put it upon a pole, and it came to pass, that if a serpent had bitten any man, when he beheld the serpent of brass, he lived."

(Numbers 21:8,9)

It is not difficult to trace the parallels of this sign of Christ's salvation. The serpent's association with sin at the beginning—suggesting disobedience, and framing the lie concerning God—makes it a fit symbol of the flesh, which from the day of transgression has had a law in its members, hindering the will to do good by the "evil present". "In me, that is, in my flesh, dwells no good thing", said Paul. That mode of thinking, modelled on that of the serpent, is by a figure, the serpent in us. All are bitten; the virus of the serpent bringing forth death in all.

Doubly emphasizing this aspect, not only was the means of salvation formed in the likeness of the destroyer, but the material used teaches the same lesson, as though proclaiming that not only in outward form, but in substance there must be identity with the sin-stricken nature. Brass (or copper), in colour suggestive of the flesh, is associated with the flesh in other types. Form and substance unite in teaching that the Saviour lifted up must wear the flesh of sin in which Sin was to be condemned. The apostolic language is emphatic: God sent His own son in the likeness of sinful flesh; God hath made him to be sin for us who knew no sin.

"Who knew no sin"; the serpent lifted up was not a struggling, biting, dangerous creature, spreading death while being nailed to the tree. It was harmless, and unresisting; as also was the one who was led as a lamb to the slaughter, and who, as a sheep before her shearers is dumb, opened not his mouth. No guile was found in his mouth, who his own self bare our sins in his body to the tree, by whose stripes we are healed.

There was an element of the improbable, from the human point of view. How could an image of the destroyer be the source of life? What virtue was there in the brazen serpent held up to view? None in itself, but as a divine appointment there was. Faith found the reward which was only to be obtained by faith. Where unbelief reigned, there death also reigned; but where faith in God triumphed over any doubt of the efficacy of the means, healing and life followed. So it is with the antitype. A crucified king was to the Jews a stumblingblock, and to the Greeks foolishness. What is there of value to others in the nailing of a Jew to a tree in a Roman province some nineteen hundred years ago? So say the scoffers of every age; but they die, overcome by sin, which reigns unto death. But faith, instructed by the word of God, sees in him one whom God has made unto us sanctification, even wisdom and righteousness and redemption. In the death of Christ the wisdom of God, the righteousness of God, and the redemption of God are all revealed. It was not simply the crucifixion of a man—the thieves, too, were crucified. But in the death of Jesus certain moral principles were shown, which God required to be set forth as the ground for the exercise of His forgiveness and healing power.

The voluntary setting forth of the righteousness of God was required, as Paul declares (Romans 3:21–26), and for this it was essential that the redeemer should partake of our nature. The denial of this strikes at the root of God's plan; hence the insistence by John that those who deny that Christ has come in the flesh are antichrist, and must not be received. The material and the shape of the typical serpent lifted up by Moses attest the truth insisted upon by John.

Jesus understood this foreshadowing of his work. It was clear to him before his ministry began. It was gradually, and later with greater insistence, pressed upon the unwilling ears of the disciples, who failed to comprehend it until after his resurrection. His own ears had been opened to the instruction of God: "The Lord hath opened mine ear, and I was not rebellious, nor turned away back". Therefore he spoke of the temple of his body being destroyed, and also of this lifting up. As he said later, "When ye have lifted up the Son of man, then shall ye know that I am he". "And I, if I be lifted up, will draw all men unto me." It is still possible, when the true nature of man is understood, and the need for healing perceived, to turn in faith to the one who was lifted up in weakness, and find peace and rest and the confidence begotten by faith in God's word, and to look to that lifting up in power as an ensign upon the mountains of Israel for all Gentiles to turn unto, in hope of sharing his rest which shall be glorious. For this lifting up of the Messiah, Nicodemus doubtless looked. He had to learn of the cross that came before the crown.

REFLECTIONS (3:16–21)

WHY should the "lifting up" of the Son of man be necessary that men might have life? John answers in the most frequently quoted, best known verse of scripture: "God so loved the world, that he gave his only begotten Son, that whosoever believeth in him should not perish, but have everlasting life." Yet how little is its significance appreciated, and its doctrinal bearing considered. Because God loved the world, He gave. The moral principles of righteousness and justification are explained by Paul in his epistles. Here John goes back to the motive that caused God to do what He has done, not indeed by setting aside any of His attributes, but finding a way in harmony with them. Beyond our power to

65

grasp in its height and depth, it is yet expressed in terms illustrated many times in human life.

God gave—it was not ours by right, no claims at all could be made; and all the glory is to God. Paul does not neglect this phase, but finds a place for this with all the other aspects of the subject. "God commendeth his love toward us, in that while we were yet sinners, Christ died for us." "The love of Christ constraineth me." "He loved me and gave himself for me." This love was seen in God's care for Israel:

"In all their affliction he was afflicted, and the angel of his presence saved them; in his love and in his pity he redeemed them; and he bare them, and carried them all the days of old." (Isaiah 63:9)

But the angel of His presence gives place in this to the only begotten Son. We are reconciled by the death of His Son. He that spared not His own Son, how shall He not with him freely give us all things?

There is a condition governing the receipt of the gift. From the Lord's reference to the faith of the Israelite in connection with the uplifted serpent is taken the phrase "that whosoever believeth in him". It supplies the necessary condition apart from which there could be no fitness, or appreciation of, the gift of life in the Son.

The perishing contrasts with everlasting life. By the contrast the former clearly denotes death, as also does the analogy of the serpent-bitten dying Israelites. The full force of this is sometimes evaded by pointing to the use of the same word in the parables of the "lost" coin, and the "lost" sheep. It is sufficient answer to say, that while so described the coins and the sheep had ceased to exist as possessions to the woman and the shepherd, and the limitations of their knowledge caused the coin and the sheep to be described as "lost". But there is no such limitation with God, and those who do not believe cease to exist, an end to which all would have come unless God had given His Son.

The primary purpose of Christ's coming is thus seen to be man's salvation. There is no racial limit to this as the Jew supposed. Therefore by a threefold using of the phrase "the world" John rebukes the narrow view of the Jew who restricted Messiah's salvation to his own race, but reserved Messiah's judgments for the Gentiles. To this John makes answer that "God sent not his son into the world to condemn the world; but that the world through him might be saved". Jew and Gentile are equal in this matter. Not that judgment is by this statement excluded. It follows of necessity where there is rejection of the Son.

This is explained in the next four verses. The believer is not condemned—he is saved. But the rejecter, by his rejection is condemned already; the sentence has not been formally pronounced, but the act of rejection has determined an issue which will be declared. When light comes, men's response determines the future. The reaction that allows its searching rays to reveal the defects and to cleanse and lead away from the love of evil, decides the test. Light and Truth are both expressive of the revelation of God, and the one who responds shows the divine influence in his life (verses 18–21).

FINAL TESTIMONY OF THE BAPTIST TO JESUS (3:22–30)

JOHN mentions a ministry of Jesus in Judea, evidently of but a few weeks duration, about which the Synoptists are silent. Jesus taught and practised baptism, the rite itself being administered by his disciples (4:2). Greater numbers responded to the call of Jesus than to that of John; and this appears to have led to a dispute with the Jews (or, a Jew, RV) upon the relative values of the two baptisms. The disciples of John approach their master and say to him: "Rabbi, he that was with thee beyond Jordan, to whom thou barest witness, behold the same baptizeth, and all men come unto him". The answer of John (verses 27–30) reveals in all its greatness the nobility of John.

He witnessed that the baptism of Jesus, and his office, was of God, and that he had before testified that he was but the forerunner of the Christ. He was, in a changed figure, the friend of the bridegroom, and not the bridegroom himself; yet his was the joy of the friend. Finally he testified to his own inevitable decline, and the advance of Christ, even as the morning star declines before the rising sun.

The figure of the bridegroom is found in the prophets, and is based upon the divine method of the creation of the woman. It is used of Israel after the flesh, but more particularly of the higher relationship of Israel after the spirit, who, joined to the Lord, are "one spirit" with him (Isaiah 54:5; 61:10; Jeremiah 3:14; Hosea 2; Ephesians 5; Revelation 19:21; 1 Corinthians 6:17).

This answer of John seems to have been known to Jesus, for when John's disciples came to Jesus and asked why his disciples did not fast, Jesus answered:

"Can the children of the bridechamber mourn, as long as the bridegroom is with them? but the days will come, when the bridegroom shall be taken from them, and then shall they fast." (Matthew 9:15)

It recalled the answer of their own master concerning the bridegroom, and had they caught the meaning of John, they would have seen why the disciples of Jesus should not follow the self-imposed fast of the Pharisees. But the words of Jesus contain another hint that shows that the shadow of the end was ever across his path. The bridegroom had to be taken away, and in the trials to come his disciples would fast of necessity and not of choice.

"He must increase, but I must decrease." It is not easy for all who have been the centre of some work to lay down their task for another to take it up. To accept what has been called "the discipline of obscurity", to consent to the passing of influence to another, to recognize that as strength fails the hill that was once climbed with zest has now become a burden, to say "I must decrease"—it has been said, "There are few harder words". But John knew the joy of the bridegroom's friend, knew the greatness of the one to come after him, felt the satisfaction of a duty almost done, a task drawing to its close. Like all the men of God concerned with critical events, he was humble, recognizing that in the presence of the divine, there is no room for human boasting. The last word on John was said authoritatively by Jesus: "Among them that are born of women there is none greater than John".

FURTHER REFLECTIONS (3:31–36)

THE last six verses of this third chapter are closely allied in thought and expression with earlier verses, particularly verses 15–17, and can be received as another inspired meditation of the gospel-writer on the words he had just written. Jesus must increase, John said. The reason was to be found in the fact that coming from above, he was above all. Others, of earthly origin, spake of "earthly things" and were limited to them. Jesus himself had spoken of "earthly things" to Nicodemus (verse 12), but heavenly things were within the range of his discourse. As Paul says, God spake by the prophets "in divers portions and divers manners", but now He had spoken in a Son. The partial, the fragmentary, yet at no time inaccurate, passed to the perfect and the complete.

The knowledge of Jesus was of a more direct character than that of the prophets, even as Jesus bore a closer relationship to the Father. They were servants, he a Son. And the matters of his testimony were within his experience—"what he had seen and heard". When and under what conditions we do not know. The ministering of angels at his call was only one privilege of God's Son; the words of John suggest revelations and visions, and a knowledge passing that of all others. He was the "true light", not a reflector as the prophets; yet his own received him not; "No man (that is relatively) receiveth his testimony".

The rejection was not universal, for some received the testimony of the Son; and John adds, that to receive the witness of Jesus is to believe God, for Jesus "speaketh the words of God". This statement disposes of the whole of the Modernist attack upon the Bible. If the words of Jesus are the words of God, he is in the completest sense the prophet of whom God said, "I will put my words in his mouth". His endorsement of the scriptures is divine, and puts all the rejecters of his teaching in a serious position, for God has also said, "Whosoever will not hearken to my words which he shall speak in my name, I will require it of him". John repeats this solemn thought; the Son of God has come: God loveth the Son and hath given all things into his hand. These divine acts have brought everlasting life near to man, and have also established a new responsibility. Believing, life is attained; rejecting and disobeying, life is missed. But the mere failure to attain is not the only result. To refuse the approaches of God, to "disobey" God's words spoken by Jesus, leads to God's "requiring" an account of it, or as John puts it, "the wrath of God abideth on him". The wrath of God, the only occurrence of this terrible phrase in the gospels, is the counterpart and necessary complement of the love of God, of which Jesus had been speaking. The "everlasting life" and the "abiding wrath" will be revealed in the day when God judges the secrets of men by Jesus Christ.

AMONG THE SAMARITANS (4:1–42)

FOR a short period John and Jesus were preaching and baptizing at the same time. John was at Ænon, that is, Springs, a place of uncertain identification, while Jesus was in Judea, probably at the Jordan, since sufficient water for baptism was available there. The news of the success attending the preaching of Jesus was brought to the authorities, and knowledge of this came to Jesus. This led him to leave Judea—he "let go" Judea, suggesting that the attitude of the authorities made further labours there undesirable for the present—and to turn northward to Galilee. There were two routes, the direct one through Samaria, usually only undertaken by Jews travelling in companies, and the route which took the traveller across Jordan, and up the eastern side of the river.

The feud between the Jews and the Samaritans was of long standing. The Samaritans were the descendants of the colonists settled in the land when the Assyrians took the ten tribes into captivity. These colonists intermarried with the few Jews left in the land, and claimed racial affinity with Israel. They wished to help in the rebuilding of the temple in the days of Ezra, but were repulsed. A rival temple was built on Mount Gerizim, and one whom Nehemiah expelled was made their first high priest. The hostility between the two races never abated, the fires of hatred being fed by the provocative acts of either one side or the other. Thus, for example, about the time when Jesus visited Jerusalem as a boy, a party of Samaritans travelled secretly one night to Jerusalem, and when the temple gates were opened at dawn, entered the sacred courts and strewed the place with dead bodies. No worse pollution could have been conceived.

John says Jesus "must needs go through Samaria". He took the direct road, but the "need" seems to have been less geographical than caused by the attitude of the Jews in Judea. He "let go" Judea, and found a welcome in Samaria, and a promise of the harvest of the Gentiles to be gathered in by the apostles in later years.

The party of travellers halted in the valley which divides Ebal and Gerizim, at a well dug by Jacob, near the village of Sychar. It was the sixth hour, either noon or approaching evening according to which mode of reckoning John employed. Much has been written on both sides of the question, and while of interest, such points can be discussed to the neglect of matters of much greater importance.

While the disciples went to obtain food—it was permissible to buy certain foods from the Samaritans—Jesus rested by the well side. Two little touches are of human interest. He was wearied; the Son of God partook of the nature of all men, and experienced the limitations of strength which others feel. Then the woman recognized him as a Jew, a detail worth remembering when we think of the national bias usually given by artists in their impressions of the scenes and episodes in the life of Jesus. But though wearied, Jesus was ready to forget his physical needs in the consideration of the needs of others, and the approach of a Samaritan woman to the well brought a fellow-being in need.

Jesus opened the conversation with the request for a drink. It would be made in a friendly and courteous way. The woman looked at him, in part surprised at his friendliness, partly amused at the request having to be made by a Jew to her, and pertly and drily she reminds him of the Jewish attitude which did not allow dealings with Samaritans, and still less with a woman who was a stranger.

She knew he was a Jew; her answer showed that; but she did not know the Jew who was talking to her. So Jesus said, "If thou knewest the gift of God, and who it is that saith to thee, Give me to drink; thou wouldest have asked of him, and he would have given thee living water".

"Living water" was a usual description of running water or a bubbling spring. To talk of giving to her living water when he was at the same time making a request for a drink was perplexing. She was puzzled, but the sincerity and gravity of the speaker did not permit the answer to be lightly dismissed. There was a depth of meaning in the words of Jesus, unperceived by her at the time. A spring of water was sometimes called "a gift of God"; she knew this gift, but did not know that the stranger was God's gift with a thirst-quenching power of an entirely different kind. Neither as yet had she fully discovered that in spiritual things she was the tired and thirsty soul standing at a well of life. Jesus proceeded to rouse her to a recognition of it. Her answer showed that her thought was fixed on the literal water, but with all her perplexity, respect for the stranger was felt. "Sir", she said, "thou hast nothing to draw with, and the well is deep: from whence then hast thou this living water? Art thou greater than our father Jacob, which gave us the well, and drank thereof himself, and his children and his cattle?"

Jesus answered: "Whosoever drinketh of this water shall thirst again: but whosoever drinketh of the water that I shall give him shall never thirst; but the water that I shall give him shall be in him a well of water springing up into ever-lasting life". Her mind still on the natural water, she sees obvious advantages in the gift the stranger says he can bestow. Still bewildered she is yet eager to get the proffered blessing, and replies: "Sir, give me this water, that I thirst not, neither come hither to draw".

The conversation had gone far enough to humble her, to remove the pertness with which she first made answer, and to awaken a lively interest. She was now sincere, but bewildered. The true nature of the gift must now be understood before further conversation would be profitable. Jesus makes a simple request: "Go, call thy husband". It were reasonable that if the gift be bestowed, he must share. The effect of the request was known to Jesus, for the life of the woman was not hidden from him, and his simple direction was designed to bring to light her sins and to reveal her need. "I have no husband", she faltered. "Thou hast well said", Jesus answered, with a little emphasis on the word husband, "I have no husband". And he told her of the number of husbands she had had, and of the present illicit character of the state in which she was living. The words were piercing, penetrating the secrets of the heart. Like Nathanael she discerned that she stood in the presence of one who could read all secret thoughts. Her respect passes to awe as she says, "Sir, I perceive that thou art a prophet".

The situation now can be understood in somewhat this fashion. For a moment or two she stands irresolute; had she to go for the man? She decides not, and instead, asks Jesus, whom she has just acknowledged as a prophet, to decide the disputed question between Jew and Samaritan of the true place of worship, whether Jerusalem or Gerizim? It has been thought that her question was an endeavour to divert the course of the conversation which was becoming inconvenient. But it is better to regard her words as a sincere request on a matter in which, despite her mode of life, she was keenly interested. The answer of Jesus contains one of his profoundest utterances, thrown into the greater relief because of the strangeness of the situation and the hearer.

"Woman, believe me", thus with quiet emphasis Jesus began, "the hour cometh, when ye shall neither in this mountain, nor yet at Jerusalem, worship the Father. Ye worship ye know not what: we know what we worship: for salvation is of the Jews. But the hour cometh, and now is, when the true worshippers shall worship the Father in spirit and in truth: for the Father seeketh such to worship him. God is a Spirit: and they that worship him must worship him in spirit and in truth."

These remarkable words, telling of coming dispensational changes, and setting forth the true basis of approach to God, made the woman think of the coming of the Messiah. While the Samaritans only accepted the Pentateuch, their ideas must have been influenced by Jewish thought and expectation, particularly in those matters which were rooted in the books which they acknowledged. In this case, the woman's words, "He will tell us all things", are clearly based upon the words of Moses concerning the prophet to come, "He shall speak unto them all that I shall command him". Is this he? she pensively wonders; and Jesus putting aside the reserve he had exercised among his own people, made the simple announcement to a Samaritan woman, "I that speak unto thee am he".

At this point the disciples returned, and marvelled that he spake with a woman, a thing forbidden to the Rabbis, but they refrained from asking him the questions they were putting to themselves. This interruption of the disciples caused her to leave. Forgetting her waterpot, she hurries back to the village, and cries, "Come, see a man, which told me all things that ever I did: is not this the Christ?"

We might profitably stop to ponder the meaning of the words of Jesus for our own sakes. The "living water" is the word of God with its fresh, vital, living message. God was the author, and the source of its living power. The figure is used of God Himself in a pathetic lament on Israel's desertion of Him. "My people have committed two evils: they have forsaken me the fountain of living waters, and hewed them out cisterns, broken cisterns, that can hold no water" (Jeremiah 2:13).

When the Assyrian in Isaiah's days tried to beguile the besieged inhabitants of Jerusalem into abandoning resistance, he invited them to return to their vineyards and orchards, and "drink ye every one the water of his own cistern". The invitation was a snare and a deceit, and the prophet called the people back to the covenant promises of God in the words: "Ho, every one that thirsteth, come ye to the waters ... Incline your ear, and come to me: hear, and your soul shall live; and I will make an everlasting covenant with you, even the sure mercies of David" (Isaiah 55:1–3). When that is fulfilled another prophecy of Isaiah will also be: "They shall not hunger, nor thirst; neither shall the sun smite them: for he that hath mercy on them shall lead them, even by *the springs of water* shall he guide them" (49:10).

Jesus is the "gift of God", and his words are a fresh spring, quenching thirst, and giving everlasting life.

His words about worship are in keeping with this. Where ought we to worship? the woman asked. The rival places were Jerusalem and Gerizim. Jesus said the truth was with the

Jews; Jerusalem was the place which God had chosen; salvation was from the Jews. But the question of place would shortly be of little consequence, and the change was in process then. Where? Jesus answered that worship would be acceptable anywhere; the necessary conditions were in the worshipper, and not in the place.

The true worshipper is the real worshipper, as against the formal observer of rites and ceremonies. In spirit and in truth contrasts with the external and the typical. The latter became very hateful to God because Israel trusted in them to the neglect of the weightier matters of the law. The Creator could not find acceptable approach in mere observance of ritual. At any time when it was appointed it must be observed, but it was only a means and not an end. It was about to be abolished, with the last vestiges of Israel's national life; and with the overthrow of Jerusalem, God's reprobation of the place for the time was definitely established.

God is a Spirit—a word for which it is difficult to find a synonym. It does not mean that God is immaterial. He is everywhere present by His spirit, while He dwells in some central place in light unapproachable. But since Jesus uses the word also of the acceptable worshipper of God, we might extend the thought in this way. God is holy: so must His worshippers be; He is perfect: so must they be; He is true: so must they be. He is the ultimate reality, and they must manifest those aspects of character which have abiding value, being in themselves all that was signified by the typical things connected with the ritual of the law. Paul has some interesting contrasts between letter and spirit in Romans 2:26–29, and 2 Corinthians 3:6, which are closely connected with the thought of Jesus.

These words of Jesus must have provided much comfort for the people of God in times of trial and conflict. Pagan and papal persecutions have driven men to seek the seclusion of dens and caves, woods, and other hiding places, that they might worship their God. Marble domes and costly spires add nothing to the worship of God, but have become the mark of departure from true worship. "The Father seeketh" as His worshippers the humble and contrite; and such are the children of God.

When the woman had gone, the disciples, remembering his wearied state when they left him, urged Jesus to eat. But physical needs are forgotten in times of mental stress or elation. The joy of service, and the satisfaction attending the response of the woman, had taken the place of food for the moment. He told them: "I have meat to eat that ye know not" (RV)—his experience was unknown to them as yet. His words were not understood; they wondered if others had provided him with food. Looking up at the Samaritans streaming out of the village, he said:

"My meat is to do the will of him that sent me, and to finish his work. Say not ye, There are yet four months, and then cometh harvest? behold I say unto you, Lift up your eyes, and look on the fields; for they are white already to harvest. And he that reapeth receiveth wages, and gathereth fruit unto life eternal: that both he that soweth and he that reapeth may rejoice together. And herein is that saying true, One soweth, and another reapeth. I sent you to reap that whereon ye bestowed no labour: other men laboured, and ye are entered into their labours."

(John 4:34–38)

Jesus uses words which recall Isaiah's language concerning the gathering of Zion's children in the day of her exaltation: "Lift up thine eyes round about, and behold: all these gather themselves together, and come to thee" (49:18). Even then the Lord himself was realizing the joy of sowing and reaping, and gathering fruit unto life eternal. He was the sower, and he called them to be fellowlabourers with him.

The work is one of toil and sometimes hardship. The clouds and the rain may discourage going out into the fields; but it has to be done at the cost of present advantage and comfort. It may even entail the suffering of present loss for future gain. In the words of the Psalmist,

"They that sow in tears shall reap in joy. He that goeth forth and weepeth, bearing precious seed, shall doubtless come again with rejoicing, bringing his sheaves with him."

(126:5,6)

It is a picture of taking that which the farmer would fain use as food, and casting it into the earth. Hunger must be faced and endured, but the harvest will turn weeping into joy. But if the hardship of the present is avoided by using the seed as food, the harvest cannot be reaped, and the short present gain is at the cost of greater future good. The gratification of the present inevitably brings the famine which spells death.

The Samaritans on this, as on other occasions, made a response which put the Jews to shame. Jesus had left Judea, and Samaria opened its doors. The Jews rejected the testimony of the prophets, of John, and of the Son of God; while a woman's testimony leads a village to entertain the Lord for two days, and to find in him the Saviour of the world. It was an illustration of the sowing and the reaping and the fellowship of the work of which Jesus had spoken.

THE SECOND SIGN: HEALING THE NOBLEMAN'S SON (4:43–54)

JESUS went from Samaria to Galilee, testifying that a prophet had no honour in his own country. The remark is obscure in this connection, but may perhaps refer to the want of response in Judea which had led him to go north to Galilee. Here he was received, the Galilean pilgrims having seen the miracles in Jerusalem. Arriving at Cana, the scene of the first miracle, a king's officer came to him, whose son was sick at Capernaum, some twenty miles away, and besought him to heal his son. The man appears to have regarded Jesus as a wonder-worker, and had the limited view that Christ's presence was necessary to perform the cure. But Jesus was not only a performer of wonderful things; he was the prophet of the Lord. The miracles were not his primary work, but were attestations of his claims. The man was in a state of nervous stress, and the apparent repulse had a steadying effect, giving thought opportunity to assert itself. But he was in earnest, and his impassioned appeal brought the response, "Go thy way; thy son liveth". Could he rise to the faith that the word of Jesus had healing power at that distance? He did, and believing, went his way, and found that healing had come when Jesus spoke the word; and he and his house believed.

John marks this as the second sign. It exhibited that healing which was to attend the work of the Word made flesh.

THE THIRD SIGN: HEALING THE LAME MAN (5:1–18)

IN chapter 5 we meet another of the omissions of the RV. In a note to verse 3 the Revisers tell us that "many ancient authorities insert wholly, or in part", the last phrase of verse 3, and verse 4. Against this evidence, the Revisers have felt it necessary to omit about a verse and a half. Can we follow their guidance here? or must we, as on a previous occasion, hold fast to the AV? It would be convenient to accept the decision of the Revisers, as it would remove a difficulty; as A. T. Robertson says of verse 4: "It is clearly not a part of the gospel of John. The periodicity of this miracle made it troublesome for interpreters. But they are now relieved of this burden". But the question of text depends upon evidence.

We have before referred to the work of A. C. Clark. A classical scholar, his work on the text of Cicero led him to the conclusion that omissions usually consisted of one or more lines dropped by the copyist, often through two lines ending with the same word; and this led him to the conclusion that the rule laid down by Griesbach, and accepted by most textual critics, that the shorter reading was always to be preferred, was false. It had no foundation in fact. Afterwards he applied his methods to the Gospels and Acts, and using the arithmetical test of counting letters, came to the conclusion that the Revisers had followed faulty manuscripts in their deletions from the text of scripture. "The primitive text is the longest, not the shortest."

Attention has been directed in previous notes to the character of the Vatican and Sinaitic Manuscripts in this respect. Clark says: "It is obvious that the scribe of the Sinaitic, or of an intermediate ancestor, was particularly prone to these omissions". Of the Sinaitic Syriac Version he says "it omits with the greatest freedom". He quotes with approval the words of Salmon: "It would seem as if in the judgment of the new editors, *any* evidence was good enough to justify an omission". Salmon points out the inconsistency of the Revisers with regard to the Bezan text, which is usually treated as of light weight, but which is regarded as a good witness and of value in its omissions.

On the value which Hort attached to the Vatican MS we quote some words from Salmon's little book, *Some Criticism of the Text of the New Testament*, in which he makes merry over Hort's weakness for "B". Salmon says:

"Hort, if consulted upon what authority should be followed, might answer, 'Follow B—Aleph: accept their readings as true, unless there is strong internal evidence to the contrary, and never think it safe to reject them absolutely'. But suppose B has not the support of Aleph? 'Still follow B, if it has the support of any other MS.' But suppose B stands alone? 'Unless it is clearly a clerical error, it is not safe to reject B.' But supposing B is defective? 'Then follow Aleph.' What about adopting the Western reading ? 'What about killing a man?'"

But what authorities omit the words now in question? As might be expected from the foregoing, the fourth verse is omitted by the Sinaitic (Aleph), the Vatican (B), Ephraemi (C), and the Bezan (D); and the character of these MSS does

not encourage us to put trust in them. The advice of Sir
Robert Anderson in his *Bible and Modern Criticism* is very
good:

"The advice I venture to offer to readers who cannot
revise the RV for themselves, is this: Read the Gospels
always in the AV, using the RV only as a book of reference;
and when the text differs, assume that the AV is right, for
in the great majority of cases it is so".

The words omitted in John 5 contain the number of letters
that correspond to a number of lines in a MS, as A. C. Clark
shows; and there is every probability that the omission has
come about through careless copying.

All this being said, verse 4 remains to be explained. There
was a pool called Bethesda—House of Mercy—at which a
great crowd of ailing people gathered to be ready to step into
the water when it was "moved". The water appears to have
been an intermittent spring, having certain medicinal
qualities which were more efficacious after a movement had
agitated it. This apparently natural phenomenon was
popularly accredited to an angelic visit; and by the addition
of a parenthesis to verse 4, as suggested in *The Companion
Bible*, to the effect that it was so thought, the difficulty is
met. John explains the reason of the gathering at the pool,
and the popular explanation of the ebullition and the
curative properties of the pool: "For (it was said that) an
angel went down at a certain season".

The visit of Jesus was on a sabbath day, and the usual
throng was present. Among them was a case of very long
standing. For thirty-eight years, as Jesus knew intuitively,
the man had dragged himself there, but others were always
quicker in getting into the pool. Jesus asked him, "Wouldest
thou be made whole?" The man would, but his only hope of
healing was by means of being placed in the water, and none
had given him the assistance which he required. Jesus spoke
again, commanding him to rise and walk, and take with him
the mat upon which he was lying. The word took effect;
vigour entered into the man; and he got up and walked. "On
the same day it was the sabbath", John adds, pointing to this
as the explanation of the following discussion, and also
providing the key to the sign.

The Sequel to the Sign (5:9–30)

SINCE the man who was healed was a chronic case, there was no urgency about his need. The following day would have done equally well. The act of Jesus we may therefore conclude was deliberate, and intended to draw the attention of the rulers to himself.

On the way to his home carrying his mat, the healed man was noticed by the rulers, and was at once accosted and charged with a violation of the sabbath. He replied that the one who had healed him had commanded him to carry home his mat. The narrow outlook of the rulers, their Pharisaic prejudice, is seen from the fact that no concern was shown about the miraculous healing, but interest centred in the breaking of the sabbath law. They do not ask, Who healed thee? but, Who ordered you to carry your mat? But the man did not know, and Jesus had withdrawn himself because of the multitude.

Jesus had not finished his work with the man. His suffering was the result of a life of excess, and Jesus would have him realize the need for reform, and a life in keeping with the wholesome change in his bodily condition. He therefore found him in the temple, and quietly addressed him when alone: "Behold, thou art made whole; sin no more, lest a worse thing come unto thee".

The next act of the man has given rise to very different opinions. He has been accused of base ingratitude in at once repairing to the rulers and telling them that it was Jesus who had healed him. This is unjust. Had he gone to them and said that it was Jesus who had told him to break the sabbath, we might have concluded that he was currying favour with the authorities. But he was concerned with his cure, and in all good faith would have the rulers know of the wonderful man who had healed him. His presence in the temple also suggests his desire to reform and to recognize God and to give thanks to Him. Added to this, the solemn warning of Jesus that a worse thing would befall him if he continued in sin, would deter him from so base an act as the betrayal of his benefactor.

The rulers had no such reserve. So blinded by their prejudice that the miracle was lost on them, they determined on the death of Jesus, and as birds of prey swooped down upon him. The event is a turning point; it marked the beginning of a persecution which continued to the end of his life; it marked also their recognition that the attitude of Jesus to the law was not the same as theirs; and his view of the sabbath as illustrated in his acts on that day came to be a cause of constant conflict. Twice within a short time of this event we find them disputing with him. It was on a sabbath that his disciples rubbed corn as they passed through a field, and according to the Jewish interpretation had worked, threshing the wheat. Jesus cited the precedent of David, and also claimed to be lord of the sabbath (Matthew 12:1–9). They then put forward in the synagogue, when Jesus was present, a man with a withered hand, to provoke Jesus to heal him on that day. He showed their inconsistency in that they were willing to lift a sheep from a pit when their possessions were affected, but were not willing that he should lift a fellow-being from the pit of suffering by the kindly ministration of his healing power (Matthew 12:10–13).

In this dispute recorded by John, he takes the highest ground of all. He was the Son of God, and his actions were a copy of the Father's. "My Father worketh until now, and I work." The rest of God had followed the creative activities, but there had been no cessation of His beneficent acts, and no stay of His plans for man's salvation. Even the sabbath itself was a figure of that rest which will come when the week-days of human toil and suffering pass into the Millennial "keeping of a sabbath" which remains for the people of God. The preparation for this was proceeding in the foundation being laid for sins to be forgiven, and sickness and death to be swept away. Even then, the toil and sorrows of sin could be forgotten in that "rest for their souls" which Jesus invited all that labour and are heavy laden to find in him.

The assertion of these facts—the relation of healing to the sabbath of God—was made by Jesus in this sabbath miracle and discourse.

The effect upon the Jews was to harden their resolution to slay Jesus. He had added to the sin of breaking the sabbath law the blasphemy of claiming to be the Son of God, and so claiming to be divine. The conflict had reached an irreconcilable stage, and nothing but the death of Jesus would satisfy the Jews.

Although their feelings took such definite form, it did not close the discussion. Jesus explained his relationship to the Father. There was perfect unity between the Father and Jesus, but the latter was dependent upon the Father; he had knowledge of the Father's acts, and the Father's will was his guide. He had the most intimate relationship with the

Father, who made full disclosure to him of His purpose. The Son "sees"; the Father "shows"; and they are knit together in love. And "greater things" are in store, which will cause them to marvel with fear and astonishment (verses 19,20).

This fear will be felt when, raised from the dead, they stand before Jesus as their judge. He proceeds to speak of this. The ultimate source of resurrection power is of God, but He has commissioned the Son to exercise it, and also to act as judge. The honour thus conferred by the Father requires that honour be given to the Son, to refuse which is to honour not God (verses 21–23).

Even then and there the life-giving power of the Son was being illustrated on the plane of faith and morals. Hearing his word, and believing on God who sent him, gave the privilege of heirship to that life which was so certain that Jesus said it was already in possession. By the act of faith men passed to a life-giving relationship to him and the Father. With the solemnity of the repeated "verily" Jesus said that the dead—those living apart from the life of God—should by hearing his voice begin to live. This quickening power was in the Son as in the Father, given to him by the Father with the authority to execute judgment because he was the Son of man. The Son of God was also a man, even the son of man God visited, the son of man made strong, but yet a man. Inheriting the nature shared by all other men, he was obedient to God, and as death had come by man, so by a man came the resurrection of the dead. His work as the Saviour qualified him to be the judge.

To discharge this office of judge requires power to call to life those who are literally dead. Jesus therefore points to the greater cause of marvel, even the awakening of the dead who are in the graves, and the bestowal of life or the passing of condemnation according to deserts. Some have stumbled at the word "all"— "all that are in the graves". But Jesus is not speaking of universal resurrection. He has just spoken of hearing his words then; such a hearing brought responsibility to his judgment. The "all" embraces all responsible hearers, without regard to the issue of the judgment; all without distinction of whether the end is life or death; it prevents the limiting of the resurrection to those only who attain to life in that day. To press it to mean all without any exception is to disregard the context of the saying.

Such a claim must have produced astonishment in the hearers; our familiarity with it hinders our appreciation of the startling nature of the words uttered by one who to his hearers was a village artisan. But Jesus at once expresses his dependence on the Father, his learning of Him and the consequent righteousness of his judgment. There was no variance with the Father, but a habitual surrender of his own will to the will of Him who sent him. His obedience to the Father, and the harmony between them, provided the means for the full expression of His purpose, whether in mercy or in judgment, to be made through him.

In this discourse Jesus speaks with a marked personal emphasis, focussing attention upon himself. From the description "the Son", (verses 19–23) he passes to "my word" (verse 24); he returns to "the Son" (verses 25–29), and then the spotlight is thrown upon himself in verse 30: "I", "mine own self", "I hear", "I seek", "I judge". We note that while he stresses his relationship as the Son, and the harmony and correspondence in the works of Father and Son, he also keeps before them that his position is a dependent one. He can do nothing of himself; the Father shows the Son what He does; the Father has given to the Son to have life in himself; He has given to him authority. The Son honours the Father, while he asserts his claims as the Son.

A Threefold Witness (5:31–47)

SUCH tremendous claims required attestation. He anticipates the objection based on the legal maxim that one's own testimony must have the corroboration of others. In claiming such a relationship to the Father, the only possible witness could come from the Father. Without that support, every other form of witness might be suspect, if not pronounced as untrue. But the Father had given him three witnesses, which was the full requisition of the law.

(1) The first witness was John, a faithful and true witness. They had appealed to John and his testimony stood, for his witness was not a personal one, but the witness of God through him. Had it originated in John, it would not have proved the case of Jesus; but John was "the lamp that burneth and shineth", lit by God, and the flame was a divine light. They had been to him, listened to him for a while, but, alas, did not continue (verses 32–35).

(2) The second witness consisted of his miracles. This was greater than that of John, for John did no miracle. But the "works" given Jesus to do covered more than the works of healing, etc. They included the whole of his work mentioned

in verse 17, and the "greater works" of verse 21: his words, his moral power over others, the enlightenment that followed hearing his words, the raising of the dead, and at last his own resurrection.

Here again the Jews failed. They had neither heard God's voice at any time nor seen His shape. Yet God's voice was speaking to them then, and God was present in their midst; and the discerning, the pure in heart, saw God manifested in Jesus. But not so the rulers. They had not God's word abiding in them, and the proof of this was their rejection of Jesus. They might know the scriptures, and with trained memories have at call large portions of it, but the word did not abide, it did not live and have its home in them. There was no understanding of God's purpose of grace and mercy in Jesus.

(3) The witness of scripture. To say that God's word did not abide in them appeared to contradict the facts of their whole schooling and life. Jesus explained; they indeed searched the scriptures—"the word" of verse 38. They sought to find the justification of privilege and title to life which was a blinding influence in all their thinking. The scriptures testified of Jesus, and failing to understand the scriptures they refused Jesus, and failed to attain to life. "Ye will not come"—that was the trouble; they nourished false doctrine, and closed their eyes to the true. Yet in wishing them to come to him Jesus did not seek honour from men; that was their fatal weakness, the love of God was not in them, they were too full of the love of themselves. As a consequence they turned from Jesus who came in the Father's name, having no spiritual kinship with him. They could not understand Jesus, his freedom from self-seeking, his fearless loyalty to God. Did one come in his own name, their affinity was at once revealed, as was indeed illustrated in the response to false Messiahs during the following generation. Their moral outlook and love of honour made it impossible for them to understand Jesus. "How can ye believe" sadly expresses the terrible blight that afflicts self-centred lives, and the moral impossibility of such responding to the influence of a life that labours to honour God.

This is the climax of Christ's analysis of their failure. They turned from John; they failed to see the Father in Jesus; and now Jesus lays bare the reason for it. Such an indictment was not his alone. Their last hope was taken from them when Jesus said that Moses would be their accuser. Their trust in him would be in vain; their hopes in the great law-giver would be without avail; they had not accepted his teaching while professing to be his disciples. The corollary was the rejection of Jesus. Moses' writings and Christ's words are knit together, and cannot be separated. No middle ground is possible either for the Jews who paid lip service to Moses and rejected Christ, or for those moderns who talk of Jesus as Master and reject Moses.

The sabbath sign provided Jesus with the opportunity to assert his claims as the Son, with power to perform all healing in everlasting life according to God's will wrought through him. It also led to the citation of the threefold witness to himself, with a corresponding laying bare of the threefold reason for their failure.

THE FOURTH SIGN: FEEDING THE MULTITUDE (6:1–14)

AT the Passover season twelve months before the crucifixion, Jesus fed the five thousand and gave the discourse at Capernaum, which John records in chapter 6. John marks the time: "Now the Passover, the feast of the Jews, was at hand"; and in so doing points to the significance of the miracle as being connected with the typical meaning of the feast. In an incidental way the season of the year is indicated by the allusion to the "much grass in the place". Matthew notes that the people sat down "on the grass", while Mark gives a picturesque touch—"they sat down by companies upon the green grass"; arranged in groups of fifty they looked like neatly laid out garden beds, with many-coloured flowers. But the grass is only present during a short season in the spring, after which the brown earth is bare.

It has been suggested, with great probability, that this Passover followed a sabbath year, and it therefore preceded the first harvest after the fallow-year, when food would be getting scarce; the miracle of Jesus thus meeting a very real want. Both Tacitus and Josephus mention the Jewish practice at this time, of allowing the land to rest during the seventh year. With singular perversity, they did not keep the sabbaths when they were a free people, but insisted upon doing so when under Gentile rule.

We learn from the other gospels why Jesus crossed the Lake of Galilee, seeking retirement for himself and the twelve. John had been put to death by Herod, and John's disciples had brought the sad news to Jesus. The Forerunner had been a faithful servant of God, and his death was a poignant reminder to Jesus of his own end. Then the twelve returned to him from the preaching tour on which he had sent them, full of news of what they had done. A season of rest was needed by both Jesus and the apostles, and with the rush and excitement in Capernaum this could only be got by leaving for some desert place. Jesus therefore said, "Come ye yourselves apart to a desert place, and rest awhile". They therefore took a boat, and crossed the lake to Bethsaida Julias.

The multitude, however, had seen them go, and they hurried by land round the head of the lake to find Jesus on the other side. The heart of Jesus was moved as he saw them approaching; they were as sheep without a shepherd, and as the true shepherd he must needs do what he could. There were many sick who had toilsomely dragged themselves by road to find him, and Jesus healed them.

As evening approached, the disciples suggested that the hungry people should be sent away, that, scattering among the villages, they might get food. The disciples themselves would also be feeling the need for food, and since the people had interfered with the rest they were to have with their Master, a touch of impatience might be traced in the suggestion. Jesus said that they need not depart, and proposed that the disciples should find them food. To do good, to feed the hungry who had deprived them of the refreshment they needed, was the antidote to impatience. It was Christ's way. John tells that before this Jesus had raised the question with Philip, the apostle who was perhaps in charge of the catering arrangements of the band, of how bread could be purchased for so many. Jesus was testing Philip's faith, for he knew what he intended to do. Philip made a quick calculation— two hundred pennyworth of bread would not suffice. Andrew pointed to a lad with a basket containing five barley loaves and two fishes—the food of the poorest, which the boy may have been offering for sale; but as he drew attention to him, the hopeless inadequacy of the supply struck him; what were they among so many? What indeed! so little that a hungry boy might have disposed of them; it has even been suggested that the food was the boy's own.

Jesus told the disciples to get the people seated, and they obeyed. They were grouped to help the distribution of food. Jesus then offered thanks, and gave portions to the disciples, who served the people. All four gospels record the giving of thanks; the first three saying that "he blessed and brake", words which have a prophetic import. That the miraculous provision of food was a figure of himself and his work becomes clear from the discourse which follows. The supply was ample, some portions which Jesus had handed to the disciples remaining untouched. These the apostles gathered, and filled the food wallets which they carried, and nothing was lost.

The immediate effect upon the people was to lead them to exclaim, "This is of a truth the prophet that cometh into the world". This was true, but they had no comprehension of the work of that prophet; they wanted to make him a king at once.

The situation was full of danger. The disciples had returned flushed with success from their preaching; the people were excited. To Jesus the circumstances provided an external stimulus to the same thought that had been quelled in the wilderness trial, that he should use the power at his call to establish at once his Kingdom. He ordered the disciples to take the boat and cross the lake, and as they were loth to obey, he "constrained them" to go. He then dismissed the multitude, using the power that he had over a crowd to enforce his will. He then betook himself to the mountain for prayer, alone with the Father. It was a crisis in his life; the morrow would see the beginning of the decline of popular support, and onwards there would be growing opposition for another year, until the next Passover witnessed the end of the conflict.

THE FIFTH SIGN: WALKING ON THE WATER (6:15–21)

THE apostles yielded to his compulsion, although the popular feeling fitted well their own desires. Jesus put them out of danger, while he sought the unfailing shelter of communion with the Father. "I would haste me to a shelter from the stormy wind and tempest", was the Psalmist's prayer (55:8); and this was the practice of Jesus, and the source of his strength. But as yet the apostles had not learned this lesson, and they must needs be taught of the power greater than the storm. Taken from the circumstances where they were subject to an unwholesome influence, and which they were not sufficiently instructed to resist, they are brought into other conditions where another needed lesson could be given to them. The literal stormy wind and tempest would lead them to know of that power which sheltered Jesus in the conflicts of his life.

The lake is peculiarly liable to sudden storms. Thomson describes such a storm as that with which the apostles battled as they crossed the sea (*Land and Book*, chapter 25).

All the night they laboured. In the early morning Jesus rose from prayer; and half-way across the sea could be seen the ship. John says they were about twenty-five or thirty furlongs from the shore, which coincides with Mark's phrase "in the midst" of the sea. Jesus went to them to their alarm, walking on the water. The miracle of the loaves had not taught them of his great power, and any spiritual lesson could not have been perceived in their state of mind. But the assuring tones of Jesus gave them confidence as he said, "It is I, be not afraid". They gladly received him into the ship, and the wind ceased, and their efforts soon brought them to land. It was an astonishing experience, filling them with a stupefying wonder—"they were amazed beyond measure", for as Mark relates, their hearts were hardened.

Looking back on the whole of the circumstances of the two miracles, we have little excuse if we fall into a like error. There was displayed the power that belongs to the Creator in the multiplication of the loaves. It is His power which endows the grain with life, and power of growth and multiplication of grains, thus providing food for man. Rightly viewed, this is a wonder no less than the instantaneous increase in the hands of Jesus. To walk on the water, and to control the winds and waves, are aspects of that might which belongs to God, who has subjected all things to the laws of their being, but who can use or modify all laws according to His will.

But the miracles are signs in John's gospel, and their import is disclosed in the discourse which occupies the remainder of chapter 6. But apart from the discourse there is a hint in the record of the miracle of the loaves. Jesus took the loaves and gave thanks and distributed them. Matthew says that Jesus "took the five loaves and the two fishes, and blessed, and brake, and gave the loaves to the disciples". Matthew also describes the scene at the last supper: "Jesus took bread, and blessed, and brake it, and gave to the disciples, and said, Take, eat it; this is my body". Is this an accidental correspondence of description, or was the miracle of the loaves designed to teach the same lesson as the emblems of the supper? In the light of Christ's own explanation, the same undoubtedly, even that Jesus was the Son of God, and the sacrifice for sins. The loaves, blessed and broken, are representative of his body broken for our sakes. Of him we must partake if we would attain to life.

What then is the meaning of his walking on the sea? Jesus has gone away after giving his life in sacrifice; he has gone to the Father, as he sought the Father after the miracle. His followers toil amidst the storms of life, in the midst of the nations. But Jesus will return, the storms will cease, and the haven will be reached in the company of the Lord. If the first sign tells of his death, the second tells of his resurrection, and of the life which is above and beyond the conditions and limitations of the present mortal state, and of his second advent, and peace for the troubled world.

Jesus will gather together his friends, who are members of his Body; none will be lost, as no broken portion of the bread was allowed to remain. All are gathered by apostolic labours; all are part of the twelve tribes either by birth or adoption. "Gather up the portions that nothing be lost", he said; and he gives the explanation, "This is the Father's will which hath sent me, that of all which he hath given me I should lose nothing, but should raise it up at the last day".

THE CAPERNAUM DISCOURSE (6:22–71)

IN the discourse based upon the miracle of the feeding of the five thousand, which Jesus gave on the following day in Capernaum, we find the key to the meaning of the miracle. The significance of the signs was largely lost upon his hearers, the inner circle of the followers of Jesus alone appearing to have laid hold of the meaning of his words, and in their case very imperfectly. This failure was not unforeseen by Jesus; and his words, like some of his parables, were probably intended to discourage the attentions of the crowds which took an unwelcome form.

The multitude had seen the departure of the disciples, urged to take to the boat by Jesus; they knew that he had not entered the boat himself, for he had later exercised the strange power which he occasionally showed, to compel them to disperse to buy food. On the morning following, after a fruitless search for him, they took boats and crossed the lake to Capernaum, and found him there. They accosted him with the enquiry, "Rabbi, when camest thou hither?" The question involved more than When; there was also implied How? But Jesus did not answer. Other and more serious matters had to be presented to them.

It was a time of crisis for all: for Jesus, in that he had now to order his steps with the cross always in view; for the disciples, in that the teaching of Jesus took a more sombre hue, the kingdom being less prominent in his teaching, and the coming crucifixion receiving continual emphasis. But it was also a crisis for the people. Their excitement about Jesus was a danger; they were talking about making him a king, and a popular movement to attain that end would have been disastrous to his plans. He therefore gave them an address which had the effect of repulsing them. It presented truths which were only faintly perceived and were very unpalatable, and which caused them to turn from him. This marked the time from which there was a steady decline in popularity. The address also tested those nearer to Jesus, bringing them still closer, with a little clearer grasp of the significance of his words.

The address is one, yet it is divided by the information of the effects it produced upon the different classes of hearers, the offending features being more and more stressed by Jesus.

TO THE MULTITUDE (6:25–40)

"WHEN camest thou hither?" they asked. Jesus answered: "Verily, verily, I say unto you, Ye seek me, not because ye saw the signs, but because ye did eat of the loaves, and were filled". The answer went to the root of their motive in following Jesus; all they cared about was the satisfaction of hunger in so easy a way. The purpose behind the miracle, and the lesson contained in it were not considered. They were prepared to toil in their search for him, but not in an endeavour to understand his words or his actions. "Work not for the meat which perisheth", he exhorted them, "but for that meat which endureth unto everlasting life, which the Son of man shall give unto you; for him hath God the Father sealed". The situation closely resembles that when Jesus met the woman at the well. There he spoke of water; here of food; but in both cases the result of partaking is eternal life, which the Son of man has power to bestow. The Son of man would indeed some day be their King, but he had now other work to do; he had to be "lifted up", as he said when he used the same title in his conversation with Nicodemus, "that whosoever believeth should have everlasting life". And this "lifting up" was not far from his thought now.

The ability of the Son to give life is confirmed by the fact that "him hath God the Father sealed". "To be sealed meant in the papyri to be imperially protected and retained for imperial use. Seals were set on sacks of grain to guarantee the correctness of the contents, and there was a mark containing the Emperor's name and the year of his reign, which was necessary upon documents relating to buying and selling, and this mark was technically known as the seal. It was the credential of the royal document making it legal." So Jesus was sealed by the Father; the testimony of Scripture, the voice from heaven, and the works Jesus did, were a three-fold witness that God had sent him, and that his words were true.

They asked: "What shall we do, that we might work the works of God?" Jesus answered: "This is the work of God, that ye believe on him whom he hath sent". This work is essen-tial—to believe the words of Jesus, and have faith in him; but they were thinking of "works", while Jesus points to faith from which works spring. They had followed him, but not with understanding and faith. Now they could not under-stand him, such claims were too great. They wanted creden-tials, and in asking for them showed their failure to grasp his meaning. "What sign showest thou then, that we may see, and believe thee? what dost thou work?" "Believe thee", they say; "believe on me", he had said—a world separating the two ideas. The limit of their thought is also seen in the challenge that he should continue to provide them with food. For forty years their fathers had been fed in the wilderness, as the scripture witnessed: "He gave them bread from heaven to eat". They were making a comparison between Moses and Jesus, which was wrong in the elements of the analogy. As Jesus answered, it was not Moses who gave them bread from heaven, but God; and the true analogy was between the manna which was God-given, and Jesus the Son of God. Jesus points to this by saying: "My Father giveth you the true bread from heaven". He was the true, antitypical bread from heaven, in that he was the Son of God, provided to give life. "For the bread of God is that which cometh down out of heaven, and giveth life unto the world" (verse 33, RV).

The "bread of God" has a double allusion to the types; but for the present the words of Jesus concern only the manna. They thought of the wilderness manna only; Jesus, of himself as one foreshadowed by it. In the wilderness the people had to partake of the manna or perish; so his hearers (and all others) must receive him in faith or perish. But having only the literal in mind they asked him to give to them this bread for evermore. They were at the stage reached by the

Samaritan woman when she wanted the water which would remove the need for going to the well, but *they* did not advance further.

Jesus now for the first time points definitely to himself as the bread: "I am the bread of life: he that cometh to me shall never hunger; and he that believeth on me shall never thirst". There is a progressive parallelism here:

He that cometh—shall not hunger.

He that believeth—shall never thirst.

To come is to believe; hunger is then at an end, thirst is assuaged. The reference to thirst is a preparation for the second aspect of the figure of the "bread of God"; there may be also, since it was the Passover season, an allusion to the Passover when they partook of both bread and wine.

They had come after Jesus, but had not come to him in the meaning of his words; Jesus did not mean physical nearness, but a spiritual appropriation of his teaching. Their failure in the higher sense is indicated by Jesus: "But I said unto you, That ye also have seen me, and believe not". They had asked for a sign, that "we may see and believe"; Jesus answers, Ye have seen me, but do not believe. He was a sufficient sign for discerning eyes.

There was a reason for their failure—a reason with two aspects. There was a choice by God, and there was a fitness in the chosen. "All that the Father giveth me shall come to me; and him that cometh to me I will in no wise cast out." He would not cast out because he had come to do the Father's will, which required that of those given to him, none should be lost (words which alluded to the instruction of the previous day concerning the gathered portions that nothing be lost), but he would raise him up at the last day (verse 39). This gives the divine side, and the totality of the response; Jesus adds the human side (verse 40) which consists of seeing him, and believing on him, with the end everlasting life. To this aspect is also added the words, "I will raise him up at the last day".

To Jewish hearers this expression was equal to a claim to Messiahship on the part of Jesus. The "last day" was the day when the Messiah would be revealed. If Jesus raises up at the last day, he must be the Messiah.

At this point Jesus is interrupted by the Jews, that is, the rulers who were listening among the crowd. They murmured as their fathers had done in the wilderness (1 Corinthians 10); and, as faultfinders usually do, they perverted his words, putting the crudest construction on them. They knew him, or thought they did: was he not Joseph's son? They had made diligent enquiries about him; they knew of his ancestry. How then could he talk of coming down from heaven?

DISCOURSE TO THE JEWS (6:41–51)

JESUS turned to the murmurers, and as his manner was on such occasions, spake words which tested them, and if they failed in the test, confounded them. He rebuked them, and affirmed again the central position that he held in God's plan. "No man can come to me, except the Father which sent me draw him: and I will raise him up at the last day" (verse 44). He had said before that God gave some to him; now he added that God draws, apart from which none can come to him. He next shows the means by which this drawing is done. In Isaiah's prophecy of Zion's children of the resurrection, their qualification is described: "They shall all be taught of God". Jesus quotes this, and adds, "everyone that hath heard from the Father, and hath learned, cometh unto me" (RV). There is hearing without learning; seeing without beholding. The Father was speaking in Jesus, and so speaking, was drawing those with willing and honest hearts to him. That the teaching of God was not by direct communication Jesus makes clear: "Not that any man hath seen the Father, save he which is of God, he hath seen the Father". He had knowledge and experience of God which none other had; hearing him, men were taught of God, and found in Jesus the Father in manifestation; seeing Jesus they saw the Father (14:9).

From the rebuke implied in these words (6:44), Jesus proceeds to emphasize those points which had led them to complain. He asserts that life can only be obtained by belief in him who was the divinely provided bread, not for the sustenance of the natural life, but for the bestowal of everlasting life:

"He that believeth on me hath everlasting life. I am that bread of life. Your fathers did eat manna in the wilderness, and are dead. This is the bread which cometh down from heaven, that a man may eat thereof, and not die. I am the living bread which came down from heaven: if any man eat of this bread he shall live for ever: and the bread that I will give is my flesh, which I will give for the life of the world."
(6:47–51)

The bread of life is now identified with himself as the living bread, and this brings the assertion that *he* came down from heaven. Whereas verse 33 is only a statement of fact in connection with the bread of God, he now places the coming of the bread into historic connection with himself. As "living bread" he has life to give; as the bread of life he is given: as the "living bread" he is the giver; and as the giver he passes to the other aspect of the bread of God as a type—"the bread that I will give is *my flesh*, which I will give for the life of the world".

A stormy scene followed as the Jews disputed among themselves. His words were taken literally, and they said, "How can he give us his flesh to eat?"

FURTHER DISCOURSE TO THE JEWS (6:52–58)

IN the miracle-sign Jesus had "broken" the bread, an act which signified the giving of his flesh. But this aspect was not foreshadowed by the giving of the manna. We must remember that it was Passover season, and the Paschal lamb had its lessons for Jesus, and of him to others. But the Passover rite does not particularly connect with the bread of God. In what way then can the offering of sacrifice be connected with the bread of God?

The answer is that the altar sacrifice is described in the Old Testament by this very phrase. Moving backwards in the Old Testament, we find Ezekiel describing the temple of the future, and telling of the Prince, who is the manifestation of the Lord God of Israel, "eating bread" in the eastern buildings of the Sanctuary. The prophet then calls upon Israel to observe these new arrangements, and to turn from their abominations, from breaking God's covenant in having allowed strangers in His house when they offered "My bread, the fat and the blood" (44:7). "My bread"—God's bread—was the portion consumed on the altar or poured out beside it. This usage of the phrase occurs in Leviticus. The portions burned on the altar were "the food of the offering made by fire", therefore they had not to eat either "fat or blood" (Leviticus 3:11,16,17). More explicitly these offerings are called "the bread of thy God", "the bread of their God", "the bread of his God" (21:6,8,21); they must not take from a stranger's hand "to offer the bread of your God" (22:25). The Law, as a part of its symbolism, forbade the partaking of God's bread; by this showing that the offerings on the altar did not bring reconciliation and fellowship with God. They could not share His "bread". In marked contrast to this Jesus insists,

> "Except ye eat the flesh of the Son of man, and drink his blood, ye have no life in you. Whoso eateth my flesh, and drinketh my blood, hath eternal life; and I will raise him up at the last day. For my flesh is meat indeed, and my blood is drink indeed. He that eateth my flesh, and drinketh my blood, dwelleth in me, and I in him."
>
> (verses 53-56)

Negatively stated—no eating of his flesh and drinking of his blood, and there is no life; positively—by eating his flesh and drinking his blood, life is attained in Messiah's day. In no stronger terms could Jesus assert that as the Messiah he must be cut off that his flesh was the true, the real ("indeed", verse 55) offering; and that the closest friendship is by it established ("dwelleth in me, and I in him"). The life of God becomes the life of the eater: "The living Father hath sent me, and I live by the Father; so he that eateth me, even he shall live by me". Life has its source in God, to whom the description "living" belongs; the Son derives his life from God, and those who eat his flesh share his life.

The discourse is rounded off by a statement that combines the two types, yet by way of contrast: "This is the bread which came down out of heaven; not as the fathers did eat—and died: he that eateth this bread shall live for ever".

At every stage Jesus insists upon the impossibility of everlasting life apart from him. In the earlier verses he connects belief in him and life (46,47); he passes to the statement, "he that eateth shall live" (51), and this becomes at the end "eateth my flesh" (54).

Attaching a terrible literalness to his words, they were horrified at his speech. The idea of drinking blood, forbidden by the law, was in itself repellent; much more so the suggestion of drinking a man's blood. Yet they should have understood to some extent. Jeremiah had spoken of eating God's words. Their Rabbis spoke of "eating the Messiah" in the sense of enjoying his reign, and since they saw in the days of Hezekiah a picture of Messiah's days, they said they had devoured the Messiah in the days of Hezekiah.

But underlying the language of Jesus are to be found deeper matters; basic principles connected with the subject of everlasting life for man are indicated. The flesh and blood of Jesus was the same "flesh and blood" as that of all the children given to him. So Paul affirms with great emphasis (Hebrews 2:14). God's object was the destruction of sin which had the power of death. This object was achieved by a perfectly obedient life, and a voluntary death by crucifixion in which God's righteousness was declared. Those who deny that Jesus had the same nature as those he came to save, as all the members of the race, or deny that all flesh is corruptible because of sin at the beginning, destroy the principle involved in Jesus giving "his flesh". The "blood" to be drunk expresses the same truth from another angle. The blood is the life, and the blood shed is the life given. Jesus laid down his life when "his soul was made an offering for sin"; and we drink of his blood when we receive for his sake forgiveness of sins, and share his fellowship with the Father. Apart from his having given his flesh, and apart from our receiving by faith what he has done, and entering into the fellowship of his sufferings, there can be no everlasting life. As the eating of the Paschal Lamb introduced the Paschal feast of Unleavened Bread, so our acceptance of the sacrifice of Jesus introduces us to the Paschal feast of fellowship and communion. The typical bread of God was forbidden the worshippers; but the perfection of the offering of Jesus is figuratively indicated by all partaking of him, and the feast of the covenant ratifies the bond of union.

John does not tell of the further effect of these words of Jesus upon the Jews. Presumably they remained disputing among themselves, while the centre of interest passes to the disciples of Jesus, who also found the words of Jesus hard to accept. "This is a hard saying. Who can hear it?"

CONVERSATION WITH DISCIPLES (6:66–71)

JESUS knew their thoughts and their murmurings. They were not willing to receive this doctrine concerning everlasting life. They stumbled at his teaching. "What then", asked Jesus, in an unfinished sentence, "if ye shall see the Son of man ascend up where he was before?" How shall the sentence be finished? If when he was a living man in their presence, they found it hard to understand what he meant about eating his flesh, how would they treat his words when he ascended to the Father in that same flesh raised from the dead and made incorruptible? Would it then be possible to take his words so literally? Would they, when that happened, still stumble?

He explains: "It is the spirit that maketh to live, the flesh profits nothing". That is, the actual eating of his flesh would not give life; but the spirit, the meaning of his words, the doctrine of his sacrifice, believed, would give life. That this is the force of the word "spirit" is established by the added explanation; "The words that I speak, they are spirit and they are life". His teaching must be accepted in faith, and his words are found to have life-giving power. But even the disciples numbered among them many who lacked faith, and so failed to share the benefits of his work. "There are some of you that believe not", and were therefore outside the Father's purpose. Jesus recalled his words concerning the divine aspect of these issues: "For this cause have I said unto you, that no man can come unto me except it be given unto him of the Father" (verse 65). Though so near him, they had not been with him; this now became evident by their leaving him. "They walked no more with him."

It is a lesson in the unresponsiveness of human nature to God's approaches. For over two years Jesus had taught, cured their sick, journeyed with them; and when he states a new and unwelcome doctrine they go back to their old haunts and ways. More sad is the reflection that among the apostles there was a betrayer. He was not as yet revealed; he continued with them although it must have been evident even at this time that something separated Judas from the rest. Jesus knew who would betray him (verse 64). In speaking in the discourse so pointedly of his sacrifice was he ignorant of how the sacrifice would be made?

Looking sadly at the retreating crowds Jesus asked the twelve, "Will ye also go away?" Peter revealed some understanding of the words that Jesus had been speaking. "Lord, to whom shall we go? Thou hast words of eternal life. And we have believed and know that thou art that Christ, the Son of the living God." Peter spoke for the twelve; but one of them did not know these truths confessed by Peter, but Jesus knew him. "Have not I chosen you twelve, and one of you is a devil?" The seeds of betrayal were even then germinating in the heart of Judas; not defined as such yet, but shortly to grow and reveal themselves. The episode ends on this sad note. The Son of man gives his flesh, and is the sacrifice for sin, and in the course of it sin reveals its malignancy in the friend of the Saviour becoming the betrayer.

AT THE FEAST OF TABERNACLES (7:1–52)

BETWEEN the sixth and seventh chapters of John's gospel there is an interval of six months, the opening phrase, "After these things Jesus walked in Galilee", describing the activities of Jesus between the Passover and the feast of Tabernacles. John's note of the season is a guide to the meaning of the address and the claims of Jesus. He healed on the sabbath, and said he was Lord of the sabbath. He fed the multitude at Passover, and directed attention to the manna and the sacrifices as types of himself. And Tabernacles is connected with the idea expressed by John in his first chapter: "The word was made flesh and *tabernacled* among us"; and on this occasion Jesus asserts that he and his doctrine are of God.

CONTROVERSY WITH HIS BRETHREN (7:1–9)

THE feast of Tabernacles was in the autumn, when the harvest had been gathered. It was thus a feast of thanksgiving. It was also designed to keep in memory the time when their fathers had sojourned in the wilderness, dwelling in tents; God therefore appointed that for seven days they should dwell in booths (Leviticus 23:42). Jesus had not attended the Passover of that year, and since attendance at one of the festivals was required, it was naturally expected by his brothers that he would attend the feast of Tabernacles. They urged him therefore to go into Judea and there perform the works he had done elsewhere. We can imagine their perplexity at the events which had come to pass in connection with their brother. Was he the Messiah? They did not believe he was, but they desired some decisive test. It seemed inconsistent to do mighty works in secret, when the issues demanded the widest publicity.

There is a certain similarity with the occasion when his mother would have him do something at the marriage feast. The motives of his mother and his brethren were different, but in each case there was a desire for action on his part. His works however could not be performed to serve the desires of others: human counsel could not determine a course which had purposes at that time altogether beyond their understanding. Jesus therefore answered: "My time is not yet come: but your time is alway ready. The world cannot hate you; but me it hateth, because I testify of it that the works thereof are evil" (7:6,7).

"Show thyself to the world", they had said. By "the world" they meant their fellow Israelites. Jesus takes up the word and gives it a deeper meaning. The world was hostile to him since it was the embodiment of evil, and his words and his ways were a reproof of the evil. Then his time had not come for the manifestation to be made at the hour which was determined by the Father. Till that time the full revelation of the evil opposition would not be exhibited, and his faithful manifestation of righteousness be shown. His brothers, as part of that Jewish world, knew little of the antagonism felt by Jesus; for he and they sustained different relationships to it.

In due course he went to the feast, avoiding any publicity such as he invited on a later occasion, when he rode into the city and challenged a comparison with the prophetic pictures of the coming of the Messiah. How necessary such carefulness was is evident from the agitated discussions in the city concerning him. The authorities sought for him, while the crowd was divided upon whether Jesus was a good man or a deceiver. But open discussion was avoided because of the known opposition of the rulers.

DISCOURSES AT THE FEAST (7:10–52)

WHILE Jesus had avoided any display which would have precipitated a storm concerning his Messiahship, yet his action in suddenly appearing in the temple in the midst of the feast, and teaching, might well have provoked a recollection of the words of the Old Testament prophets concerning "the Lord, whom ye seek" coming "suddenly to the temple" (Malachi 3:1). But then he was not recognized as the messenger of the covenant; neither could it be said that he was one "in whom ye are delighted".

What Jesus said as he taught in the Temple Courts, we are not told. The effect upon the rulers is noted—"they marvelled". In this, as well as in their contemptuous remark— "How knoweth *this man* letters, having never learned?"— they unconsciously reveal a recognition of the power of Jesus as a teacher. His exposition of the Scriptures would have an attractiveness and a warmth that was lacking in their own laboured dissection and citation of the opinions of their teachers of the past. They knew he had not graduated in their schools; he had not spent the years usually occupied in study before a pupil was solemnly ordained a Doctor of the law. Where then had he got the qualifications that so excited their rage, and which they would willingly have denied, but had to acknowledge in spite of themselves?

Jesus heard their question and answered it in what at first appears to be a series of disconnected statements, but which on examination are found to be four closely connected reasons.

(1) Rabbinic practice was to quote the teacher from whom they had received their sayings. Jesus was not "taught" of the Rabbis but his teaching was not therefore his own. It had a higher source than theirs, with the greatest of authorities. "My doctrine is not mine, but his that sent me" (verse 16). Both in form and content his message was of God. His words were God's words (8:47).

(2) The teaching of Jesus was for faith and action. It called for a trial on the part of all who heard him. It was for them to "prove what is that acceptable will of God". They asked for signs in support of his claims, but they neglected the test of personal experience of the teaching he gave. "If any willeth to do his will, he shall know of the teaching, whether it be of God, or whether I speak from myself." The will must be called into action, and the resolute effort to do God's will, with the inclination bent to delight in God's law, brings a realization that the teaching is divine. There may be both negative and positive aspects of this recognition: negative, in that the very demands of the law, as Paul recognized, marked it as holy, just and good; positively in that every conquest of holiness brings a sense of the "profitableness" of godliness even in this life. Conversely, apart from the moral conditions being met, it is impossible to know this truth Jesus proclaimed. As he sadly said: "How can ye believe, which receive honour one of another?" (5:44). The words of Jesus indicate an experimental knowledge based upon a right understanding and a patient effort to obey, which is not to be discounted by the many false claims of knowledge based upon some fancied "light within".

(3) The third point in Christ's answer was an appeal to the evidence of his own life. A man who proclaims his own message seeks his own glory; but if a man claims to be a messenger from another and still seeks his own glory, he is manifestly unfaithful to him who sent him; and also false in himself, since he represents as his own that which is another's. But if a messenger seeks only the glory of the sender, his

personal disinterestedness is evident; he is shown to be a
faithful man. By this test Jesus is shown to be a faithful
witness, and this the most clearly to those who are striving
themselves to be faithful.

(4) The last point was a counter-thrust. They accepted the
law of Moses as the law of God. Yet they failed to keep it. So
flagrant was their disregard of it that Jesus on more than one
occasion told them that Moses in whom they trusted would be
their accuser. If they failed to live up to the standard of what
they professed to acknowledge, they could not possibly go
forward to the understanding of further revelation. Their
failure unfitted them to understand Jesus; and while such
failure may arise from inability, in their case it arose from
culpable disregard of the light they had received.

Jesus added a particular illustration of their failure with
regard to the law. Provision was made for ensuring that the
prophets whom God sent could be distinguished from the
false prophets. Jesus was pre-eminently the prophet like
unto Moses, with all the evidence for which they should look,
and yet they had not only rejected him in their minds, but
were endeavouring to give effect to that decision by seeking
the opportunity to kill him. "Why seek ye to kill me?" Jesus
asked.

There were many provincials present at the feast, and on
more than one occasion a difference in their attitude to that
of the inhabitants of Jerusalem is discernible. In the policy
of the authorities to Jesus the Jerusalem multitude was
better informed, as appears from verse 25. Some, from the
provinces, probably, gave the answer that Jesus must be possessed of a demon to entertain such a thought. This answer
brings into bolder relief the guilt of the rulers—the people
could not consider the idea of slaying Jesus as rational.

Jesus recalls the indignation that had been shown when
he had healed on the sabbath (5:1–16), when the rulers had
settled among themselves that Jesus must die. This miracle,
performed on the sabbath day, had caused a revulsion of
feeling which had not in any way changed in the interval.
The "one" work on the sabbath had produced such results. Yet
constantly the sabbath law was broken by the rulers without
offence because of another law which had greater importance. Thus even Moses, as they, his followers, showed by
their acts, allowed that on occasion precedence over the
sabbath must be given to other things. Jesus says that the
inculcation of this lesson was designed by the law. *"For this
cause* hath Moses given you circumcision (not because it is of

Moses, but of the fathers); and ye on the sabbath day circumcise a man". The rite was of the fathers, and was the token of the covenant made with Abraham. If the eighth day fell on a sabbath, the law of circumcision was followed even though contrary to a rigid interpretation of the sabbath law. The covenant relationship was more important than the sabbath. This was a right instinct on their part, although the lesson does not appear to have been learned. For if circumcision, which was based upon the promise which was prior to the law, took precedence over the sabbath based on the law, then obviously the promise was greater than the law. But the application of this principle in the case of Jesus would have justified him who had made a man "every whit whole on the sabbath day" (verse 23). But instead of "judging righteous judgment" they were angry with Jesus.

The contrast implied by Jesus between the circumcision, which was outward in the flesh, and the "wholeness" in every part—body and soul—which Jesus had given the man healed at Bethesda, leads us to the significance of that act on the sabbath. Jesus was the true rest—"I will give you rest"; and the healing on the sabbath was designed to connect the sabbath type with himself, and the rest from works to be found in him.

At this point some of the dwellers in Jerusalem express their surprise at the boldness with which Jesus is speaking in view of the rulers' purpose to kill him. Their bewilderment is seen in the conflicting thoughts—Do the rulers know Jesus is Messiah? But, said others, we know he cannot be, for he will appear suddenly from his hiding place.

Jesus perceived these conflicting thoughts. They truly knew, as they had said, whence he was, so far as his family associations went—that he was son of Mary, that he had lived in Nazareth; but other matters they did not know—that he was God's son, that God had sent him. They did not know God; Jesus knew Him, having come from Him. By not knowing Jesus they showed they did not know God (verses 28,29).

This language could not be endured; his claims were unmistakable. They attempted to seize him, but there was a difference of opinion among the crowd which frustrated it. The ultimate cause of the failure to touch him was not to be found in human disputations, but in the purpose of God—"his hour had not yet come".

The differences among the people, with evident support for Jesus among some of them, led to an official attempt to arrest him, the Sadducean rulers being supported in this action by the Pharisees.

On the arrival of the officers Jesus addressed to them a warning, followed by a claim addressed to all, that caused what must be one of the strangest explanations for failure to make an arrest ever put forward by the police of any age or country. Returning without a prisoner to greatly angered authorities they said, "Never man spake like this man", an answer which evoked a derisive "Are ye also deceived?" What led to such an excuse?

The approach of the officers must have been an indication that the rulers were determined to take drastic action against him. He knew also the time had not yet come when he would be delivered into their hands. He therefore said: "Yet a little while am I with you, and then I go unto him that sent me". His ascent to the Father, whatever the rest made of his words, was clearly in his mind: and this helps to fix the meaning of the next sentence. "Ye shall seek me, and shall not find me: and where I am, ye cannot come" (verse 34). John records in verse 30 that they *sought* to take him; but such a seeking is not now in the thought of Jesus. It is one of a different nature altogether. There sounds in the words of Jesus an increasingly sombre note as his ministry nears its close, in which he warns his opponents of a day of judgment in which their positions will be reversed, when they will be rejected and driven away. To that Jesus refers. They will yet seek his protection, and claim acquaintance based upon his preaching in their midst, but it will then be too late: "Where I am, ye cannot come".

These simple words have a deep meaning. He does not say, "Where I shall be", because he is not thinking of place, but of relationship. His future relationship to the Father already existed then—that of other men would be decided for ever at his judgment seat. Theirs was declared beforehand—they would not attain to that friendship and fellowship with God which is the true basis of everlasting life. They would seek him in the future desiring his favour, but without avail; they were not seeking him then to receive what he had to give.

They avoid the obvious allusion to God, who had sent Jesus, and with bitter sarcasm ask if he is going to the Gentiles, and contemptuously ask, "What is this word, Ye shall seek me?" (verses 35,36).

John, conscious when he wrote his gospel of the terrible irony of their saying, records the words which, like other unconscious prophecies he narrates, came to pass. The gospel preached by Jesus and his apostles, rejected by the Jews, was taken to the Gentiles.

These events happened on the last day of the feast. During the feast a priest brought water in a golden vase from the pool of Siloam and poured it upon the altar. The ceremony was attended with the sounding of trumpets and demonstrations of joy. To this Isaiah alludes (12:3): "With joy shall ye draw water out of the wells of salvation", uniting in a sentence the natural and the spiritual. For Siloam, as we shall presently see, represented the Messiah, and the drawing of water the provision by him of the water of life. By it Israel commemorated the provision of water in the wilderness, in which again Christ as the antitype of the smitten rock is before us.

There was thus a wonderful appropriateness in the proclamation made by Jesus, when he stood and cried: "If any man thirst, let him come unto me and drink. He that believeth on me, as the Scripture hath said, out of his belly shall flow rivers of living water". John adds an explanation that by this was meant the giving of the Holy Spirit.

The absence of a scripture which exactly answers to the words used increases a difficulty concerning the meaning of Christ's announcement. The substance can be discovered in many references besides the one already quoted from Isaiah. The same prophet says, "I will pour water upon him that is thirsty, and floods upon the dry ground". Ezekiel tells of living waters that flow from the temple, and Zechariah witnesses to the opening of a fountain in Jerusalem, in all of which there is reference in one form or another to Christ. The description in the Psalms of the smiting of the rock seems also to find echoes in the language of Jesus.

"He clave rocks in the wilderness, and gave them drink abundantly as out of the depths. He brought streams also out of the rock, and caused waters to run down like rivers."
(78:15,16)

From whom do the rivers of water flow? From whom did the Spirit come? Answering the first question by the second we are led to Jesus as the source of the life-giving stream. These considerations have led to the suggested punctuation: "Let him drink, he that believeth on me; as the Scripture hath said (concerning me), Out of his belly shall flow rivers of living water."

Jesus is the smitten rock, the source of water in the wilderness. The Spirit gifts given when Jesus was glorified were a foretaste of that fulness of power which will be bestowed on those who now partake of the water of life. John therefore cites that which was already given as at once an illustration and earnest of the fulfilment of the words of Jesus.

Further strife and division followed this announcement. Some said Jesus was the prophet (Deuteronomy 18), others that he was the Christ, to which the objection was made that Jesus came from Galilee, but Christ must be born in Bethlehem. Some would have helped to arrest him; but others hindered; and he remained unmolested, while discomfited officers returned with the difficulty of accounting for their failure.

In the discussion that followed among the rulers Nicodemus interposed. The people were despised as ignorant of the law. The teacher who nearly three years before had interviewed Jesus, now reminds his fellow rulers of the law they were disregarding, which required trial before judgment. They resorted to the customary weapon of beaten men and returned abuse instead of arguments to the protest of Nicodemus. In these incidents we see the restraints which prevented the rulers taking Jesus at this time: first the crowd, then the officers' failure, and last a fellow-councillor. Jesus was hid in the Father's hand, and all assaults beat against him in vain while he faithfully went on until the time appointed of the Father for him to be offered up.

A QUESTION OF TEXT (7:53—8:11)

THE RV puts the section 7:53—8:11 in brackets, and separates it by a space before and after from the rest of the gospel. We are told that "most of the ancient authorities omit" these verses. It is a fashion to-day to regard them as not belonging to the Gospel of John at all. Some recent writers on this Gospel dismiss the verses with a casual remark to that effect. Moffatt has a note that "it is uncertain to which, if any, of the canonical gospels the fragment of primitive tradition originally belonged". It has been suggested that it was written by Luke.

But despite all the doubts that have been cast on these verses we believe they are in their right place. Occasionally a voice is heard in their favour. For example, A. C. Clark, who has been quoted before, regards the omission as probably due to a page being lost in an early codex. His conclusions, based on the counting of the letters in the lines of writing, are opposed to the decisions of the Revisers and to the trustworthiness of the two MSS (Vatican and Sinaitic) on which the Revisers, led by Hort, placed an unwarranted confidence. Burgon left an unfinished paper on this section, which is printed in a collection of his writings published with the title *Causes of the Corruption of the Traditional Text of the Gospels.* McClellan in *The Four Gospels,* marshals the evidence for and against with care, and says in his conclusion: "Taking therefore the external and the internal evidence together we have a body of proof in favour of the Section which is perfectly irresistible"; and he expresses the expectation that as the evidence comes to be better understood, assertions of spuriousness will cease to be heard. He wrote in 1875; since then the weighty influence of Westcott and Hort has through the Revised Version caused doubt to persist, although signs are not wanting that their influence and the thraldom to the two MSS named are beginning to pass.

The Christadelphian, 1933, page 405, contains a review of the internal evidence, showing from the place and persons mentioned, and the structure of the record, that the verses cannot be removed, and are in their proper context. The *Companion Bible* gives a summary of the evidence of the MSS and Versions.

The omission of the paragraph leaves an obvious gap. John has recorded the conflict of opinion among the crowd; the return of the officers sent to arrest Jesus; the expostulation of Nicodemus on their disregard of the law, and their retort, "Art thou also of Galilee? Search and look: for out of Galilee ariseth no prophet". We are asked to believe that John's next words are, "Then spake Jesus again unto them, saying, I am the light of the world". What is meant by such a connection of words? The one was spoken in the office of the Priests, the other in the temple.

But take the text as we are familiar with it, with the proviso that the first verse of chapter 8 is the conclusion of chapter 7. The retort to Nicodemus ends the meeting of the rulers: "And every man went into his own house: but Jesus went unto the Mount of Olives." They conclude their meeting and go home: Jesus finishes his discussion in the temple, and, being homeless, goes to rest in the open on the Mount. Then 8:2 begins the story of the following day: "And early in the morning he came again into the temple, and all the people came unto him; and he sat down and taught them". We are back in the temple—it is early in the day—and the story moves on in sequence.

The Woman Brought to Jesus (8:3–11)

JESUS was engaged instructing the crowd that had gathered round, when he was rudely interrupted by a group of Scribes and Pharisees dragging with them a woman whom they thrust before Jesus. It was an unseemly thing to do—an outrage on decent feelings. Had they wanted his advice a private approach on such a matter would have been fitting. But his advice was neither wanted nor sought; their object was to beguile him into some statement which they could use to incriminate him. Their brutality and indelicacy were shown in their speech, as they blurted out the charge against the woman, adding the details which left the need for witnesses out of the question. They remind him of the law of Moses— the woman should be stoned—what did he say?

John says that this they did "tempting him, that they might have to accuse him". Their motive thus revealed, the snare is not difficult to discover. Had he said, "Stone her", they would have accused him to the authorities of inciting to an act forbidden by Roman law; if he said, "Do not stone her", he contradicted Jewish law, and gave them opportunity to raise an outcry amongst the people. Perhaps they stood stone in hand—if so the situation was capable of being at once used to stir up the people—either answer, with the excitement which the circumstances had produced, could be made by adroit handling to lead to a disturbance. In many ways the position resembles that when they raised the question of the tribute money.

But Jesus was never ensnared, and his answers prevented further discussion. He first stoops and writes on the ground. What he wrote has been a matter of speculation. There was a writing required by that law which the Scribes had invoked in their question to Jesus, in connection with the remarkable arrangements for "the trial of jealousy". The priest took "holy water in an earthen vessel", and mixed some of the dust of the floor of the tabernacle with the water. The accused woman was "set before the LORD", and the priest holding in his hand the "bitter water that causeth the curse" charged the woman with an oath of cursing. He then wrote the curses in a book, blotting them out with the bitter water, of which he made the woman drink. The guilt or innocence of the woman was revealed by its effects upon her (Numbers 5:11–31).

Now, in the midst of Israel, the Word made flesh, bringing the holy water of divine truth in the earthen vessel of human nature, meets the adulterous rulers of God's nation. Their unfaithfulness to God had been denounced by Jesus and the prophets in the terms of this sin; but their lives were notoriously corrupt, also. Did Jesus by his action endeavour to remind them of the curse of the law for that sin? Did he write the curse? Whatever it was, he was not suffered to continue; they persisted with their enquiry, pressing for an answer. He lifted up himself and gave an answer that startled with its unexpectedness. How foolish they were, and slow to learn his power of making their attacks recoil! "He that is without sin among you, let him first cast a stone at her."

It was an appeal to conscience; it was also a sentence of condemnation. He knew their lives, and policy and shame combined to make withdrawal advisable. The elder led the way and all went away. Meanwhile, Jesus continued to write; then looking up, the woman alone stood before him. The crowd for the moment are simply awestruck onlookers, a living ring in the midst of which this amazing thing has been enacted. Jesus asked her of the accusers; had none condemned her? She answered, No. To which he answered: "Neither do I condemn thee: go, and sin no more".

Strange conclusions have been reached from this answer. Jesus does not condone sin: he bids her sin no more. But he does not condemn—it was not his province. "The censuring and judging this woman", says J. Lightfoot, the Talmud scholar of three centuries ago, "belonged to a judicial bench at the least of twenty-three judges; and it would have carried a fair accusation against him, had he gone about to judge in such a matter." He asks also where was the woman's companion in sin? Why had they not brought him? How much higher than human is the Lord's handling of the situation; how much better than a wordy strife, inconclusive in its results, concerning the illegalities of their action and of their request.

THE LIGHT OF THE WORLD (8:12–20)

THE feast of Tabernacles (7:2) was over; and the ceremonies of the feast were finished for another year. One ceremony consisted of the lighting of four large candelabra in the Court of the Women, which, from their elevated position, shed a radiance over all the city. As the "drawing of water" (7:37) celebrated the provision of water from the smitten rock, so these lamps were lit as memorials of the "pillar of fire" by which Israel's God led them in the wilderness. There is some uncertainty how often the lamps were lit during the week, but all authorities agree that during the last evening it did not take place. The omission provided Jesus with the opportunity to draw attention to himself as the true light, and the counterpart of the divine manifestation in the wilderness.*

"I am the light of the world: he that followeth me shall not walk in darkness, but shall have the light of life". The words are based on the record of the pillar of fire: "And the LORD went before them by day in a pillar of a cloud, *to lead them in the way*; and by night in a pillar of fire, *to give them light*; to go by day and night" (Exodus 13:21). Thus were they led to the land that God had promised them.

The Messiah was traditionally called The Light, not without scriptural authority. "The people that walked in darkness have seen a great light" said Isaiah, in introducing the prophecy of the one upon whose shoulder had to rest the government (9:2,6). God's servant is given for "a light to the Gentiles" (42:6) as well as being the light of Zion (60:1).

Israel had to follow the cloudy pillar; and the fiery glory led them by night. But the journey's end was a mortal inheritance, lightly held at first, more securely grasped in David's day, but later lost altogether through disobedience. But Jesus leads the way to that which Paul calls by contrast, "the eternal inheritance" which is based upon better promises and secured by better sacrifices (Hebrews 9:15,23).

Following Jesus is a "walk" in light: mentally enlightened concerning God's truth, morally exercised concerning God's commandments. Such is a "walk in newness of life" now, and leads to a new life which partakes of the divine in its perfection from every side, morally and physically. This is involved in the possession promised by Jesus: he "shall have the light of life". It is a light that leads to life, and becomes a light which is life.

There is a challenge to Jewish narrowness in the title "light of the world", which increased Jewish hatred of Jesus. The sun in the heavens cannot be limited to one country or people; neither is there restriction with the Sun of righteousness. He is truly Zion's light, but his healing beams embrace the world.

How high Jewish feeling ran immediately the rulers came into contact with Jesus may be judged by the interruptions, which reveal an increasing tension. And his words were evidently well discussed in their council. They now turn back

* For account of this ceremony, see Conder, *Handbook*, page 120. Edersheim, *Temple*, page 246.

on Jesus his own words about bearing witness to himself (5:31), and say that by his own rule his record was not true (verse 13).

Jesus rebuts this; it would be true of fallible man, but he was the manifestation of the Eternal. He spake God's word, hence his witness was true. He knew his origin; he knew where he was going; but they did not know him, his origin and destiny. He was the Son of God, begotten of the Father, and would go to the Father. He knew these things; they "knew not" (RV, verse 14).

What was the cause of their failure? An error in the ground of their judgment. They judged after the flesh, by outward appearances. He, himself, did not judge, but his sentences were the Father's judgments pronounced through him. "I am not alone, but I and the Father that sent me". The law, upon which they trusted, testified that the witness of *two men* is true; how much more certain is the witness of God and the Son of God, whose joint testimony they were hearing in the words of Jesus. "I am one that bear witness of myself, and the Father that sent me beareth witness of me" (verse 18).

It was a high claim, that his one voice contained a double witness; but they were unwilling to seek his meaning. "Where is thy Father?" they ask: as much as to say, "You stand there alone; we only see one person and hear one voice". It was an illustration of that judgment after the flesh, of which Jesus had spoken immediately before. It was evidence of a complete lack of understanding of the Father and the Son. Had they recognized him as the Son of God, they would not have asked their question: they then would have reached an understanding of the revelation of the Father in him.

These words were spoken in the temple, in the citadel of the rulers. They had determined upon his death, yet in their awe of him they do nothing. Hid in the shadow of the Father's hand, they were powerless to touch him yet; as John adds: "His hour was not yet come" (verse 20).

DISPUTES IN THE TEMPLE (8:21–59)

THE RV rightly begins a paragraph at verse 21, thereby making a break in the narrative. John's words, "Then said Jesus again unto them", serve to indicate an interval of time, without showing whether long or short; and at the same time marking a connection in thought in the resumed conflict which John now records. Because "no man laid hands on him" Jesus resumed, as the opportunity arose, his teaching about himself as the "Light" that leads to the inheritance, corresponding to the type of the pillar of fire which led them in the way out of Egypt.

The feast had ended; many had left already, others were about to go away. So Jesus said, "I go away, and ye shall seek me, and shall die in your sin: whither I go ye cannot come". Here was a "going" clearly of greater significance than leaving the feast—a "going" from which his hearers were excluded. They had not sought him then in faith, but the time would come when they would desire to be acknowledged by him. With a similar ominousness he had said before (7:34), "Ye shall seek me and shall not find me": and such a fruitless seeking—fruitless because too late—is now in his mind. The final issues of life and death would be in his hands—their present course of action determining what his would be then. Since they refused him now, he would not accept them then; their sins unforgiven, he could do no other. "Ye shall die in your sin." They had made sin the environing condition of their life—in it they would die.

Jesus is not speaking of the death that happens to all, terminating this present life: a judicial death to which they were individually responsible is in his thought. And the connection between sin and death in this teaching of Jesus might be noted, a connection to be found in the writings of the prophets and apostles, but altogether at variance with the speculations of men concerning the soul's deathlessness.

But whither was Jesus going? He was going to God very shortly: but an ascent to heaven like that of Jesus is not promised to any, and there would be no point in the exclusion of his adversaries. But, keeping to the thought of a leading to an inheritance implicit in the language, we can see that exclusion from the Kingdom of God is intended. As Jesus said on another occasion, "Ye shall see Abraham, Isaac, and Jacob in the kingdom of God, and ye yourselves thrust out". To that Kingdom they could not enter. In 7:33 he had spoken of going to God, and of his fellowship with God. That fellowship already existed, "Where I *am*, ye cannot come". While there is some connection, the difference in his thought in this discussion and that of chapter 7 is seen by careful attention to the language used.

They once more refused to understand, preferring to seek for some other meaning in his words than he intended. On the previous occasion they asked, "Will he go to the

Gentiles?" Now they say to each other, with sarcasm in their tones, "Does he mean to commit suicide? What true Israelite would think of thus ending his life? We cannot follow him there".

Such an answer revealed the character of his hearers. As James says of "bitter envying and strife": "This wisdom descendeth not from above, but is earthly, sensual, devilish" (3:14,15). Such was the state of Israel's leaders—of the earth, earthly. But Jesus was an embodied wisdom that is from above, the result of a paternity that was heavenly. This difference, illustrated in the contrast between Jesus and his opponents, he points out in parallel lines which are mutually explanatory.

"Ye are from beneath;
    I am from above:
Ye are of this world;
    I am not of this world".

They by choice followed the course of this world, making their own the spirit that worketh in the children of disobedience. He had chosen to follow the counsel of God. His life illustrated his divine sonship; their lives exhibited the ungoverned ways of natural men. Because they had made their choice they were culpable, and deserving of that which he had before pronounced, and now repeats, that they should die in their sins. There was one way of escape from this, but one only: "If ye believe not that I am he, ye shall die in your sins" (verse 24).

There is a connection indicated here between belief and an acceptable relationship to God that is very foreign to modern sentiments. Belief of particular doctrines is regarded as a relic of a narrower and more fanatical generation. Believe what you like and do as you please is the general rule to-day. But the testimony of Jesus is emphatic—"except ye believe, ye shall die".

The particular phase of belief emphasized at this time by Jesus is stated in the simple words "that I am he": the phrase "I am" or "I am he" (the same in the Greek) occurs three times in this chapter, verses 24, 28 and 58. But who was he? He had just said, "from above", "sent of the Father", "the light of the world"; in all these phrases he claims to be a manifestation of God. The point in dispute is variously expressed, but it was not perceived by them, moral perversity having blinded their

111

eyes; and not being perceived, "ye shall die in your sins" is a sentence of death.

Their next question is to be understood in a scornful, derisive, sense: "Who art *thou*?" Perhaps they desired him to say more plainly what was implied in his previous utterance. It may be that both the words and the tone in which they were said expressed only the bitter dislike they felt towards Jesus. The meaning of verse 25 has been much disputed; the meaning of every word but "you" having been doubted. The interpretation of the early Greek writers, to whom Greek was the mother tongue, is given in the margin of the RV, and fits the circumstances well. "How is it that I even speak to you at all?" If we accept the AV, with which the RV practically agrees, we must then understand Jesus to say that he was in his life all that he had claimed in his speech all the time. And he adds that his testimony had not yet come to its end: he had many things to say to them, things that in view of their attitude must be of judgment. They might reject them, but that did not affect their truth: the world—their world (verse 23)— must have the message, "which I have heard of him".

Jesus saw that they had not perceived his meaning in these words about the One who sent him; and John records their failure to understand so that the reason for the next words of Jesus may be understood. Their failure may be surprising; but that it was blameworthy is evident from the words which follow.

"Jesus therefore said, When ye have lifted up the Son of man, then shall ye know that I am he, and that I do nothing of myself; but as the Father has taught me, I speak these things. And he that sent me is with me: the Father hath not left me alone; for I do always those things that please him."   (verses 28,29)

The "lifting up" refers first of all to the crucifixion, which was a Jewish responsibility although performed by the "wicked hands" of the Romans (Acts 2:23). But it was a necessary step to another "lifting up", as an ensign on the mountains of Israel, when all the world will hear him. For the suffering of death he has been crowned with glory and honour; and this will yet be as widely recognized on earth as it now is in heaven. When this takes place they will perceive the truths which Jesus gives in the three clauses: (1) "that I am" (the Son of man, Psalm 8:4; 80:17); (2) that he was dependent on the Father; (3) that his message was received from the Father. To this he adds that there was continual co-operation between Father and Son, the Father being always present with him, and he being always obedient to the Father.

The effect of these words upon two classes is noted; "many believed *on* him" (verse 30); and some Jews—that is, some of the hostile rulers—believed him. The different reaction, one a more complete acceptance than the other, distinguished by the use of "on" in the first class, is clearly brought out in the RV. To the second class Jesus addresses himself in words which encourage further trust in him if they were willing, but which call for a decision. They must go forward, or return to his enemies. The sequel reveals a collapse of faith.

"If ye abide in my word, then are ye truly my disciples; and ye shall know the truth, and the truth shall make you free." Here was a test of discipleship; for such a relationship requires that the teacher be followed from one element of doctrine to another. His word was truth, as he was the Truth; and to be his disciples in truth they must accept him as the Saviour from sin and from death. This aspect of his work was not appreciated by them, yet it was constantly the subject of his teaching; he had only a little while before told them they would die in their sins apart from belief in him. But their thoughts were far away from these ideas; political freedom was of greater consequence to them. Therefore with a complete disregard for truth, they answer, "We be Abraham's seed, and were never in bondage to any man: how sayest thou, Ye shall be made free?" To be Abraham's seed and to be in bondage may be discordant ideas; Abraham's seed are a royal race. Sarah "shall be a mother of nations, and kings of peoples shall be of her" (Genesis 17:16). But the promise was not yet fulfilled; were they even heirs of the promise, and their present bondage a passing phase? That was dependent upon whether they were true heirs; pride of race continually preventing them from seeing that flesh descent *in itself* gave no title to the everlasting features of the covenant. These features were necessarily bound up with the removal of sin. The answer of Jesus thus gets to the heart of the matter, when he says: "Verily, verily, I say unto you, Whosoever committeth sin is the servant of sin. And the servant abideth not in the house for ever: but the Son abideth for ever. If the Son therefore shall make you free, ye shall be free indeed".

These relationships of the servant and the son to the house are general terms, behind them of course being the suggestion that they were servants and he the Son. The servant sustains no permanent relationship to house and inheritance, the son does. Behind the figures used may be traced the lines of the domestic affairs of Abraham, which, as Paul shows, were an allegory. Ishmael was a son of Abraham, but born of a servant, and not the heir. Such was their case, the terms being used on the moral and not the physical plane.

Jesus admits their flesh descent from Abraham: "I know ye are Abraham's seed"; but he denies there is any spiritual kinship with Abraham, for they sought to kill him, because "his (Christ's) word hath not free course in you". And, adopting the margin of the RV, which gives excellent sense, Jesus makes another appeal that they should follow his example. "I speak the things which I have seen with the Father: do ye also therefore the things which ye have heard from the Father"—an invitation to accept his words as the Father's and to obey them.

But their hearts are hardening to the appeal: and with that their minds are becoming unreceptive. They miss the reference to God, and answer with the old racial infatuation, "Abraham is our father". This had been admitted as true in one sense: it must now be denied when "doing" is the test. They did not follow Abraham's faith and obedience, but were seeking to kill him. Abraham listened to God's word and looked for Christ. They refused God's word and would kill the messenger. Tested thus, what parentage had they? For "ye do the works of your father". Some light breaks upon them— Jesus has spiritual descent in view. They do not hesitate to claim the highest standing—they were unpolluted with idolatry, they had "one Father, even God", yet in formulating their claim, may they not have intended a sharp thrust at him about whose parentage they had made some investigation (6:42), and about whom in the second century the vilest slanders were circulated?

Jesus once more challenges their claims and applies again the test of actions. If they were sons of God they would love the Son of God; for he was loved of God, having come from God, his birth, character and mission being of God. And here also is the secret of their failure continually to understand his teaching. "Why do ye not understand my speech? even because ye cannot hear my word." *Speech* refers to the form; *word* to the substance, the meaning, the thought. They did not understand his language because they were ignorant of the truth it expressed. Such failure called for the bluntest of expressions, hence he told them they were sin's children, with a pedigree going back to the lie in Eden, and their words and deeds were the characteristic modes in which sin was to be found (verse 44). The lie in word in Eden had been trans-

114

lated into a lie in action ever since; but in Jesus both word and action were transcripts from the divine. His life was a foreign tongue to them which they did not understand, but which was really the highest proof that he was the Son of God. In a statement that would be impossible from other lips he said: "Because I tell you the truth ye believe me not. Which of you convicteth me of sin? And if I say the truth, why do ye not believe me?" There was only one answer: "He that is of God, heareth God's words: ye therefore hear them not, because ye are not of God" (verses 45–47).

Their only answer is abuse, saying that only a Samaritan and a demoniac would thus talk. Of these accusations the second was the more serious—were it true it would invalidate his witness. He therefore denies it, asserting that even in the claims made he was honouring his Father, while they by their accusations dishonoured Him. This did not disturb him, since he did not seek his own glory and God would decide the issue, vindicating him, judging them (verses 48–52).

The thought of judgment is the link with the next verse, and the key to its meaning. There was one way and one way only in which they could escape the death that would follow their judgment. "If a man keep my saying (word) he shall never see death." Separated from context it would be a promise of immunity from death now; but if the thought is carried on from the preceding verse, it is then rightly seen to have reference to the second death which will not "hurt" those who have kept the word of Jesus (Revelation 2:11)

Such language seemed to them proof of madness. They misunderstood him; regarding his words as promising an escape from death now, they change "behold death" to " taste death". Since Abraham and the prophets were dead, what did he claim to be?

He was not glorifying himself, he answered; personally bestowed honour availed nothing: but God glorified him in the works He had given him to do. This, however, they had not learned. But Jesus knew God, knew Him by experience, as he indicates by a change of word to distinguish his knowledge from theirs; and if he denied this he would lie. But he was to God what he demanded the believer must be to him, "I know him and keep his word" (verses 55,51).

Having answered the insinuation about himself he turns to the comparison suggested with Abraham. He was greater than Abraham, inasmuch as his day was before Abraham as a matter of hope and rejoicing. Through him Abraham would inherit the Kingdom. But taking his "day" as being the duration of his life they consider it a sufficient refutation to point out he was not yet fifty. On their understanding of his words he must have lived for two thousand years. To which Jesus rejoins, he was in the Father's purpose long before Abraham: "Verily, verily, I say unto you, Before Abraham was born, I am". His place in God's plan ante-dated Abraham, for as the apostle says, he was foreordained before the foundation of the world (1 Peter 1:20).

Such claims called not for wordy answer; he deserved to be stoned, and then and there they would have killed him. Building material about supplied them with missiles, but as they took them in their hands Jesus was swallowed up in the crowd, some of whom were not unsympathetic, and he left the temple.

SIXTH SIGN: GIVING SIGHT TO THE MAN BORN BLIND (9:1–7)

IN the days of Hezekiah, when the Assyrians invaded Palestine, preparations were made in Jerusalem to withstand a siege. Foremost among these was the provision of an adequate water supply for the city. Before this time Jerusalem had depended on rock-cistern storage for rain water, and the fountain of the "Virgin's Spring" outside the walls of the city. But Hezekiah "made a pool, and a conduit, and brought water into the city" (2 Kings 20:20). By this means the water was made available for the city; and by stopping "the waters of the fountains which were without the city" they cut off the supply of water for the enemy: "Why should the kings of Assyria come and find much water?" This rock-cut watercourse has been discovered in modern times, in much the condition it was left by Hezekiah's engineers. It winds for some 1,700 feet from the Virgin's Pool to the Pool of Siloam. In 1880 the Siloam inscription was discovered, telling of the meeting of the miners who had begun at opposite ends.

But before this tunnel was made by the men of Hezekiah there had been an aqueduct, or "conduit of the upper pool" to convey the water to the city. It was here that Isaiah met Ahaz (Isaiah 7:3); and from this softly flowing stream he drew his parable of the divine covenant of the throne which was despised by Ahaz. "Forasmuch as this people refuseth the waters of Shiloah that go softly, and rejoice in Rezin and Remaliah's son; now therefore behold, the Lord bringeth up upon them the waters of the river, strong and many, even the king of Assyria, and all his glory: and he shall come up over all his channels, and go over all his banks" (8:6,7).

When the same waters of Shiloah flowed into the city, and the waters of the Gentile powers roared and were troubled as they broke in fury against the divine protection of the Holy City, again the Psalmist used the stream as a figure of God's covenanted protection and care. "There is a river, the streams whereof shall make glad the city of God, the holy place of the tabernacles of the Most High. God is in the midst of her; she shall not be moved; God shall help her at the dawn of the morning" (46:4,5).

Hezekiah had experience of such help when the angel of the Lord smote the Assyrians, "and when they arose early in the morning" the dreaded army had passed into the sleep of death (Isaiah 37:36).

The same waters of Shiloah were connected with the ceremonies of the feast of Tabernacles, as we have already seen. The annual ceremony of the drawing of water was kept as a memorial of the water from the smitten rock, and was associated with the words of Isaiah: "Therefore with joy shall ye draw water out of the wells of salvation" (12:3). In these allusions we find a connection between the "water of Siloam" and the divinely provided son of David, who should occupy David's throne and also be the salvation of all who would accept the water of life.

All these associations must be kept in mind as we consider the sign of the healing of the blind man.

As Jesus and the disciples "passed by" (presumably) one of the temple gates, Jesus noticed the man who had been born blind. The disciples observing his interest asked him a question which reflected one of the subjects discussed by the Rabbis. Starting from the position that all sickness and suffering is the result of sin, they had to find an explanation for the disabilities of those born blind or lame or in any way defective. A number of theories were held; one related to the idea of the migration of souls, but was without many adherents; another recognized that the sins of the parents are visited on the children, the grim fact of heredity explaining some cases of sickness; still another view was that a child could sin before birth, and thus be born with the penalty of such sin. Seeing the man born blind, the disciples asked Jesus, Who did sin, the man, or his parents, that he should be born blind?

117

Jesus did not answer the question, but said that this man was so born that "the works of God should be made manifest in him". The answer was not a denial of the fact of sin or of the effects of sin, while it does deny the thought that all suffering is directly connected with the specific sin of the individual or his parents. The man was there in such a condition as enabled a great spiritual lesson to be taught in connection with his restoration of sight. The physical cure was a representation of the giving of spiritual sight which it was the work of Jesus to perform. Isaiah had written that the Messiah would be "for a light of the Gentiles; *to open the blind eyes*" (42:6,7). The words and work of Jesus point to the connection between himself and the water of Siloam and also with the prophecy of Isaiah. "I must work the works of him that *sent* me, while it is day: the night cometh, when no man can work. As long as I am in the world, I am the light of the world." John explains that Siloam, to which the man was sent to wash his eyes, means *Sent*; and by the work of Jesus the man saw the light of day; and it was a sabbath.

The method employed by Jesus was symbolic, in keeping with the practice of the prophets of illustrating by action the lesson they wished to teach. It was a recognized practice to use spittle for anointing sore eyes: but this was forbidden on a sabbath: and Jesus did not use spittle but clay mixed with spittle. With this he daubed the man's eyes, an action that would have taken away vision from one who could see, and sent him to Siloam. Jesus can blind as well as give sight; but those who are blind can only receive their sight by an act of faith which takes them to the One who is sent of God.

SEQUEL TO THE SIGN (9:8–41)

WHEN the beggar now healed of his blindness was seen by his neighbours they were naturally surprised. He was a familiar figure, but the change in him led them to doubt his identity. But he quickly removed doubt, and in answer to the question how he had received his sight, said, "He that is called Jesus made clay, and anointed mine eyes, and said unto me, Go to the pool of Siloam, and wash: and I went and washed, and I received sight". His answer shows he knew the identity of his benefactor, and the phrasing suggests that he felt the action was in keeping with the healer's name.

They asked him the whereabouts of Jesus. But the man did not know. The next step is a strange one: it has been called a shameful one. The neighbours take the man to the authorities, who had decreed that anyone confessing that Jesus was the Messiah should be excommunicated. Whatever their motive in taking the man to the Pharisees, a lack of appreciation and understanding of Jesus is evident from their action. The miracle had been performed on a sabbath, one of seven miracles which Jesus had done on a sabbath, and this had become a grievous offence on the part of Jesus in the eyes of the Pharisees. The sequel might well have been expected by these people who would seek the favour of the rulers in bringing the man to them.

The Pharisees questioned the man. They did not attempt to deny the miracle but were divided among themselves how to explain it. The ceremonialism and sabbath-keeping rules blinded many to the obvious explanation; they started from the necessity of keeping their sabbath laws, and hence denied that Jesus was of God. Others started from the fact of the miracle, and concluded that Jesus could not be a sinner. They asked the man, who had none of their hesitancy about facing the issue. "He is a prophet", he answered.

At this stage it would seem higher authorities intervened. The man was brought to the Pharisees, but now the Jews, by which John indicates the rulers of Israel, took part in the enquiry. They first cast doubt on the statement that the man had received sight, and called for his parents to confirm that he had been born blind, and to say how his sight had been given to him. The parents were wanting in courage, and for fear of being expelled from the synagogue, shifted the responsibility of answering to the son.

Called again before the rulers, they treated him as a criminal called upon to confess: "Give glory to God; we know that this man is a sinner". But the man was a careful witness. He did not argue with them either about what they knew, or whether their statement concerning Jesus was correct; he was concerned with what were facts in his own experience. He was blind, now he saw. His simplicity condemned them—he stuck to facts which they could not brush aside or explain away.

Baffled, they sought for a flaw in his evidence. They asked him to state again what had happened; but their scornful attitude concerning Jesus and their want of judicial fairness, provoked the retort, I have told you once; do you also wish to be disciples?

Taking his words as a confession that he was a disciple, they reviled him and contemptuously contrasted discipleship

119

of "that man"—Jesus—with that of Moses. God had spoken to Moses; but they knew not whence Jesus was, and therefore he should not be followed. The weakness of their position is shown alike by their rising tempers and the confession of not knowing who Jesus was, when it was their duty to test his claims and make a decision.

The courage of the man grew, and his faith increased as he realized how ill-founded was their case. He retorted with a fine irony, lashing them with their own scourge, that here was a marvellous thing that they did not know whence Jesus was, and yet he had opened a blind man's eyes; the power must be of God, and Jesus could not be a sinner or God would not hear him; the miracle was evident and its character exceptional; the man must be of God.

With the superior attitude of the self-righteous, and infuriated by his logic and his scorn, they turned on him, and with marked inconsistency after denying the miracle, now threw his previous calamity in his teeth as an evidence of his sinfulness, confirmed as it was by his perversity in answering them: "Thou wast altogether born in sins, and dost thou teach us?" And they thrust him out.

Jesus heard what had happened, sought out the man, and asked him, "Dost thou believe on the Son of God?" The RV (margin) changes this to Son of man, chiefly on the evidence of the Sinaitic and Vatican MSS, and against the great weight of evidence in favour of the AV. And the context harmonizes with the AV. The man had been arguing that such powers as his healer had shown witnessed that he had a divine mission. Jesus would lead him on to an understanding of his relationship to God. The man did not perceive that Jesus was speaking of himself, but he was willing to be guided by Jesus. Jesus therefore said, adding the fact of sight to the evidence that his voice would have to the man, that he was none other than his healer, "Thou hast both seen him, and it is he that talketh with thee".

The gratitude of the man grew to faith, and faith passed to worship as he confessed, "Lord, I believe".

The believing seeing man contrasted with unbelieving blind Pharisees, and Jesus expressed in the terms of this paradox the effect of his mission. His coming would issue in a judgment giving sight or blinding according to men's response to him: "For judgment I am come into this world, that they which see not might see; and that they which see might be made blind". The man illustrates the first physically and spiritually: the vaunted knowledge of the rulers would lead them to a position as unseeing as eyes besmeared with the clay of human perversity.

Some hearers were quick to see the parable in his words, and to apply the lesson. Jesus implied that sight depended upon coming to him. Were they then, who had not responded to his teaching, blind? Jesus answers, they were not utterly blind, unable to use eyes and judgment in connection with his works and words: in such a case there would be no sin. But since they claimed to be able to see, their sin remained, inasmuch as they did not come to him to learn of him.

THE ALLEGORY OF THE SHEPHERD AND THE SHEEP (10:1–21)

THE Gospel of John does not record one parable spoken by Jesus. The word "parable" indeed occurs in this chapter but it represents another word than the one translated "parable" in the other Gospels. The two words are used in the Septuagint to represent one word in the Hebrew text, so the distinction cannot be pressed too hard. The RV has made a distinction by the marginal suggestion of "proverb" in this place, but reverses the position in John 16:25 where the revisers suggest "parables" in the margin where "proverbs" is used in the text. The other two occurrences are in John 16:29 and 2 Peter 2:22 where we find "proverb" in the text.

The shepherd was a well known figure in Palestine. Clad in the simplest and roughest of garments, equipped with the club and the staff, he led his flock into the desert for pasture during part of the year. He faced hardship and danger continually. The straying sheep, fallen maybe down from some cliff-edge, must be found and carried to safety. The wild beasts, the lion, bear, leopard, jackal and hyena, were an ever-present danger. There were also human enemies, the wandering children of the desert, whose hand was against every man, ready to plunder and to rob whenever opportunity came. The shepherd's calling required courage and strength, patience and endurance.

The club and the staff were for the defence and guidance of the flock. The staff corresponds to the crook, used to guide and rule the flock. The club, a formidable weapon in experienced hands, was for protection of the flock against all foes.

Moses was a shepherd—first of Jethro's flocks, and then of God's people. "Thou leddest thy people like a flock by the hand of Moses and Aaron", writes Asaph (Psalm 77:20); while

Isaiah, in language which provides Paul with the words he uses concerning Jesus, says,

"Then he remembered the days of old, Moses and his people, saying, Where is he that brought them up out of the sea with the shepherd of his flock? where is he that put his holy spirit within him? that led them by the right hand of Moses with his glorious arm, dividing the water before them, to make himself an everlasting name?"

(Isaiah 63:11,12)

Paul's application is in his prayer that "the God of peace that brought again from the dead the Great Shepherd of the Sheep through the blood of the everlasting covenant" would make the Hebrews perfect in every good work" (13:20,21).

The Mediator of the first covenant thus foreshadowed the Mediator of the Abrahamic. And David also, the first king of divine choice, was a shepherd, first of his father's flock, and then of the sheep of Israel. The lion and the bear met a dauntless defender of the flock in Jesse's son. God, who judges after the heart, took him "from following the sheep to be ruler over Israel", and he prefigures his greater Son who will yet fulfil the word of God through Ezekiel:

"I will set up one shepherd over them, and he shall feed them, even my servant David, he shall feed them, and he shall be their shepherd." (34:23)

God was the Great Shepherd of His people, whether of the individual or of the nation. "The Lord is my shepherd", the shepherd-king wrote in the well known twenty-third Psalm, and God was everything unto David that David would be to his sheep.

Micah prays to God:

"Shepherd thou thy flock with thy rod, the flock of thine inheritance" (Rotherham);

and God answers:

"As in the days of thy coming out of Egypt will I show him wonders." (7:15)

This day of the second Exodus will reveal Messiah the Prince, the Shepherd of Israel, who, Jacob foretold, would be the Son of God. "From the mighty God of Jacob is the shepherd and stone of Israel" (Genesis 49:24). Both sonship and office of shepherd are brought together in the Lord's decree (Psalm 2).

"My son thou art,
I today have begotten thee:

122

> Ask of me, and let me give
> Nations as thine inheritance,
> And as thy possession the ends of the earth:
> Thou shalt shepherd them with a sceptre of iron—
> As a potter's vessel shalt thou dash them in pieces."

Asaph pleads: "Give ear, O Shepherd of Israel, thou that leadest Joseph like a flock", and petitions that His hand would be upon the son of man made strong for Himself (Psalm 80:1,17). By that means they would be "quickened" and be saved.

This same figure Isaiah again uses of God in a context which shows that it is bound up with Israel's restoration and Jerusalem's exaltation, when the glory of the Lord is revealed and all flesh see it together. One comes to Zion with the good tidings, "Behold your God", and the prophet continues:

> "Behold, the Lord GOD will come with strong hand, and his arm shall rule for him: behold, his reward is with him, and his work before him. He shall feed his flock like a shepherd: he shall gather the lambs with his arm, and carry them in his bosom, and shall gently lead those that are with young." (40:10,11)

This application of the shepherd-figure to God and to His Son in the prophets gives great force and meaning to the words of Jesus when he describes himself as the "good shepherd". In the light of Old Testament references he claims that he was the manifestation of the God of Israel, the Son of God, and the Messiah. The discussion that arose out of it concerning the status of Jesus—"that thou being a man, makest thyself God"—was therefore strictly relevant.

It is unfortunate that the chapter division dissociates the shepherd allegory from the discussion reported in chapter 9. Jesus has convicted the Pharisees of blindness and incompetence in dealing with the flock of God. As bad shepherds they had cast out the healed man, but the good shepherd had found him.

The first five verses are quite general and no application is made to the work of Jesus in them. The sheepfold was an enclosure sometimes of stone walls or of palings, with a doorway. A porter was in charge. Several shepherds might drive their flocks into one fold.

Jesus begins his allegory by saying that a man who tries to get into the fold by a way other than the door has some evil purpose. "But he that entereth in by the door is a shepherd of the sheep" (verse 2, RV margin). The porter opens to the shepherd, who calls his sheep by name "and leadeth them out". By the use of a word Jesus contrasts the good shepherd with the Pharisees who had "cast out" (9:34) the man who had been healed. They "put out" of their congregation the one who has entered the good shepherd's flock. "When he *putteth* forth his own sheep, he goeth before them, and the sheep follow him for they know his voice"; but the stranger they do not follow.

From verse 7 onwards Jesus makes an application to himself of the figure, but without working out a close and detailed parallel. He does not, for example, bring out any analogy to the porter, unless the word "know" used of the Father in verse 15 is intended to connect with the use of the word concerning the porter. Brother Roberts finds a counterpart to the porter's duty in the work of Moses and John.

In the interpretation Jesus is the door as well as the shepherd, different aspects of his work being thereby represented. As the door he is the way out to pasture: as the shepherd he has under-shepherds—in Peter's words, he is the Chief Shepherd.

Others had come before making claims to be the way; of these false Messiahs Jesus says: "All that ever came before me are thieves and robbers, but the sheep did not hear them" (verse 8). Such try to enter the fold by unlawful ways, having personal interests. But there were other men associated with Jesus who use the door, and who entering in shall be saved, and shall lead others to salvation, going in and out and finding pasture.

The figure changes from door to shepherd, and the contrast is made between the thieves and himself. The thief cometh to steal, to kill, and to destroy. "I came that they might have life, and that they might have it more abundantly." The wolf destroys, tearing the sheep: but Jesus excels the ordinary shepherd in that he not only finds pasture but gives life to the sheep. This thought leads to an extended account of his relationship to the sheep (verses 11–16).

He is the good shepherd—there is nothing that is foul or mean or wicked in him; he is noble and beautiful in thought and act, which is seen in his laying down his life for the sheep. The rulers were plotting to take his life; but he presents his side of the issue that was drawing ever nearer. He contrasts himself with the hireling, a man even worse than the thief, in that his regard for his own life is a dereliction of duty. With him profession is belied by act: he is a wolf clad as a sheep; a false teacher who does not defend the truth when personal interests are involved (Acts 20:3,29,30).

The beauty and the development of thought of the next lines can be best exhibited by indicating the parallelism that underlies them:

> I am the good shepherd,
> and know my sheep,
> and am known of mine.
>
> As the Father knoweth me,
> even so know I the Father:
> And I lay down my life for the sheep.

Because Jesus is the good shepherd he knows his sheep, and they know him. But this close friendship and trust is a reflection of a similar friendship that exists between himself and God. May we not carry on the figure to him? If he is "the lamb of God", can we not add to the sacrificial aspect of that phrase this thought also, that God is *his* shepherd, and the twenty-third Psalm is the Lord's expression as well as David's? His trust in and obedience to God's voice is the example for his sheep to trust and obey him. Springing from that knowledge of the Father is his readiness to lay down his life.

Jesus knew his work was not limited to the Jews. There were "other sheep", of the Gentiles, who also must be led by him and "hear his voice", and being joined to the Jewish sheep become "one flock", an enlargement of the idea of the union of the divided Israelites into one flock with the One Shepherd over them chosen by God (Ezekiel 34:23; 37:22). There is a remarkable confidence in the continuation of his work after his death in these words of Jesus which should be noted. It shows a faith in resurrection after he has laid down his life, as quiet and assured as a healthy man speaks of resuming his work after rest in sleep. The thought at once follows: "Therefore doth my Father love me, because I lay down my life, that I might take it again".

The decision was his—he had power of choice. The Jews might plot, but apart from his acquiescence in the purpose of God, they could do nothing, just as they were powerless to prevent his taking up of life again. The whole matter was of God, from whom the commandment had come to him.

Claims such as these provoked the most diverse reactions. Strife and division among the Jews followed as they discussed his words. He is mad, some said; but others remembered the miracle of giving sight, and drew other conclusions. But the incident was not closed: the words, with all their graciousness, rankled in their minds, and their implications were considered. A short interval of time passes (probably two months), and when Jesus is again teaching in the temple the discussion is resumed. The connection of subject matter is so close that John, after a brief time note, continues his narrative in a way that links the two discourses together.

AT THE FEAST OF DEDICATION (10:22–42)

THE feast of Tabernacles, the third of the annual feasts appointed by the law, was held when the work of gathering in the harvest in the seventh month of the year was completed. This corresponds to our month of October.

Two months later, in the month of December, the feast of Dedication was kept. This feast was observed to commemorate the purification and restoration of the Temple after its desecration by Antiochus Epiphanes, in 170 BC. From the illuminations with which it was celebrated it was also called the feast of Lights. This feast did not require the presence of the worshippers at Jerusalem, which may supply the reason for John's statement that Jesus was at Jerusalem during the feast. His added words, abruptly interposed as in the RV, "it was winter", may be understood as an indication not merely of the time when the feast was held, but also of the wintry reception given to Jesus. It was a time of growing difficulty, of storminess, when the gales of opposition were blowing stronger. It was the winter of Jewish unbelief, when the temple was defiled, not by a pagan Antiochus, but by the Jewish rulers by their apostasy.

The rulers saw Jesus walking in the covered colonnade which bore Solomon's name, and gathered round him. His discourse of two months before on the shepherd and the sheep had rankled in their minds for two reasons. It contained an indictment that they were thieves and robbers, hirelings, and false shepherds; and it was a claim of a unique position for Jesus in relation to God, and a work to be done by him appointed by the Father, which contrasted only too forcibly with their shortcomings. But the exclusive and reciprocal knowledge of God, who was described by Jesus as "my Father", implying a close and exceptional relationship, which Jesus had proclaimed, appeared to them to be blasphemy and therefore a grievous offence.

The differences among the rulers made it difficult to make a definite charge. They were confused as a body, as many individuals were confused in their own minds. They therefore ask, with varying motives, "How long dost thou hold us in suspense? If thou art the Christ, tell us plainly". Some may have wanted a pronouncement that would help them to a decision; many doubtless wanted him to say something which would incriminate him. From the answer of Jesus we might infer that they added to the question which John records some reference to his claims to be the Shepherd-Messiah of the prophets.

Jesus, who knew the hearts of the questioners, did not answer in the way they hoped. He saw the spirit of the questioners was wrong, and perhaps the manner in which they put it; he therefore refers them to the addresses he had given before, and to the works that he had done. "I told you, and ye believe not; the works that I do in my Father's name, these bear witness of me". The change of tense in the RV, which is quoted, is significant. "I told you"—the claims had been repeatedly made in the past; "and ye believe not"—there had been ample opportunity to end the doubt and suspense, but they would not remove them in the only possible way, by believing him. They had in fact rejected his claims, and were then unbelieving; they were refusing to believe. Both word and deed were rejected by them.

Jesus proceeded to lay bare the reason for this. "Ye believe not because ye are not of my sheep, as I said unto you." He had before in other words explained their unbelieving attitude to him: "He that is of God heareth God's words: ye therefore hear them not, because ye are not of God" (8:47). He spoke the words of God, and the godly discerned this and listened to him. These had the character of his sheep, while the moral defect in his opponents was revealed in their rejection of his words.

By a change in punctuation verses 27 and 28, which form two triplets in the AV, may be arranged in three couplets, bringing out in the parallelism a developing relationship and blessing.

My sheep hear my voice,
   And I know them;

127

> And they follow me,
>> And I give unto them eternal life;
> And they shall never perish,
>> Neither shall any man pluck them out of my hand.

The repeated "and" knits together closely the whole statement, while the alternate lines give the position of the sheep, and the shepherd's attitude to them. They hear, they follow, and as a result they shall never perish. The shepherd knows them, gives them eternal life, and as a consequence they are safe from all human wolves who cannot "snatch" (the same word as in verse 12) them away from him.

Jesus now traces the parallel between his work and the Father's purpose. "My Father, which gave them me, is greater than all; and no man is able to pluck them out of my Father's hand. I and my Father are one." To be in his hand, is also to be kept in the Father's hand; the security which belongs to possession by Jesus, is the security which pertains to possession by the Almighty, who is also the Father of Jesus (my Father), and becomes the Father of all who belong to Jesus. Between the Father and Jesus there is perfect harmony—they are one in will, in purpose, in action, in power.

The Jews had on a previous occasion snatched up stones to throw at Jesus. They now more deliberately take hold of stones to bury Jesus beneath them as a punishment for what they regard as blasphemy. But before they throw the first stone, as the stones are poised to hurl at him, they are arrested by the question, "Many good works have I showed you from the Father; for which of those works do you stone me?"

It was his words that had infuriated them; but he calls upon them to think of his works. He describes them—they have been "good works": such works, indeed, as revealed the Father. The works endorsed the words; what fault could they find with the endorsement? They answer, brushing aside the evidence of the works, that his words were blasphemy because he being a man made himself God.

English usage here tends to mislead, giving the impression that by their answer the Jews had understood that Jesus claimed to be the Almighty. This is not the case. They saw that his claims of sonship and of oneness with God carried a claim to be divine. So it did, in his origin, his character, and purpose. What fault was there in that? Had they forgotten the prophecy of Zechariah concerning the Shepherd: "Awake, O sword, against my shepherd, and against the man that is

my fellow, saith the LORD of hosts: smite the shepherd ..."
(13:7)? Altogether forgetting the prophecy they prepared to
fulfil it, smiting the shepherd and denying that he was "the
fellow" of the LORD of hosts.

There are degrees in men's relationship to God. The rulers
appointed to govern Israel were God's representatives, and as
such bore the name of God. So the judges were called "gods"
in the law; see Exodus 21:6; 22:8,28, comparing the RV. The
last passage reads, "Thou shalt not revile the gods, nor curse
the ruler of thy people". God himself so described them in
Psalm 82, which Jesus quotes. "Is it not written in your law,
I said, Ye are gods?" From this unquestionable fact Jesus
reasons: "If he called them gods, unto whom the word of God
came, and the Scripture cannot be broken; say ye of him
whom the Father hath sanctified and sent into the world,
Thou blasphemest; because I said, I am the Son of God?"
(verses 34-36).

In introducing the quotation we notice that Jesus calls the
Psalm "your law", a description which shows that the Psalms
in his estimation had the authority of law. This receives
emphasis from the words, "and the Scripture cannot be
broken". Then further, Jesus calls the Psalm "the word of
God" which "came" unto those rulers described in it as "gods".

The Psalm was written by Asaph, probably in the days of
Hezekiah. That good king had stood in the congregation of
God, reproving the gods, or judges, of that congregation for
their injustice. Though privileged as rulers, and therefore
"gods", and therefore also "children of the Most High", they
should die like men.

But all local and immediate occasions fail to complete the
meaning of prophecy. The Psalm Jesus cited was then in
process of fulfilment. The contemporary judges were "gods" to
whom the word of God had come, first in the fulness of the
revelation in the spoken words of Jesus, and then in the life
which revealed he was the Word made flesh. As they were
"gods", so he was "God" who stood in their midst; reproving
and rebuking them for their unrighteousness in judgment.
They were in a national sense "children of the Most High";
why could they not lift their thoughts a little higher and
recognize that Isaac, the son of promise, the divinely raised
up "seed" from which their race had sprung, and because of
which they were a national son of God, foreshadowed another "seed" who would be truly Son of God and through whom
would be established an individual sonship to God by adoption. They were prepared to acknowledge that *they* were

children of the Most High, entitled to be called "gods", but they would not allow the claims of Jesus. They therefore crucified "the prince", and the words of Asaph received a terrible fulfilment when those called "gods" died like that pre-eminent "one of the princes", in being crucified in great numbers by the same Roman power they employed to crucify Jesus.

The detailed fulfilment of the Psalm in the work of Jesus is illustrated by the following extract from *The Ministry of the Prophets: Isaiah*, page 164:

"Jesus 'being a man' could nevertheless be called 'god'; especially as the Father was 'in him' and had 'sanctified and sent him into the world'. The 82nd Psalm, from which Jesus made this quotation, is very enlightening when considered with reference to 'mighty God' of Isaiah 9, his controversy with the unjust judges of Israel, and the ultimate establishment of his kingdom with 'judgement and justice for ever'. It runs as follows:

" 'God standeth in the congregation of the mighty; he judgeth among the gods. How long will ye judge unjustly (John 8:15), and accept the persons of the wicked? (John 7:48; 5:43). Defend the poor and fatherless: do justice to the afflicted and needy. Deliver the poor and needy: rid them out of the hand of the wicked (Matthew 23:14). They know not, neither will they understand; they walk on in darkness: all the foundations of the earth are out of course (1 John 2:11; Psalm 11:3). I have said, Ye are gods; and all of you are children of the most High (John 10:34). But ye shall die like men, and fall like one of the princes. Arise, O God, judge the earth, for Thou shalt inherit all nations' (Isaiah 9:5; Hebrews 1:8; John 8:26; Revelation 11:15).

"The interpolated references indicate the application of the Psalm to the time when Immanuel rebuked the apostasy of the 'gods', and declared that they should die in their sins for rejecting him (John 8:21), and also to the terrible time when they shall see Abraham, Isaac, and Jacob in the Kingdom of God, and they themselves thrust out (Luke 13:28)."

The word of God came to the judges calling for obedient service from them and describing them as gods. Jesus had been sanctified and sent into the world, bearing thereby a much higher relationship to God than those rulers who for a short time had possessed and misused the little delegated power God had given to them. If they admitted the divine basis for the title in the case of past rulers, let them consider the equally divine grounds for the claim of Jesus to be Son of God. To speak truth is not blasphemy; to reject divine testimony and evidence may be. To this witness Jesus appeals when he added, " If I do not the works of my Father, believe me not; but if I do them, though ye believe not me, believe the works: that ye may know and understand that the Father is in me, and I in the Father". They are thrown back upon a consideration of all his mighty works, "miracles, wonders and signs", which, as Peter says, marked him out as approved of God (Acts 2:22). They were of such a character, both in form and frequency, that they were ample evidence that God was in him; and since God would not have worked so mightily in any other than one who was in willing co-operation, they were evidence also that he was "in the Father".

The answer of Jesus did not alter their purpose to stone him, but for some reason not stated they had in the short respite decided to take him elsewhere to carry out their purpose. But once again they were frustrated; the power in Jesus disabled them and he left them. As he had said, to lay down his life was in his own power, and until the time appointed none could take it from him.

John closes this account of conflict with a note concerning the retirement of Jesus to the place beyond Jordan where John had baptized (1:28). There may have been several reasons for this. The end was approaching and a period of rest was necessary. This was only possible away from Jerusalem, and there the effects of John's teaching still remained and ensured a greater friendliness towards Jesus. Additionally he may have found in the environment so closely connected with the work of his forerunner, that help and comfort which he needed. The place would also recall to the Twelve the testimony of John to Jesus, and so help them to overcome the dismay which the opposition they had met must have produced in their minds.

THE SEVENTH SIGN: RAISING OF LAZARUS (11:1–54)

THE sojourn of Jesus in the place of retirement beyond Jordan (10:40) was interrupted by the news of the sickness of Lazarus, and Jesus once again visited the district of Jerusalem before the final effort of the last week of his life was made. The visit was not without connections with the closing events, for one effect of the raising of Lazarus upon the rulers was to make them determine that he must die.

Such intensified hostility caused Jesus to seek further retirement until the hour came for him to allow Jewish hatred to encompass his death.

This seventh sign is the last one before his own death and resurrection. There seems a fitness in the seventh sign illustrating his mission as the Life-giver by resurrection from the dead; it completes the series during his ministry and sets forth his completed work.

The little family in Bethany probably had influential connection with the rulers, some of whom came to mourn with the bereaved sisters. But their hearts were knit with Jesus and with his work. He must have stayed with them many times, for the love which Jesus had for them, and their love for him, indicates a close friendship. One other visit to them is recorded, in Luke 10:38–42, where the same features of character in the sisters may be traced as in John's record, a little indication of truth on the part of both Luke and John. On that occasion, Martha, busy to distraction with her household duties, found fault because Mary did not help; and the Lord gently rebuked her for her anxiety, and pointed to the greater importance of listening to him which Mary was doing. It would be most unfair to Martha to conclude from this there was any lack of appreciation of the truths Jesus taught—in fact her faith is seen in the narrative of John to have a clearer grasp of his teaching than many of the apostles at the time.

The greatness of their friendship and trust in Jesus is seen in the simple message they sent to him. They make no request either that he should hasten to their home or exercise his power from where he was; it is enough that he be informed that the one whom he loved was sick. They were content with whatever action he chose to take.

Jesus was moved by the news. Behind it he traced the Father's hand, for His glory and the glory of the Son. This was brought about in two ways—immediately, in that the resurrection of Lazarus itself exhibited the glory of God, as Jesus said to Martha, when she hesitated to remove the stone, "Said I not unto thee, that, if thou wouldest believe, thou shouldest see the glory of God?" And a little remotely, it led to his own death and resurrection, in which also, and in greater fulness, Father and Son were glorified.

Jesus tarried two days; and Lazarus died. If the messenger heard his words that the sickness was not unto death, and carried back to Martha and Mary what Jesus said, it must have aggravated the trial of the sisters that in the meantime Lazarus had died and been buried. What could Jesus have meant in view of the distressing fact of death? Yet John would have us understand that behind the action of Jesus in staying away, was love for them. "Now Jesus loved Martha, and her sister, and Lazarus. When he heard therefore that he was sick"—and who would not expect the conclusion to be, he left at once to go to them? But divine ways are not as we expect; "he tarried two days"; and so doing, they knew the joy of a brother restored to them from death, and that the delay with all its consequences sprang from a love wiser and more far-reaching than ordinary human love.

The two days having gone, Jesus said to the disciples, "Let us go into Judea again". It surprised them; only recently the Jews had tried to stone him, and he had to flee; now he proposed to return. Jesus replied by a figurative reference to walking in light and not stumbling; while walking in the night would end in disaster. While the light of his day continued he would continue to work, and the Father's care was sufficient to protect him while he did the Father's work. With the coming of the night his work would end—the hour of his enemies and the triumph of darkness would then have come. He then said that Lazarus was sleeping and he would go to waken him. Uncomprehending, they remarked on the value of sleep, thinking probably that the visit to Judea would be unnecessary; then Jesus said plainly, "Lazarus is dead. And I am glad for your sakes I was not there, to the intent that ye may believe; nevertheless let us go unto him".

Then Thomas, the Twin, twin in the double characteristics of doubt and courage struggling within him, proposed they should end their uncertainty and go with him, even if it meant death. It was the despondent saying of a brave man, who felt that with the death of their Leader all hope was destroyed and they too had better share his fate.

The fashion among the Jews required seven days of mourning for a near relation, and that at least ten persons should join in condolence with the bereaved. These ceremonials were interrupted by the appearance of Jesus in the village. Hearing of his coming Martha hurried to meet him, accosting him with words which later Mary also used, and which must often have been on their lips as they tended their sick brother, "Lord, if thou hadst been here, my brother had not died". It was an expression of regret, telling of mingled sorrow and unrealized hope. And yet hope was not dead; for Jesus had restored others to life—would he do the same for

Lazarus? Without shaping the thought in words, she added, "But I know, that even now, whatsoever thou wilt ask of God, God will give it thee".

Jesus responded to the unexpressed thought and said, "Thy brother shall rise again". There was ambiguity in the answer, designedly so to try her faith. She does not dare to apply it to her immediate wish, and responds, "I know that he shall rise again in the resurrection at the last day". Her hope was clear and true. The last day was the day of Messiah, of the Great Prince who would stand for the people of God, when many that slept in the dust would awake, some to everlasting life, and some to shame and contempt. Her faith was the faith of the prophets; did she as clearly connect the work with Jesus? He leads her to this, saying, "I am the Resurrection, and the Life; he that believeth in me, though he were dead, yet shall he live; and whosoever liveth and believeth in me shall never die". He is the Resurrection to those who are dead, and also their Life: but his work embraces living and dead, and the believing who live in the day of his revelation as the Messiah will never die. Did Martha understand his relationship to this purpose—and the essential place in it which was his? Her answer is marvellous in its grasp and comprehension. "Yea, Lord: I believe that thou art the Messiah, the Son of God, which should come into the world".

How uncertain and hazy were the men who companied with Jesus beside this woman. She declared his Messiahship, his Sonship, and that he was the Coming One of the prophets' promises and of Israel's expectations. Coupled with his question, she saw him also as the source of life for the prisoners of hope who would turn to the King when he comes to the daughter of Jerusalem. Did she also see that in the message of the prophets there was reference to the "blood of the covenant", to the "giving for a covenant", to the "cutting off" of Messiah? It may be doubted; but we may conclude that such a faith as hers would quickly find the true place for the sufferings of Messiah when the next few months revealed him as the Risen Lord, and the Resurrection, and the Life, which was only partly illustrated in her brother's restoration to mortal life.

Martha secretly sent for Mary, her action showing her carefulness; and her words having almost prophetic import in this connection: "The Master is come, and calleth for thee". Mary rose to meet Jesus, accompanied by the mourners, who were ignorant of her object, thinking she went to the grave.

Falling at the feet of Jesus she uttered the words her sister had used, her grief making more impossible.

The intense grief of the sister and the conventional display of mourning on the part of others produced an agitation in the mind of Jesus which was evident in his distress. He asks where the grave is, and at the tomb his emotion finds outlet in tears.

His sorrow thus shown, as with most of the actions of Jesus, lead to discussion and dispute. While some remark on his evident love for Lazarus, others sneeringly scoff, and say that a man who could give sight to a blind man should have saved his friend, thus casting doubt upon that work of healing and the power of Jesus.

The reactions of Jesus to human sorrow and need are revealed in this chapter with peculiar fulness. The divine power at his disposal did not interfere with his acute distress and personal anguish. He entered into a fellowship with human suffering, not only in his sympathy for his friends, but by his own personal suffering. "He groaned in himself" as he approached the sepulchre.

He then ordered the removal of the stone; but Martha with practical sisterly feeling for the effects of time upon her brother's body, disfiguring and marring the loved form, would have prevented it. But Jesus recalled her expression of belief in him, and his promise that the glory of God should be seen. He then prayed to the Father in words which show his dependence but also his continual fellowship with the Father. "Father, I thank thee that thou hast heard me. And I knew that thou hearest me always: but because of the people which stand by I said it, that they may believe that thou hast sent me". Then raising his voice, he called Lazarus from his sleep of death, and ordered the unbinding of the grave clothes.

John adds no more about the family thus blessed. Jesus is the centre of his theme, and the effect of the miracle is briefly told. The mourners with the sisters believed on Jesus when they saw what had been done. But others of the rulers who were with the crowd hurried off to the authorities at Jerusalem to report.

A meeting of the rulers was called at once. Reproaching themselves for not having taken action, but in their rage acknowledging that Jesus had wrought many miracles, they expressed the fear of increased popularity leading to tumult, and the Romans taking away the freedom they still had, and destroying their temple. The words are an unconscious prophecy, the irony of it all being in the fact that what they feared was brought about by their own action towards Jesus. Caiaphas, the high priest, intervened, revealing his utter heartlessness and selfishness as he haughtily exclaims, "Ye know nothing at all, nor consider that it is expedient for us that one man should die for the people, and that the whole nation perish not". It was a callous enunciation of the doctrine, Save yourselves; never mind if he perishes as you do it.

John points out that in his high priestly office the words of Caiaphas were overruled. He little appreciated the ultimate truth of his words that Jesus would die for the nation, and in a larger sense for all the people of God. God can and does use human actions to further His plan: He can guide the words of a man so that they declare a purpose beyond the speaker's intention.

The words of Caiaphas settled the policy to be followed. Jesus must die. But since the time was not yet, Jesus withdrew; he knew that the resurrection of Lazarus was his own death-warrant; but the issue was in his hands, and he retired until the appointed hour to the wilderness.

THE LAST PASSOVER AT HAND (11:55–57)

THE raising of Lazarus was separated by only a few weeks from the death of Jesus. The retirement of Jesus (11:54) in face of the hostility and the determination of the rulers that soon he must somehow be removed out of the way, must therefore have been only brief. The short rest over, he spent the last week of his life in a final appeal to the nation. The last scenes were witnessed by the companies representing the whole nation, the time and circumstances in a unique way making this possible. John shows the preparation for the last acts (11:55–57).

The passover was approaching, and a number of days earlier than the feast many who needed to perform ceremonial rites of purification went to the city of Jerusalem. They were expecting to see Jesus there, and John records their eager questioning among themselves whether Jesus would attend the feast. They were friendly in their attitude to Jesus, contrasting with the set determination of the rulers that the feast must not go by without the arrest of Jesus. The warrant for his arrest was issued—it was, as John states in a phrase expressing more than the surface meaning, the Passover *of the Jews* (verse 55).

CHAPTER 12 SUMMARY

IN the 12th chapter John groups three incidents which present three vivid and dramatic contrasts:—the anointing at Bethany (1–11); the triumphal entry (12–19); and the visit of the Greeks (20–36). In the first is seen the love of Mary and the hatred of the Jews; then the triumph of Jesus is opposed to the discomfiture of his enemies; and in the third incident we find Gentiles seeking Israel's light while Jews walk in darkness. John concludes the record of the ministry with a summary of the attitude of Israel (37–43) and an epitome of the teaching of Jesus (44–50).

THE ANOINTING AT BETHANY (12:1–11)

SIX days before the Passover, that is, according to the general view, on the Friday, Jesus came to Bethany. While there a supper was made in his honour, but where and by whom John does not say. It is sufficient to say that Lazarus and his sisters were present. The importance of the incident centres in the act of Mary, who took "a pound of ointment of spikenard, very precious", and anointed with it the feet of Jesus, wiping his feet with her hair.

The weight would be about 12 ounces, its value about £25; and the use of such costly ointment is the measure of Mary's love for Jesus. The discussion which it provoked revealed the character of Judas, and the significance of the act.

No contrast could be greater than this action of Mary and the spirit of Judas. John emphasizes the latter by two remarks: first that Judas was the one about to betray Jesus, (although at the time John did not know this), and then by the further comment that he was a thief, and stole from the small store of money belonging to the band, which was in his keeping. His complaint, "Why was not this ointment sold for three hundred pence, and given to the poor?" sprang from no love of the poor, but from a covetous mind. With a simple directness John lays bare the motive: "This he said, not that he cared for the poor; but because he was a thief, and had the bag, and bare away what was put therein".

The answer of Jesus indicates that a certain symbolism attached to the act of Mary. How far any other than Jesus saw this at the time is not indicated. "Let her alone: against the day of my burying hath she kept this. For the poor always ye have with you; but me ye have not always". We catch again the sombre shadow of the death that had been before the mind of Jesus for so long. The language of Jesus is somewhat enigmatic. Had Mary caught a glimpse of the impending end, but in overwhelming emotion, indicated by the loosing of her hair, used the spikenard at once? Or it may be that, as yet, the significance was only understood by Jesus. It was felt by him to be preparatory for the end.

There may be a designed contrast in the record of the *anointing* of the feet of Jesus, and the washing of the disciples' feet in chapter 13. Both trod the same way of life, but Jesus needed no cleansing for any defilement contracted in the walk. He needs must die, but anointing was the fitting prelude to that in his case.

There is also a lesson in proportion, in the remark that the poor are always present. We may be sure that the ears of Jesus were never closed to human need, but poverty cannot be eliminated in the day when mortals earn their bread by "sweat of face". The giving of alms affords some relief, but on occasion may do harm; indiscriminate giving on a large scale has been known to demoralize a district; in any case it provides no permanent cure for the problem of poverty. There are times when great issues demand all the resources, with which even the claims of poor and needy may not interfere. Such an occasion produced the loving gift of Mary. Only then had she the opportunity to anoint the Lord; and the opportunity knew no return.

The sharp distinction between the action of Mary and the attitude of Judas finds a reflection in a cleavage among the rulers. "Much people of the Jews" were attracted to Bethany to see Jesus, and Lazarus whom he raised from the dead (verse 9). And since by "the Jews" John describes the rulers, we must understand the officials and holders of the lesser offices of the state are here indicated as showing more sympathy towards Jesus than before. But the leaders are hardened in their determination to crush the movement associated with Jesus, and plan to put Lazarus also to death. The moderate Jews separated themselves, unable to follow the leaders in their hatred of one they could not believe to be other than true and good.

THE TRIUMPHAL ENTRY (12:12-19)

ON the first day of the last week of his life, Palm Sunday as the anniversary of the day is called, Jesus issued a challenge to the authorities by an action which he took. It was written in the prophecy of Zechariah:

"Rejoice greatly, O daughter of Zion; shout, O daughter of Jerusalem: behold, thy King cometh unto thee: he is just, and having salvation; lowly, and riding upon an ass, even upon a colt the foal of an ass." (9:9)

By his dramatic entry into the city riding upon an ass, Jesus identified himself with the One of whom the prophet had spoken. It was an enacted claim that he was Zion's King.

The people also played a part in the scene. The news quickly spread among the companies going to the feast who crowded the roads, that Jesus was going to the feast. Most of these would know little of the policies of the rulers in Jerusalem, and with a simple faith in the coming of the Messiah and in the teaching of Jesus concerning the Kingdom of God, were ready to hail Jesus as their deliverer. A Psalm, familiar because it was sung at the feasts of Passover and Pentecost and which was interpreted of the Messiah, gave them the words of greeting. Taking palm branches, commonly used at the festival, and which were associated also with the blessings of the Messiah whose advent was looked for at the Pentecost season, they went to meet Jesus, shouting, "Hosanna; Save now; Blessed is the King of Israel that cometh in the name of the Lord".

The application of the Psalm to the Messiah was undoubtedly right. It was quoted by Jesus of himself in dispute with the rulers. In his indictment of them that they were plotting to kill "the heir" and seize the inheritance for themselves, he asked them if they had never read that prophecy of the rejected stone which became the head of the corner by the Lord's action (Psalm 118:22; Matthew 21:42).

The Psalm concerns one given over to death but who yet lives; thrust at sorely by the people, yet helped of God—but one to whom would be opened the temple gate provided for the righteous to enter in, and at whose command the sacrifice is bound to the horns of the altar. Who is this one with right of entry to the temple of God, with authority to sacrifice? Not simply a king, or he would be a transgressor as was Uzziah. Evidently he is a priest-king, rejected by man, but exalted by God. And in that day of his exaltation, the people will rejoice in it and be glad. They will return to the once rejected but now glorified Deliverer with the petition:

"Save now, we beseech thee, O Lord;
O Lord, we beseech thee, send now prosperity;"

And acclaim him with the words:

"Blessed be he that cometh in the name of the Lord".

To this comes a response from the new temple rulers:

"We have blessed you out of the house of the Lord."

Then follows the order for preparation of the sacrifice, and the people as one join in praise to God.

It is evident that the Psalm is concerned with some formal recognition of the King of Israel when the temple is rebuilt, and its services inaugurated.

The action of the people and the words they used, with the evident challenge of Jesus in accepting the homage as he acted the role of the King as described in the prophecy, very naturally disturbed the rulers. In their dismay the Pharisees, with an unconscious irony so often noted by John, said among themselves, "Perceive ye how ye prevail nothing? Behold, the world is gone after him". On the other hand, the people witnessed to his works, having seen the miracle of the resurrection of Lazarus. The disciples saw it all in an uncomprehending way: but after his resurrection the significance of the testimonies of the Old Testament concerning Jesus was perceived, and the teaching of Scripture became plain to them.

THE VISIT OF THE GREEKS (12:20–36)

THE bitter comment of the Pharisees that all the world was gone after Jesus had a wider significance than they thought. The world includes Gentiles as well as Jews, and the work of Jesus was for all men. An immediate illustration of the Gentiles seeking while the Jews rejected Jesus is given by John.

Among the visitors to the Holy City at the feasts were a number of Gentiles, and since they came up to worship it might reasonably be concluded that they were proselytes. We know that "Jews and proselytes" made up the multitude that were present at Pentecost some two months later (Acts 2:10). The Ethiopian eunuch is an example of those who, dissatisfied with pagan worship, turned to the pure ethical teaching of the Law and the Prophets, and adopted in part the ceremonies of Israel, becoming what were known as "proselytes of the gate". These Greeks had heard of Jesus, and had probably heard him, but they desired to meet him. They therefore approached Philip, with the request, "Sir, we would see Jesus". The respectful tone used to the follower of Jesus helps us to understand the spirit in which they came, and the reverent attitude they would show to his Master. This is in keeping with the response of Jesus.

There is little to indicate why Philip was approached. Perhaps his Greek name gave them confidence to speak to him, or since John mentions that he was of Bethsaida of Galilee, perhaps they had met him before in his home town. Philip seeks Andrew—the two being also mentioned in close contact on an earlier occasion (6:7,8), suggesting a companionship between them. Andrew is always mentioned among the first few in the lists of the apostles, and may have had a closer contact with Jesus. Together they inform Jesus.

John does not tell us anything more of the Greeks, what they said to Jesus, and what he said to them. John finds in the words Jesus spoke to Andrew and Philip, and which we might infer were spoken in the hearing of the Greeks, the lesson he wishes to give.

The request of the Greeks seems to have deeply moved Jesus. He sees in their hunger for knowledge of him the promise of an ingathering of Gentiles into his fold; and this leads him to speak of the means by which this would be accomplished. The hostility of the rulers would in a very short time lead to his death. While rejected by his own, his work would not be in vain, and would bring forth fruit. But it needed the giving of his own life, just as the seed must be lost by sowing it in the ground before it can be increased manifold.

There is something very touching about the courage and faith and self-sacrifice of the small farmer who, when sowing time comes, must take of his little store of seed and give it up, sacrificing it beyond recall when he places it in its bed of earth. The loss may mean less food for many days; but to hold it back would mean permanent loss, for if it is saved to be eaten there will be no harvest, and no seed for further sowings. Such experiences of the conflict of present need and future good would be known to almost every generation of Israelites with their recurring periods of drought and bad harvests. On occasions the seed was sown with tears in the acuteness of a felt hunger. But the Psalmist says,

"They that sow in tears shall reap in joy. He that goeth forth and weepeth, bearing precious seed, shall doubtless come again with rejoicing, bringing his sheaves with him."
(126:5,6)

The time for tears was near—"strong crying and tears", and sweat as it were of blood; for the agony and anguished cry from the cross. But before that Jesus tasted the joy of the harvest, of reaping of precious sheaves unto life everlasting. "The hour is come", he exclaimed, "that the Son of man should be glorified." The glory of the Son is to be found in the successful issue of his obedient life, in his resurrection, ascension, and ultimate exaltation upon earth. The burial closes the door upon his sufferings, his resurrection opening the new and living way to fulness of joy in the possession of all power in the Father's presence, everything else—his coming in glory and power, his filling the earth with the Father's glory—being assured. To him shall the Gentiles seek, and his rest shall be glorious.

The Son of man, whom God visited, and who was made a little lower than the angels, because of the suffering of death has been crowned with glory and honour, as Paul says in his exposition of Psalm 8, in Hebrews 2:5–9. So Jesus combines this suffering of death with the glorification. "Except a corn of wheat fall into the ground and die, it abideth alone: but if it die, it bringeth forth much fruit." Here is a natural law with a counterpart on the spiritual plane. Jesus himself came under the law, he was one with us, dying representatively. He restates the rule in terms of human life. "He that loveth his life shall lose it; and he that hateth his life in this world shall keep it unto life eternal". A man loves the present and clings to it, and loses all; another, prepared to sacrifice the present life, finds life complete and abiding in the coming age. It is a divine paradox that destruction is the means of preservation.

The rule is of universal application: "If any man serve me, let him follow me; and where I am, there shall also my servant be: if any man serve me, him will the Father honour". That fellowship with the Father which Jesus enjoyed ("where I am") could be shared by his servants, upon the conditions of service and following his example. It was not restricted in scope to race—"any man" could enter the service; and the service passes to sonship—the Father honours all his sons, the only begotten, and the adopted sons in him.

The thought is familiar in the other gospels, but is founded upon the idea of crucifixion, and not of a sown grain. "If any man would come after me, let him deny himself, and *take up his cross*, and follow me. For whosoever would save his life shall lose it; and whosoever shall lose his life for my sake shall find it." And Jesus asks his hearers to consider a man facing the Judge when eternal issues are to be decided, having acquired possession of all the world, but with no right to life—what then would life be valued at?

"For what is a man profited, if he shall gain the whole world, and forfeit his life? or what shall a man give in exchange for his life? For the Son of man shall come in the glory of his Father with his angels; and then he shall reward every man according to his deeds."

(Matthew 16:26,27)

The thought of Jesus concerning exaltation was never separated from the necessary steps to it, as we have already seen. His exultation at the coming of the Greeks brings the thought of the wheat grain which must die. So with a slight pause between verses 26 and 27 we can understand Jesus saying, "Now is my soul troubled; and what shall I say?" How in his anguish shall he express himself? His life-long discipline of obedience finds the way: "Father, save me *out of* this hour". It was an anticipation of the prayer in the garden to Him who was able to save him *out of* death. God would save him, and at once the assurance of that guides the next thought, "But for this cause came I to this hour"; and that being so, God would save him. Therefore all he needed to do was to seek the Father's glory, and the petition is added: "Father, glorify thy name."

A voice, loud and awe-inspiring, in that some mistook it for thunder, answered the prayer: "I have both glorified it, and will glorify it again". The work of Christ now nearing completion had glorified God; a future work would glorify God yet again. If the sufferings yielded glory, how much more the glory to be revealed.

The people's disputes about the nature of the noise was settled by a word from Jesus: it was God's voice, but uttered for them and not for himself. They needed to be instructed that what appeared defeat was victory; the shame was glory; the yielding to death, the conquering of death. "Now is the judgment of this world: now shall the prince of this world be cast out. And I, if I be lifted up from the earth, will draw all men unto me". Sin was enthroned in the world; sin, in the persons of the Jewish rulers, was judging him; in reality sin was judged and cast out. His death by "lifting up" would be the means of men of all races gathering to him; "all" without distinction of race, speech, colour, would be drawn to him.

The preaching of the cross has always been foolishness in the eyes of many; but to those who believe it is the power of God unto salvation.

The crowd catch the idea of death in his words, and to them it conflicts with the idea of Messiahship. How could Jesus be the Messiah and yet speak of his death—would not Messiah abide for ever? Was he the Messiah? Who was the Son of man to be lifted up?

Jesus does not answer the contemptuous enquiries, but utters a solemn warning. Not for long would they be able to hear his instruction The light was still shining—only by following would they escape the overtaking darkness; believing on him, the Light, they would become enlightened, and themselves lights, or, in Hebrew idiom, they would become "sons of light".

Their response must be inferred from the action of Jesus. He "departed and did hide himself from them". The light left them; darkness closed about them; and the public ministry of Jesus was closed with this symbolic act.

THE REFLECTIONS OF JOHN (12:37–43)

THE close of the public life of Jesus called for some estimate of results. It was indicated by the withdrawal of Jesus and the abandonment of the nation to its chosen darkness. Very briefly John recounts their failure. "Though Jesus had done so many signs before them, yet they believed not on him." The accredited messenger of the Holy One of Israel, His Son who had done more mighty works among them than any of the prophets, was rejected. Jesus had fulfilled his part as revealed in the scriptures; and their treatment of him was also foreseen. Isaiah's saying in the 53rd chapter had been accomplished in that generation: "Lord, who hath believed our report? and to whom hath the arm of the Lord been revealed?"

Their attitude to Jesus was a ground of judgment, which became in itself a divinely inspired judgment. They turned from him, and, choosing darkness, lost the power of sight; hardening their hearts against Jesus, they lost the power of response to the good and the true. Their choice became their sentence: and another prophecy of Isaiah was fulfilled in them.

Isaiah had a vision of the millennial throne, with Christ as priest-king, attended by the children of the resurrection; all made equal unto the angels (chapter 6). In response to the invitation, "Whom shall *I* send, and who will go for *us*?" the prophet, as a man of sign, responds "Send me". He is then given the message which John quotes. Jesus himself had given this message, citing the words of Isaiah as a reason for speaking in parables. That form of teaching was designed to enlighten the honest-hearted, but to confound the unbelieving. Paul repeats it, following the Jewish rejection of his teaching in Rome (Acts 28). The multitudinous unity of which Jesus speaks in John 17 is before us in Isaiah's vision. Jesus was "sent" for them; but the nation rejected him, and their unbelief became blindness as Paul says, echoing Isaiah's language, "Blindness in part is happened to Israel, until the fulness of the Gentiles be come in" (Romans 11:25).

There was a portion which believed; blindness was only in part. The true believers were very few, so few that they are unnoticed by John. He mentions the number who were not engulfed in the darkness, but had not as yet the strength of conviction to come to the light with boldness. They saw the vision of glory, and believed on Jesus: but human fears, threats of excommunication from the synagogue, hindered their advance. The heavenly glory was eclipsed by the earthly glory of men. "For they loved the glory of men more than the glory of God."

EPITOME OF THE TEACHING OF JESUS (12:44–50)

THE ministry of Jesus so clearly ends in verse 36, the end being emphasized by John's statement that "Jesus departed and did hide himself from them", that it is at first difficult to understand the abrupt introduction, "Jesus cried and said", to another short address of Jesus. Were the words spoken in public? or in private to the disciples, or to the crowd? The insistence in the tone, the warning note so evident in every verse, shows that the words had a larger audience than the disciples. Carefully examined, the verses are seen to gather up the whole teaching of Jesus in relation to John's particular object in writing his gospel. The opening words, "Jesus cried and said", signify that what follows was the substance of this teaching.

"He that believeth on me, believeth not on me, but on him that sent me" (verse 44). First calling for notice is the place of belief or faith in Jesus. Without faith it is impossible to please God; and faith in God requires faith in His messengers. Jesus in fact says the ultimate object of belief is God, and that believing in him involves, not merely leads to, belief in God. Conversely, however men regard it, to reject Jesus is to reject God.

A glance at the concordance shows the conspicuous place given to faith in this gospel. In the prologue we are told that John came for a witness to bear witness of the Light, that all men through him might believe (1:7). And reception of the Light gave authority to become sons of God; and those who receive the Light are defined as "them that believe on his name", and also as being divinely begotten by the will of God by the word of truth.

Jesus is given by the Father in his love, that men might have life—but the condition is belief on him (3:16). Again, belief as a condition of attaining to life is concisely expressed in the words: "He that believeth on the Son hath everlasting life: and he that believeth not the Son shall not see life" (verse 36).

In the discussion following the healing of the impotent man, Jesus with a pronounced emphasis said: "Verily, verily, I say unto you, He that heareth my word, and believeth on him that sent me, hath everlasting life, and shall not come into condemnation; but is passed from death unto life" (5:24).

He puts his words with the writings of Moses as being alike of divine authority, and as calling for belief. There is the same insistence on belief in him and his words in all the addresses. It is the work of God to believe on him whom He hath sent (6:29). "Why do ye not believe me?" was his complaint to the Jews (8:46). Those who believe are thereby shown to be "the sheep" of whom he is the shepherd, and to whom he gives eternal life (chapter 10). He calls for belief in him for the sake of the very works that he had done among them (10:38).

Jesus claims to be "sent" of the Father. John was a man sent from God; but in the case of Jesus a more particular meaning attaches to the word "sent". This is seen by John's linking the idea that Jesus was sent by the Father (9:4) with the meaning of Siloam, "which is by interpretation, Sent". Its fuller meaning comes out in the saying, "I am from him, and he hath sent me"—"from him", in that he was His Son. And if such a thought cannot be drawn from all the references to "sent", we must recognize at least that the reiteration of the idea by Jesus points to an exceptional commission which had been given to him.

The peculiar relationship which Jesus sustained to God is clearly shown by the next statement. "He that seeth me seeth him that sent me." This is a tremendous claim in view of who the Sender was. Surely no greater claim could be made than that a man was so like God that in his words and acts, in his whole life, God was revealed. From the lips of anyone else it would provoke well-deserved scorn; but the character of Jesus upholds the claim. "Which of you convicteth me of sin?", he could challenge his ever-watchful enemies. "He that hath seen me hath seen the Father", he could respond to the request of a disciple; and his meaning is found in the next words:

"I am in the Father, and the Father in me: the words that I speak unto you, I speak not of myself; but the Father that dwelleth in me, he doeth the works."   (14:10)

As John declares in the opening chapter: "We beheld his glory—full of grace and truth". "The only begotten of the Father hath declared him."

The next words gather up a number of statements which fell from the lips of Jesus, and, again, a thought in the prologue. "I am come a light into the world, that whosoever believeth on me should not abide in darkness." The terms of the physical world are used to describe the moral conflict of righteousness and sin. In the primeval darkness light broke by divine fiat; and the same God "who commanded the light to shine out of darkness hath shined in our hearts, to give the light of the knowledge of the glory of God in the face of Jesus Christ" (2 Corinthians 4:6). And this is otherwise expressed in verse 4 as "the light of the gospel of the glory of Christ, who is the image of God". The glory of Jesus is his divine like-ness—the perfection of the idea unfolded in creation's purpose—"Let us make man in our image". It was true of the physical, potentially true of the moral. And since darkness fell, or the image was defaced, fresh creative energy was employed to scatter the darkness by new light, embodied in a developed "image of the invisible God". The prologue says, "That was the true light, which coming into the world, lighteth every man". Every man, not in the absolute sense, but every man without distinction of race—all men catching the rays of light in the apostolic testimony. So in this summary Jesus says he is come a light "that whosoever believeth on me should not abide in darkness". Faith and light are synonyms: as are also disbelief and darkness.

The coming of the light changes times of ignorance and darkness to times of knowledge and light, and therefore to

times of responsibility. If God speaks, it were an imperti-
nence for man to think he can ignore. Of this Jesus next
speaks. "If any man hear my words and believe not, I judge
him not: for I came not to judge the world, but to save the
world. He that rejecteth me, and receiveth not my words,
hath one that judgeth him: the word that I have spoken, the
same shall judge him in the last day. For I have not spoken
of myself; but the Father which sent me, he gave me a
commandment, what I should say, and what I should speak."

The words of Jesus have grave importance, for men
determine their destiny by their response to them. When
Jesus says the word judges, he means that judgment will be
based upon that word. The saying of Jesus echoes the words
of God concerning the prophet like unto Moses:

"I will put my words in his mouth; and he shall speak
unto them all that I shall command him. And it shall come
to pass, that *whosoever* will not hearken unto my words
which he shall speak in my name, I will require it of him."
(Deuteronomy 18:18,19)

The time of judgment is connected with the word spoken by
Jesus, because "the last day" denotes the day when he will
raise the dead at his appearing as the Messiah.

The point of view set forth in these verses concerning the
word of Jesus, is quite out of keeping with modern tenden-
cies. The record of the words of Jesus is treated as a suitable
subject for speculation, and its acceptance is optional. The
common view to-day makes the Fourth Gospel an impression
rather than a history. The other three gospels have been
analysed, and theories have been put forward about them
which leave the reader in doubt of what amount of fact is to
be found amidst much fiction. The saying of Jesus might well
give pause to such speculations; it will at any rate enable
the one who believes in Jesus to estimate modern critical
theories at their true worth, and to realize the necessity of
accepting and obeying without hesitation the words which
God has given through Jesus.

The last point in the summary of the teaching of Jesus
consists of a personal testimony to the Father's work—"I
know"; and the Father's purpose—"His commandment is life
everlasting". Jesus knew, because he had the continual evidence of the Spirit, the knowledge of God's word in perfection,
and the knowledge that also came from the experience in his
own life of obedience to the Father's commandments, by
which he knew the doctrine was of God. Although he has
placed so much emphasis on the consequences of rejection of

God's word, yet the end in view was the salvation of man, and not his condemnation. "Life everlasting" was the substance of God's commandment; the centre of the message given by Jesus; the bringing of it within reach of man the whole object of his life. As the Father spake, so Jesus spake. He and the Father were one: the words spoken were spirit and life.

THE GOSPEL OF JOHN

SECTION 5

THE FAREWELL DISCOURSES
CHAPTER 13

THE next five chapters (13–17) in John's Gospel concern the close and intimate contact that Jesus had with his disciples from the end of his public ministry to his arrest. For a few precious hours he is alone with them, endeavouring to reveal the Father unto them who are called by John "his own".

The storms and conflicts of the ministry are over; the company with him are his close associates; all, after the short interval at the end of which the traitor withdrew, sympathetic and full of affection for him, even though so slow to comprehend his teaching. Jesus therefore pours out his soul in affectionate act, counsel, and prayer.

AN EXAMPLE OF HUMILITY (13:1–20)

IT was the evening of the Passover, before the meal began. The festival was full of significance for Jesus, and had been so doubtless from the first occasion when at twelve years of age he had gone up to the feast with Mary and Joseph. It had significance for every Israelite, pointing back to the dark night when Egypt's first-born were slain, when God "passed over" every house where obedient Israelites had sprinkled lintel and door post with the blood of the lamb.

But the Exodus from Egypt, like so much in the Old Testament, was part of the foreshadowing of the Lord's own work. He had an "exodus to accomplish at Jerusalem" (Luke 9:31), of which Moses and Elias had spoken to him on the Mount when he was transfigured. And this exodus had its Passover Lamb, to be slain for a "blood of sprinkling" for a greater deliverance than from Egyptian bondage, even "Christ our Passover, sacrificed for us".

There was an appointed hour in Egypt for the slaying of the lamb, and the time was fixed for the "cutting off of Messiah". John finds the basis for the conversation Jesus had with the Twelve, in the knowledge of Jesus that the time had come, and as a result of this, the love of Jesus rises to its highest manifestation. He had loved them all the days of his ministry, carefully and patiently instructing them and guiding them. But the greatest manifestation of his love was about to be shown, in that he would lay down his life for his friends, so fulfilling the work which was appointed by God, which would lead to his going away to the Father. The words of John introducing the section are thus seen to be full of significance. "Now before the feast of the Passover, Jesus knowing that his hour was come that he should depart out of this world unto the Father, having loved his own which were in the world, he loved them unto the end" (or, "to the uttermost").

Two other factors in the situation are noticed by John. The first of these concerns the betrayer; a note concerning him being necessary to explain the words of Jesus in connection with the incident that marks the beginning of the gathering. The AV translation puts the incident at the end—"supper being ended"; the RV, during the meal; perhaps it would be sufficient to say the supper-hour had come. John says the devil had already put into the heart of Judas to betray Jesus. The Lord had previously told Peter that the authorities had been noticing them, to find among them a suitable tool for their work. "Satan hath desired to have you, that he may sift you as wheat". The Jewish adversaries found the man who would work with them, aiding them in getting Jesus into their power. The inner weakness of the man responded to their offer of gain: "he was a thief" and stole from the common fund of the band which was in his keeping. The lust for gain became Sin—the Devil; and, blinded for the time concerning the enormity of the consequences, he met for the last few minutes with a leader to whose undoing he had agreed. This hindrance to full fellowship had to be removed.

The other factor John notices is the knowledge that Jesus had, that all things were his by God's gift, that he was God's Son; and that he would shortly ascend to the Father. This factor provides the knowledge of the circumstances in which Jesus took the servant's form and washed his disciples' feet.

Yet the memory of it remained with Peter to the end of his life. "Ye younger", he exhorts, "submit yourselves unto the elder. Yea all of you be subject to one another, and *be clothed with humility*: for God resisteth the proud, and giveth grace to the humble" (1 Peter 5:5). In this way had Jesus "clothed" or "girded" himself, when rising from supper, he had wrapped about him a towel, poured out water into a basin, and washed their feet, using the towel to wipe them.

Peter might well remember for, appalled at the idea that the Master he loved should wash his feet, he had said to his Master, in a tone that implied he did not know what he was doing, "Lord, dost thou wash my feet?" The Lord had replied with an emphasis on his own knowledge and Peter's lack of it, "What I do *thou* knowest not now; but thou shalt know hereafter". Then had Peter wanted hands and head as well as feet washed, impulsively passing to the other extreme, and unmindful of the fact that the Lord implied that *he* knew what he was doing.

The words of Paul to the Philippians find an illustration in this washing of feet, particularly in view of John's reference to the knowledge of Jesus concerning his origin and destiny. "Let this mind be in you, which was also in Christ Jesus: who, being in the form of God, counted it not a thing to be grasped to be on an equality with God; but made himself of no reputation, and took upon him the form of a servant, and was made in the likeness of men: and being found in fashion as a man, he humbled himself, and became obedient unto death, even the death of the cross" (2:5–8). He not only washed their feet, but by the sacrifice he offered provided for the cleansing of their sins.

The mind of Peter was fixed upon the actual washing of their feet, any significance in the act being unperceived. They had assembled with Jesus for the Passover meal. Usually in attending a banquet the guests bathed before leaving home; and on arriving at the house of the friend a servant washed their feet that any defilement of the journey might be removed and the guest sit down to the banquet wholly clean. Jesus performed the servant's part in washing their feet, to Peter's astonishment and dismay.

But there was a meaning in the act, which Jesus pointed out. "He that is washed needeth not save to wash his feet, but is clean every whit: *and ye are clean*, but not all."

The teaching of Jesus had cleansing power: "Now ye are clean through the word which I have spoken unto you" (15:3). "Sanctify them through thy truth; thy word is truth" (17:17). "Cleansed with the washing of water by the word" (Ephesians 5:26). The apostles had listened to him, and responded to his teaching. Their lives had been cleansed, but they were not perfect; there was the defilement of sin in their daily walk. The boastfulness of Peter, his denial, and the faults that sprang from his impulsiveness, were so many spots in need of daily cleansing. It is so with all. The washing of baptism, when the truth is understood, and obedience rendered in faith, cleanses from sin. Thenceforward there is no need for the repetition of that rite; but there is a daily need for approach to the throne of grace for forgiveness for the slips of the day, the defilement of the road in daily walk.

"But not all" were clean. Jesus knew, says John, who should betray him: Judas was not clean. The words he had heard during the ministry had not changed his character. Perhaps we may conclude that the motives which led Judas to join the band had been less worthy in his case than in the others. The self-seeking of the man had remained. To betray such a leader as Jesus shows an utter want of appreciation of the finer things of life, and reveals the baseness of human nature when self-directed.

A comparison of the other gospels shows there was another immediate cause for the action of Jesus in washing their feet. There had been a strife among them, which should be the greatest, and in his reproof Jesus said he was among them as one that serveth (Luke 22:24,27). His humble service, usually the servant's duty, was a tacit rebuke, and this was stressed in the words he spake. The story of the strife mentioned by Luke is almost necessary for a complete understanding of the words of Jesus next recorded by John.

So after he had washed their feet, and had taken his garments, and sat down again, he said unto them, "Know ye what I have done to you? Ye call me Master and Lord: and ye say well; for so I am. If I then, your Lord and Master, have washed your feet, ye also ought to wash one another's feet. For I have given you an example, that ye should do as I have done to you. Verily, verily, I say unto you, The servant is not greater than his lord; neither he that is sent greater than he that sent him. If ye know these things, happy are ye if ye do them."

The incidental reference to the mode of address used by the disciples to Jesus is noteworthy; "Master and Lord" expressed the position he held in contrast to theirs of pupil and slave. They did well to remember it, and to use the titles. Too great familiarity in their address was not good: respect and reverence became his position. This is a feature which can be obscured by a too familiar reference in our speech and our prayers. In the gospel narratives—historical records— the Son of God is simply Jesus, the name given to him by God's appointment. In the epistles he is Jesus Christ, or the Lord Jesus, the few occurrences of the simple name Jesus having some particular purpose.

Jesus transposed the titles in pointing the lesson, the greater title of Lord coming first: and by the use of the definite article, "The Lord and the Master" (RV) marks himself out as unique in this relationship. And yet being such, he had done a lowly service; how much more should his disciples be ready to do such an act for fellow disciples. They were inferior to him, as servant to Lord. They were sowing seeds of misery and unhappiness in their rivalries for the chief places. The way to happiness was through humility and service, following the example he set before them. "If ye know"—the lesson seems so simple; "happy if ye do"—it is so hard to learn.

One had failed more than the others to learn and to do. The failure was not unknown to Jesus: and the man had been an open book to Jesus all the time they had companied together. Jesus knew when Judas was chosen what disposition he had. He knew also that a betrayer had to be one of his apostles.

The forty-first Psalm had foretold of the familiar friend, who had shared the fellowship of the table, turning traitor. David had known the defection of Ahithophel; Jesus knew the violation of the sacred ties of a meal shared, in the baseness of Judas in joining his enemies. Of both men it is written that "he went and hanged himself". Jesus knew the parallel which would be worked out between David and himself, and their followers. The Psalms had authority for him, and his life was directed to their fulfilment; hence he said, "I speak not of you all; I know whom I have chosen: but that the Scripture may be fulfilled, He that eateth bread with me hath lifted up his heel against me".

In view of the nearness of the betrayal Jesus felt no further reserve about making it known. In fact the knowledge was calculated to confirm faith a little later (verse 19). And when the time came for them to be "sent" by him, they would realize the more who had sent them, and that as ambassadors of him they would bring men to the Father, who had sent Jesus (verse 20).

THE TRAITOR DEPARTS (13:21–30)

THE words that Jesus had just uttered filled him with emotion, which increased as he solemnly declared that one of them should betray him. The disciples were perplexed at this, and Peter beckoned John to ask the Lord of whom he spoke.

Jesus indicated by giving to Judas a morsel dipped in the sauce used at the Supper. It was a gesture to John and to Judas: to John in that it answered his query; to Judas, saying in effect, "You partake of my food, be loyal to the covenant of salt", thereby making a final appeal to him.

But Judas had gone too far. The action he had already taken was apparently known to Jesus; and with the sop decision hardened beyond change. Jesus saw this and said to him, "That thou doest, do quickly".

The meaning of these last words was lost on all but Judas. They thought Jesus was instructing him to complete certain purchases at once, or to relieve someone in need. Judas obeyed: he went out immediately. He obeyed in going to the authorities. The time was short—he needs must make haste if the events of the next few hours were to see the fulfilment of all that was written concerning the way the Son of man should go. Judas knew not this; but Jesus did.

"And it was night", John adds. So it was: why, then, mention it? Because John wants us to feel that the action of Judas is one with the darkness. The light had passed from Israel, and the hour of darkness had come, and the deeds of darkness were being done.

The Last Discourse at the Feast (13:31—14:31)

THE words recorded in 13:31 to 17:26 are closely bound together, although it would appear that they were not all spoken in the Upper Room. The company leave the place after the Supper with the words: "Arise, let us go hence" (14:31). But all these chapters have the same atmosphere, and record the words of Jesus during his last few hours with the apostles.

We must remember that Jesus knew what would have happened before another day had come. He had bidden Judas act quickly. He knew also that at the end of another day the last agony would have passed, and his flesh would be resting in hope or that quickening touch of the Father's power which would bring back his life, and give him the fulness of joy that accompanies immortality. But the disciples did not. Can we not appreciate their bewilderment, their surprise at his words, their failure to grasp his meaning, as first Peter and then in turn Thomas, Philip and Judas (not Iscariot) interrupt his address with questions?

The conversational character of the words at the Supper is in keeping with the position of twelve men around a table. The more formal discourse of chapters 15 and 16 belongs to the time when they had left the Upper Room and asking questions was not so convenient.

When Judas had left on his errand to the leaders of Israel Jesus evidently felt the removal of some constraint. John notices the effect of the traitor's leaving. Jesus marks it by the word "now", as he said, "Now is the Son of man glorified, and God is glorified in him. If God be glorified in him, God shall also glorify him in himself, and shall straightway glorify him".

The words are simple; yet have a depth of meaning that we feel is beyond our grasp. Some of their import is plain enough. Judas had gone out on some deed of darkness. As Jesus said when he was arrested, "This is your hour, and the power of darkness" (Luke 22:53); and the love of men for the darkness was revealing itself in all its evil. This is a strange background for the claim, almost in triumphant strain, that Jesus was now glorified. Yet it was true; true because the triumph of darkness would be short, and its very success its own death-blow.

The death of Jesus was the limit that the evil of men could reach; sin could bruise him only in the heel. But his death was the condemnation of sin, and the appointed way for the victory over death. Now the end was near, the last steps taken which would bring the officers of the rulers to arrest him, and then, as with swiftly moving action the last events took place, he could speak of the glory as being already his.

What is the glorifying of the Son, God being glorified in him, and in Himself? What is the glory of God? An important aspect is revealed when Moses asked, "Show me thy glory". And God said, "I will make all my goodness pass before thee, and I will proclaim the name of the LORD" (Exodus 33:18,19). When the proclamation of the name was made, God revealed His character:

> "The LORD, the LORD God, merciful and gracious, long-suffering, and abundant in goodness and truth, keeping mercy for thousands, forgiving iniquity and transgression and sin, and that will by no means clear the guilty."
>
> (34:6,7)

This character of God had been revealed in Jesus, of whom John says, "We beheld his glory, the glory as of the only begotten of the Father, full of grace and truth". Here was the Son,

157

the expression of the Father, showing the mercy and grace of God, the goodness and truth of God, and in his work laying the foundation for the forgiveness of sin that the Father offered to humble and repentant sinners through him. And the outworking of this co-operation will be seen when the earth is full of the glory of God, when sin and its effects have all been removed.

Morally, Jesus was glorified in that he had been obedient in all things. Presently he would be physically glorified, the firstfruits of the harvest of risen and exalted men and women. And for the suffering of death he has been crowned with glory and honour; he has been given a name over every name, that in the name of Jesus every knee should bow ... and every tongue confess that Jesus Christ is Lord, to the glory of God the Father (Hebrews 2:9; Philippians 2:9–11). His "lifting up" in crucifixion was the necessary prelude to that other lifting up, when all nations will seek him, when his rest shall be glorious (Isaiah 11:10).

The close connection between the work and the glory of the Son and the glory of the Father is evident from the words of Jesus. If the Son is glorified God is glorified in the Son; and if this is so, then God will glorify the Son in Himself, in the Son's sharing the glory of the Father, which requires that God shall glorify him, when things in heaven, on earth, and under the earth join in one acclaim,

"Blessing, and honour, and glory, and power, be unto him that sitteth upon the throne, and unto the Lamb for ever and ever."   (Revelation 5:13)

If this is the future for the Son, what will befall the disciples? He turns to them, and uses a term for them found only certainly here and in John's first epistle: "Little children"— John had caught and treasured its tender and loving thought. "Little children", said Jesus, "yet a little while I am with you. Ye shall seek me: and as I said unto the Jews, Whither I go, ye cannot come; so now I say to you."

The record of the saying to the Jews is in 7:34 and 8:21. On the first occasion Jesus added, "and shall not find me"; on the second he had also said, "and shall die in your sins". We found that on both these occasions the "seeking" was one yet future when the favours of Jesus would be desired. It is so here; but the added words of the former occasions are not spoken to the disciples. Jesus would leave them shortly; but their interest in him, and their service for him would continue, and at last their desire for him would be gratified in the sharing of his life, and his throne and Kingdom. But to both his enemies and his friends the one ban stood: they could not follow him: ascent to the Father was for him alone.

But as their future would be found in him and with him, so they had now a duty to do. They were to continue his work: and in the absence of the Master, in the desolateness of being left alone, they were to turn to each other, and in love for one another find the comfort and help that they had found in his love for them.

Hence he gave them a new commandment: not new in itself, since it was contained in the Law; but new as the rule of the society, "his church", which would come into being immediately; and new as the motive of action. This desire for each other's good involved in the idea of love, would mark them out before all men as the disciples of Jesus. "A new commandment I give unto you, That ye love one another; as I have loved you, that ye also love one another. By this shall all men know that ye are my disciples, if ye have love one to another."

Peter was the first to interrupt. With attention fixed on the words of Jesus about his going away, indicating separation from a Master he adored, he asked whither the Lord was going. And whereas Jesus had just said, "Whither I go, ye cannot come", he also knew there was a fellowship of the way that Peter must know. But not yet: not now. Peter could not join in the death of the morrow. In fact, how different would his action then be. Jesus knew the weakness as well as the strength of Peter, and when he overconfidently said, "Why cannot I follow thee now? I will lay down my life for thy sake", Jesus foretold the threefold denial of the impulsive Peter before the cock crew.

Yet there was an "afterwards" when Peter should follow. "Converted", and comforter of his brethren, Peter was bold in his testimony for many years, until the time came to follow his Lord in laying down his life. But how little Peter knew of the interval between the night of the Lord's betrayal, and the time when men would "carry him whither he would not", by which the Lord had indicated by what manner of death Peter should glorify God (John 21:18,19).

CHAPTER 14

THE fourteenth chapter of John's gospel continues the discourse at the Last Supper, and the chapter break must be ignored. The announcement of the betrayal had been made, and an intimation of his death given. Peter's defection had been foretold, and Jesus had said he was shortly leaving them. It must have been a very troubled and perplexed group of men who fixed their faces on their Leader. Their troubled thoughts were revealed in anxious looks. Jesus speaks comforting words to them.

"Let not your heart be troubled; believe in God, believe also in me. In my Father's house are many mansions; if it were not so, I would have told you. I go to prepare a place for you. And if I go and prepare a place for you, I will come again, and receive you unto myself; that where I am, there ye may be also. And whither I go ye know, and the way ye know." (14:1–4)

There is comfort in the confident words of a strong man: and there is assurance in the counsel, "Let not your heart be troubled". But Jesus goes further and tells them how they might overcome their troubled thoughts. There was a foundation for peace in human lives, away from which there is only unrest and disquiet. The foundation was faith; faith in God, and then faith in him. The disciples had faith—but it needed to be fostered and strengthened. Belief in God must be accompanied by belief in him, the coupling together of God and himself as the objects of faith carrying an implicit claim that his words and his counsel had divine authority.

The words had great value then, but their importance would increase as the days passed by and they took his gospel to the world and found opposition and difficulty such as he had encountered. The memory of his words, spoken during the crisis of his life, would nerve them to endure with fortitude and courage. They have not lost their value yet. In the midst of difficulty, and in a world that has ceased to believe, when doubt and despair stalk hand in hand, the man of faith can still hear the words of Jesus, and believing find heart's ease.

But the words of Jesus concern the future. In fact, much of the comfort of the Bible lies in the promise of the victory over the evil, when mourners are comforted and tears are wiped away. The blessedness which Jesus pronounces upon certain states and conditions is connected with the hope of the changes which it is in his power to bring about. While, then, he points to the assurance of faith, he also directs attention to the future good, about which he speaks with a confidence that is divine. He knows: were the future otherwise he would have told them. His quiet endorsement, his certainty, is such as pertains to the Son of God.

160

What ideas did the reference to the Father's house, with its many abiding places, call to the disciples' minds? It is difficult to say; but there is exposition of his words in the writings of the apostles which shows how we must interpret his words.

The Father's house was a phrase used by Jesus of the temple. If we follow the RV we find that at the age of twelve he described the temple as "My Father's house". He should not have been *sought*—there was the place where he would be found. Then at the beginning of his ministry he cleansed the temple and told them, "Make not my Father's house a house of merchandise".

The description of the temple, past and future, as the house of God is found in the Old Testament. At its dedication "the cloud filled the house of the LORD" and "the glory of the LORD filled the house of the LORD". In the Psalms we find intense longing for "the house of my God" (84:10); a day in its courts being better than a thousand elsewhere. In the passage quoted by Jesus when he cleansed the temple the second time we have a reference to the future temple to be built in the Holy Land, when Gentiles will be brought to God's holy mountain, and made joyful in His house of prayer; and, says God:

"Their burnt offerings and their sacrifices shall be accepted upon mine altar; for mine house shall be called a house of prayer for all peoples." (Isaiah 56:7)

The Psalms breathe a hope of an everlasting association with God's house, in which we may find the thought passing from the house where men worship to a house composed of worshippers. "One thing I have desired of the LORD", wrote David, "that will I seek after; that I may dwell in the house of the LORD all the days of my life, to behold the beauty of the LORD, and to enquire in his temple" (27:4). And the well-known Shepherd-psalm concludes with the words, "I will dwell in the house of the LORD for ever" (23:6).

The prophet Isaiah gives the reason why the house of wood and marble, precious stones and gold, could not be for ever God's dwelling place. They were only for a temporary typical house. Heaven was God's throne, the earth His footstool; and all the materials that men could gather and give were of His providing: "All these things have mine hands made". As Stephen inferred from this, God dwelleth not in temples made with hands. The one thing that a man can give is his own self, in doing God's will. That only is his own; he can set mind and heart to live in obedience to God. With such an offering God is pleased, and to such Isaiah points when he adds, "But to this man will I look, even to him that is poor and of a contrite spirit, and trembleth at my word" (Isaiah 66:2). Such a willing offering was foreshadowed in the voluntary contributions made by Israel as each determined, "willingly in his heart", to "make God a sanctuary, that he may dwell among them" (Exodus 25:8). And God whose power fills all space, and whose days are timeless, is not too great to accept the offering of men for His abode:

"For thus saith the high and lofty One that inhabiteth eternity, whose name is Holy: I dwell in the high and holy place, with him also that is of a contrite and humble spirit, to revive the spirit of the humble, and to revive the heart of the contrite ones."   (Isaiah 57:15)

After the Word was made flesh and tabernacled among us, and the Son revealed the Father who dwelt in him, the application of the types to Jesus and his disciples might be expected. This we find. Jesus spake of the temple, even his body, which would be raised up on the third day (John 2:21). Paul says Jesus was "the true tabernacle, which the Lord pitched" (Hebrews 8:2). Jesus promises that he that overcomes shall be made a pillar in the temple of his God, and go no more out (Revelation 3:12). He is the builder and maker of the house, under God; and in the words of Isaiah that Jesus quotes in the letter to Philadelphia:

"He shall be for a glorious throne to his father's house; and they shall hang upon him all the glory of his father's house."   (Isaiah 22:23)

In the writings of the apostles the figure finds ample illustration. "Ye also, as living stones, are built up a spiritual house" (1 Peter 2:5), Christ being the tried and precious foundation stone. Upon this foundation the saints are built into "a holy temple in the Lord; in whom ye are also builded together for a habitation of God through the Spirit" (Ephesians 2:20–22). "Ye are God's building" (1 Corinthians 3:9).

In this house are many "abiding places", using the words of the RV margin, which provide a present-day meaning for the word "mansions", which is used in this place in a sense now obsolete. The word occurs again in verse 23, where Jesus says the Father and he "will make our abode" with the man who loves him and keeps his words.

The going away of Jesus was connected with his work on their behalf. "I go to prepare a place for you." His present work as High Priest on behalf of his people, and the direction of human affairs to the end appointed, are parts of his preparatory work on their behalf. But while it was necessary for him to go away, he promised to return and "receive you unto myself; that where I am, there ye may be also". They will be with him then for ever, and if we may give the words "where I am" the significance attached to them in earlier reference, we must understand Jesus to say they would then share his full fellowship with the Father. He was then in that position (12:26); they would attain to it at his second coming, when, approved and forgiven, they would be made like him in nature, to live for ever in the Father's house.

Incorporation in the house then, required preparation now. This had been illustrated in his own life, in the observance of which they should have learned the way to the Father. "And whither I go ye know, and the way ye know." They did not grasp his meaning that the way was a mode of life, which they had seen in him. Thus in knowing him they knew the way. A question by Thomas drew from Jesus the explanation.

"Lord, we know not whither thou goest, and how can we know the way?" The Father's house of which Jesus had spoken was associated in their minds with the temple in Jerusalem; rightly so; how then could Jesus talk of going away if he was to prepare a place for them? The place was there; the idea of separation was at once unpleasant and incongruous, and the feelings of Thomas discouraged and perplexed, are expressed in his words.

Jesus did not directly answer *whither* he went, although it is implied that it was to the Father he was going. But even here there is a double thought. He speaks of men "coming to the Father" by him as the outcome of his going to the Father. His going was physical; an actual bodily ascent, while their coming was a spiritual approach in a new spiritual relationship. Jesus focuses attention upon the way, and upon himself as the way. It is by him and through him that access to the Father is possible, and if Thomas would know the way he must know Jesus. "I am the way, the truth, and the life: no man cometh unto the Father but by me."

They were thinking of his coming separation from them; he thinks of men's separation from God, and of himself as the uniting agency. If the distance was bridged, it was bridged by him, and therefore men must travel by him. He was an illustration of the way in himself, in his obedient life and voluntary death: no other could be the way, because none

163

could perfect holiness as a qualification for the offering of himself. Hence all must accept him, or remain apart.

The separation of man from God was divinely emphasized in the lesson of the tabernacle arrangements: the linen enclosure, only entered by sacrifice; the first veil only to be drawn aside by appointed priests for daily service; the second veil which the High Priest only could pass, and only with blood and incense. The second veil effectively separated God from the nation and the priesthood. The annual entry was not made by the High Priest in his official capacity, but as a typical representative of a sinless man. When that man appeared, God's approval of his sacrifice was shown by the rending of the veil from top to bottom, and an opened way to the Father was revealed. Paul explains the significance of these tabernacle shadows in his letter to the Hebrews, exhorting them to draw near, "having boldness to enter into the holiest by the blood of Jesus, by a new and living way, which he hath consecrated for us, through the veil, that is to say, his flesh" (Hebrews 10:19,20). Here again Jesus is the way, and by means of the rent veil others come near unto God.

Jesus called himself "the truth", as well as the way. What is signified by this claim of Jesus? Paul, writing to the Ephesians, says:

"But ye did not so learn Christ; if so be that ye heard him, and were taught in him, *even as truth is in Jesus*: that ye put away ... the old man; and that ye put on the new man, which after God hath been created *in righteousness and holiness of truth*." (4:20–24)

A recent writer has said:

"It is extraordinarily easy to read the phrase 'as truth is in Jesus' without thinking clearly what it means. Yet the whole passage, and indeed much of Paul's doctrine, depends upon a clear understanding of it. Does such an expression as 'Truth is in Jesus' make any sense at all to the modern reader? What conception of Truth therefore justifies the statement that hearing about Jesus Christ, and being taught in him, will have, not an intellectual, but a moral and spiritual effect upon them? Is Truth connected with a manner of Life? Finally, what has Truth to do with righteousness and holiness?"

It is pointed out that while the Greek word for *truth* carries much the same meaning as the English word, when we turn to the Hebrew equivalent the whole emphasis is changed.

"The standard of truth not only took complete and manifest control of the noun *truth*, of the adjective *true*, and of the verb *to be true*, but also dominated the whole conception of knowledge. The Hebrew mind, in its certainty of a transcendent God, fixed upon Him as the standard of Truth ... It may be that the conception of a covenant relationship, to which Jehovah would be true, even if Israel proved false, was actually responsible. At all events, the Truth of Jehovah was regarded as an integral part of His character."

Truth therefore was revealed in all God's actions, and in His purpose: and since His purpose was sure, because He is True, the Truth of God came to express the purpose in its opposition to, and ultimate triumph over, evil in every form. Truth is thus much more than right knowledge or right speech; it includes motive and action as well. Truth is something *to be done*, as John counsels his brethren "to do the truth". And when Paul says that Jesus was made "a minister of the circumcision for the truth of God", he indicates that all God's promises were to be accomplished in Him, and the Father's purpose, which was in keeping with His character, vindicated.

"As truth is in Jesus" is another way of saying God's character is revealed in him, and God's design for His character to prevail throughout the earth is to be wrought out in him. The "new man" is a divine creation, after God's image of righteousness and holiness of truth.

Jesus claims to be "the truth" with these Hebraic concepts of the word's significance in his mind. It was a claim to Messiahship, for the Messiah in Isaiah's prophecy is "the God of truth" in whom men will bless themselves in the age to come (65:16). To the lukewarm Laodiceans Jesus addressed himself as "The Amen", that is, The Truth (Revelation 3:14); and to the Philadelphians as "he that is holy, he that is true" (verse 7), thus identifying himself with the one of whom Isaiah had spoken.

Jesus also said he was "the life". This inevitably follows from the others. The Truth of God requires that the earth shall be replenished, and inhabited by men and women of proved worth according to divine standards. They must have life—and since this is forfeit because of sin, one must be manifested who will bring resurrection and life, and not only bring it for others, but who must be in himself an exemplifi-

165

cation of resurrection and life. We know that he so described himself when Lazarus was dead. The double description was necessary in those circumstances; it was sufficient here to say, "I am the life", resurrection being involved.

The three titles together state the place Jesus had in God's purpose both in himself and in relation to others. Because he was the way, the truth, and the life, men could come to the Father.

It is interesting to observe that two of these words came to be used as descriptions of apostolic Christianity. The RV has made this clearer than the AV. Paul went to Damascus empowered to bring bound to Jerusalem any that were of *the Way* (Acts 9:2). At Ephesus the Jews spoke evil of *the Way*, and Paul and the disciples dissociated themselves from the synagogue (Acts 19:9). Then Demetrius caused trouble "concerning *the Way*" (verse 23). Paul the persecutor, became the foremost exponent of the teaching he had opposed. He persecuted "*this Way*" (22:4); but the evidence of the risen Jesus led him to worship God according to "*the Way*" (24:14). Felix had knowledge concerning "*the Way*" (verse 22).

Peter combines the two titles in his second epistle (2:2); "the way of the truth" was evil spoken of as the result of the work of false teachers.

Since the Father's purpose was so personally exhibited in Jesus His Son, it follows that, as Jesus said, "If ye had known me, ye would have known my Father also; and from henceforth ye know him, and have seen him". By this conversation Jesus had lifted their thoughts to another plane; without destroying their expectation of a kingdom to be restored, they were instructed concerning the essential personal relationships to God which all who inherit the kingdom must have first known.

Philip stumbled at the words "seen the Father". When had he seen Him? He did not perceive that since to know Jesus was also to know the Father, so also to see Jesus was to see the Father. He therefore asked for a vision of the Father. The Father's voice he had heard; he knew of past manifestations of God in his nation's history. Could they now complete their knowledge by seeing God?

The answer of Jesus contains reproof and instruction. From the time he had been with them they should have apprehended more clearly who he was; they should have known him. Their failure was shown by Philip's request. There was a manifestation of God before their eyes, fuller, greater, more complete, than ever before. The Father was there revealed in a Son, the express image of His character. "He that hath seen me hath seen the Father." Fuller revelation was not possible. How this was so Jesus explains: "I am in the Father, and the Father is in me". And if evidence were needed, words and works joined in a witness that was conclusive. "The words that I speak unto you, I speak not of myself: but the Father that dwelleth in me, he doeth the works."

Jesus turns from Philip to all the twelve, asking for their faith in his word, and should confirmation be required, he asks them to accept the evidence of his works. "Believe me that I am in the Father, and the Father in me; or else believe me for the very works' sake." What other explanation of Jesus and his works is possible? Rule out God and there is no reasonable or adequate explanation. Admit that he was the Son of God, and that God dwelt in him by His Spirit, and that the mind of the Son was in perfect harmony with the Father, and all is plain. We see the most wonderful intervention of God in human life as the means of bringing men to God.

Much help to a right understanding of the discourse of Jesus in chapter 14 is obtained from noticing to whom and of whom Jesus is speaking. In the opening words of verse 10 he speaks to Philip: "Believest thou"; he then turns to the whole company: "the words that I speak unto you ... believe (ye) me". In verse 12 we have a general statement: "He that believeth"; while in verse 13 he returns to the apostles: "Whatsoever ye shall ask".

Jesus has appealed to the "works" he had done as a basis for faith in him (verse 11). He now appeals to "greater works" which he said it would be in the power of the believer to perform. With solemn emphasis he says: "Verily, verily, I say unto you, He that believeth on me, the works that I do shall he do also; and greater works than these shall he do; because I go unto the Father". The promise is of the widest application: "he that believeth"; and it is not surprising that strange theories have been built on this and similar passages concerning the power to perform miracles.

It is not necessary to think that by "greater works" Jesus means greater miracles. Such an interpretation is excluded by the simple facts of history. No follower of Jesus has ever been able to do greater works than he did, healing the sick, giving sight to the blind, hearing to the deaf, speech to the dumb, and raising the dead. But there is a sense in which greater works have been done. Jesus was nearing the end of his life, and judged from human standpoints it seemed a failure. The popularity of the early period had passed; the crowds had grown smaller as his teaching repulsed them; only a few disciples remained, and they were full of anxiety and perplexity. The world with which Jesus had waged his conflict appeared to have won: Jesus was yielding, and even then one disciple was interviewing the rulers, arranging how his arrest might be made.

Yet the work was not in vain; failure was only apparent. His work would continue in them, and by their ministry they would change the face of the world, bringing Gentiles to the light, testifying before rulers of the work of God accomplished by Jesus. This world-wide preaching "to every creature under heaven" (Colossians 1:23) was only possible after the death and ascension of Jesus, and his words, "because I go to the Father", are at once the reason for and the guarantee of the "greater works". "They overcame him (the pagan dragon) by the blood of the Lamb, and by the word of their testimony" (Revelation 12:11).

Turning to the Twelve he continued: "And whatsoever ye shall ask in my name, that will I do, that the Father may be glorified in the Son. If ye shall ask anything in my name, I will do it" (verses 13,14). He had spoken of "the works that I do"; here is a future work he will do, but one done in and through them, as his Body. Their willing co-operation is implied, and the right relationship indicated. The phrase "in my name", here used for the first time, is not a formula to be appended to petitions to secure their acceptance. The "name" is a name of salvation, "the only name under heaven given among men, whereby we must be saved" (Acts 4:12). It is connected with the name which God gave Himself at the bush, a name which includes in its full scope not only Jesus but all who are in Christ. Such are in "the name of the Father, Son, and Holy Spirit"; they know God's name, and have put their trust in him.

It has long been a Jewish practice, and probably was so in the days of Jesus, to present petitions in the names of the men of old time who enjoyed the favour of God. Thus they joined with their prayers "for the sake of Abraham", of Isaac, of Jacob, and of David and of the prophets, all named with that tiresome reiteration condemned by Jesus. Jesus puts before the Twelve a better way, because it is the true way. "In his name" is the only approach, for he is the mediator of the new covenant; "in his name" defines and limits the range and scope of the petitions then in his mind; "in his name" is the condition upon which he will do that for which prayer is made. That Jesus is thinking of the things that pertain to salvation is further evident from the result aimed at, "that the Father may be glorified in the Son". "Whatsoever" and "anything" cannot be given an unlimited meaning, but are defined by the context. Petitions in harmony with the purpose of God in the Son are granted; and the mind of the petitioner is regarded as being in harmony with the mind of the Son, since the "works" done through them are the works of the Son.

The close connection between the Son and those who believe on him is the link with the next words of Jesus. In turn they reveal the basis upon which further favours from him may be bestowed. "If ye love me ye will keep my commandments." It is not a command but a statement of fact. Loving him they will keep his commandments, as the RV shows. To fail to keep the commandments, to ignore them or treat them lightly, shows there is not love.

There are two sides to co-operation: obedience is the condition on the part of the believer; and then Jesus for his part "will pray the Father, and he shall give you another Comforter, that he may abide with you for ever" (verse 16). "Another" comforter suggests they had one already. So they had; Jesus had been their Comforter and is so called by John in his first epistle: "If any man sin we have an Advocate (Comforter, RV margin) with the Father, Jesus Christ the Righteous" (2:1). This is the only occurrence of the word outside John's Gospel, where we find it four times (14:16,26; 15:26; 16:7).

A comforter is "one who is called to the side of another" to aid in a court of justice; one who pleads, instructs, and reasons with them; one who advocates. The Comforter took the place of Jesus with them, guiding and instructing them.

The language is that of personification, and it is easy to understand how Trinitarians have found in these words of Jesus evidence for their belief. What the Father gave to them was power from on high when on the day of Pentecost "they were all filled with the Holy Spirit, and began to speak with other tongues, as the Spirit gave them utterance". By this means Jesus was "with them", as the closing words of Matthew's gospel record: "I am with you all the days, even unto the consummation of the age". These days were the closing days of that age, reaching their end with the destruction of Jerusalem, at which time we can understand the decline in the spirit gifts, as Paul had said would come to

169

pass (1 Corinthians 13:8). This reference in Matthew may also help to define the meaning of the Spirit's "being with them for *ever*".

Jesus explains what he meant by the Advocate: "Even the Spirit of truth; whom the world cannot receive, because it seeth him not, neither knoweth him: but ye know him; for he dwelleth in you, and shall be in you. I will not leave you comfortless (desolate, or orphans, RV): I will come to you."

The Spirit was the means of revealing the Truth to them, hence it is called the Spirit of truth. As the prophets "spake as they were moved by the Holy Spirit" (2 Peter 1:21), God "testifying by His Spirit" in them, so the apostles would be guided and instructed and enabled to teach the truth. Human "spirits" are spirits of error: the speculations of the heart of man tend continually away from God's truth. Worldly wisdom does not qualify for receiving the knowledge of God; as Jesus said, "the world cannot receive" the teaching of the Spirit. But "ye know him", said Jesus: that is, the apostles would accept the instruction. The teaching of Paul in 1 Corinthians 2 is an instructive commentary on this saying of Jesus.

The word "comfortless" of the AV (verse 18) suggests a connection with the reference to the Comforter; but the verbal association is incidental. The real connection may be found in his calling them "little children" (13:33). He would not leave them without assistance when he was no longer with them, but the help would not be by his personal presence. "He would come to them" truly, in the pouring out of the Spirit upon them.

This "other comforter" would come only at the departure of Jesus, which was then drawing near. "Yet a little while", he says "and the world seeth me no more; but ye see me: because I live, ye shall live also. In that day ye shall know that I am in the Father, and ye in me, and I in you" (verses 19,20).

The world saw him for the last time when he hung upon the cross: but the chosen witnesses saw him again; and we may perhaps give an added meaning to the second occurrence of the word "see"—they saw when raised from the dead, and by the eye of faith saw him exalted to the Father's right hand, alive for evermore. In that life they found life in him now, and the hope of living for ever with him. With these experiences of Christ risen and the Spirit given they would know in greater fulness the fellowship of the Father and the Son; a fellowship established in Jesus and his Father, and the mutual fellowship of Jesus and the believer. Upon the basis of the apostles' doctrine, the apostles' fellowship was established (Acts 2:42); and John, the last of the Twelve, on behalf of all says,

"that which we have seen and heard declare we unto you, that ye also may have fellowship with us; and truly our fellowship is with the Father, and with his Son, Jesus Christ." (1 John 1:3)

This extension of the fellowship beyond the apostles is involved in the next words of Jesus, which are of wider application than the apostles. "He that hath my commandments, and keepeth them, he it is that loveth me: and he that loveth me shall be loved of my Father, and I will love him, and will manifest myself to him" (verse 21). It is a fellowship of belief and works, of thought and action, of knowing and doing the commandments. The motive of this is love to Christ, and the result of its expression is still greater love for Christ; and this leads to a greater divine response and a fuller measure of God's love and Christ's love being bestowed. Fuller knowledge results; as Jesus had once before said, "He that wills to do his will shall know of the doctrine"—so now he adds that as the outcome of obedience and love, he would manifest himself to the faithful servant, not by the sight of the eyes but by the conviction that comes with knowledge of him.

"He that hath my commandments, and keepeth them ... I will love him, and will manifest myself to him" (14:21). Jesus imposed a serious limitation upon his manifestation when he restricted it to those who have his commandments and keep them. It seemed to oppose, almost to the extent of nullifying, the idea of Jesus being the Messiah who was expected to reveal himself to all Israel and then to the nations. Judas voiced the perplexity which all probably felt: "Lord, how is it that thou wilt manifest thyself unto us, and not unto the world?" (verse 22).

John adds parenthetically, that Judas who thus spoke was not Iscariot. He had already left the upper room before the conversation at the table began. This Judas is only known to us, apart from the lists of the apostles' names, by this remark.

But Jesus had not the kingdom in mind. He knew of the long centuries that would go by while he was at the Father's side, during which the gospel would be preached among all nations to take out of them a people for His name. By this work, performed in the first instance by apostolic labours, there would be many to whom he would be manifested, not by his bodily presence, but by knowledge of him and love to him.

171

Such thoughts are evidently in the mind of Jesus as he replies.

"If a man love me, he will keep my word: and my Father will love him, and we will come unto him, and make our abode with him. He that loveth me not keepeth not my words; and the word which ye hear is not mine, but the Father's which sent me."   (verses 23,24)

The conditions of the manifestation are given by Jesus, as he answers Judas, not by direct reply, but by expanding the thought which provoked the question. These conditions are loving Christ, and keeping his word: a test which shows why the world is excluded from the blessing. The individual aspect is of essential importance: the world cannot be treated in this connection as a whole. It is to men and women who know God's purpose and render a loving response that the blessing comes. No one is excluded except he who fails to meet the necessary conditions: "he that hath the commandments", "if anyone love me", whoever he might he, is accepted. That the world at large fails to qualify is sadly true, but the absence of knowledge and obedience, which Jesus practically puts as equivalent to love, makes friendship with God impossible. Therefore the world is the enemy of God, and friendship with the world is enmity with God.

The very close association of Jesus with his Father is evident in all these sayings. The one who loves Jesus is loved of the Father; and Father and Son find a dwelling place with him. It completes the thought (verse 2) of the many "abiding places in the Father's house". If the believer finds a place in God's house, he is also himself the sanctuary of God. Isaiah had indicated this when he said that the high and lofty One that inhabiteth eternity, whose name is holy, dwells not only in the high and holy place, but also with him that is of a humble and a contrite spirit (57:15). How impossible on such a basis as Jesus lays down, for Jesus to be manifested to the world. The world keepeth not "his word", which includes "his words"; and his words are not his own, but the Father's who sent him. He is pre-eminently the prophet like unto Moses, of whom God had said, "I will put my words in his mouth".

It is this thought of the Father's revelation in the message of Jesus which provides the link with the next words. The disciples had to carry a message to the world in continuing the work of Jesus. That message must be authoritative. And thus while Jesus was not manifested to the world in the sense he was to the believer, yet there was a proclamation to be made about him; he was to be manifested in the testimony about him. In giving the message the apostles would need assurance that it was of divine power and authority. It was not possible then for Jesus to communicate all, but he could give them instruction of what would be done to fit them for their work.

"These things have I spoken unto you, being yet present with you. But the Comforter, which is the Holy Spirit, whom the Father will send in my name, he shall teach you all things, and bring all things to your remembrance, whatsoever I have said unto you."   (verses 25,26)

There is a contrast between "these things" and "all things"; the latter comprehending all the revelation to be made through the apostles. But "these" included what Jesus had said to them during his ministry.

This promise is of the greatest importance as evidence of the reliability and accuracy of the apostolic writings. The Spirit would teach them, and give infallibility to their recollection of his words. It is said that many easterners have very good and accurate memories enabling long addresses to be recalled—a power never developed in lands where newspaper reading and hurried skimming of the printed page is the rule. But the best of unaided human memories would not provide a suitable basis for faith. That must come by the word of God. Since the apostles wrote under the guidance of the Spirit, the gospels and the epistles have the authority of the word of God: in fact, they are the word of God. Paul could say with thankfulness that when the Thessalonians had "received the word of God which ye heard of us, ye received it not as the word of men, but as it is in truth, the word of God, which effectually worketh also in you that believe" (1 Thessalonians 2:13).

The time is drawing near for the final words, and the thought of Jesus goes to the real significance and value of the Hebrew salutation. Peace, said the Jew, in saluting his fellow. Now Jesus was about to give them the parting "Peace"; but it was not a formal or casual farewell word. Thoughtlessly men tossed the word which has such abiding worth to each other as they went their ways, not caring whether peace went with the leaving friend, and abode with him. Not so Jesus. He knew peace—an inward peace untouched by the stormy waves of life; and he would they should know and possess his peace. So he gives to the parting phrase, "Peace I leave with you", the emphatic addition, "My peace I give unto you: not as the world giveth, give I unto you. Let not your heart be troubled, neither let it be fearful".

173

These words are the more significant in that they were spoken within an hour or two of the closing scenes of his life, so full of suffering and anguish. They were spoken with the knowledge of the closing darkness coming upon him. Yet he speaks of "Peace, my peace": and he speaks out of knowledge and experience. Such was his faith and his courage.

It must often have recurred to them when the circumstances of their work of preaching brought peril and danger, that Jesus had this peace, and would have them share it, with hearts strong and brave. Who can doubt, as the record of their work is studied, that this benediction became a treasured possession?

The peace of Jesus had strong foundations. Peace is based on righteousness; "first pure, then peaceable" is the order of the heart's progress: the pure in heart have peace. The vain searching for peace in human life in all its phases is from want of recognition of the essential conditions.

Peace has a twin—the name of which is joy. The disciples had not yet reached either peace or joy. Jesus therefore added:

"Ye have heard how I said unto you, I go away, and come again unto you. If ye loved me ye would rejoice because I said, I go unto the Father: for my Father is greater than I."
(verse 28)

Remembering the close connection between love and knowing and keeping the commandments (verses 21,23), when Jesus says "if ye love me" he indicates more than a personal allegiance. He implies a broad recognition of his work and of God's purpose. Such a love would find joy, not in the separation from a loved leader, but in that his going away meant that he was exalted; and going to the Father was an exaltation that placed him at the Father's right hand. The Father was greater than he—to go to the Father would bring an accession of power to him, and continued progress in the work, under conditions that did not admit of possible failure. A consequence of this exaltation would be enhanced joy to them.

It must have seemed at the time that the words of Jesus had little meaning. They were removed from every thought they held and every expectation they cherished. Events seemed a stumblingblock to all faith and peace and joy. But Jesus intended that the present difficulty should be made to contribute to faith. By telling them now (verse 29) they would find in his foreknowledge and in his example a reason for trust and hope.

There must be a limit to such a method—a limit then nearly reached in the wisdom of Jesus. He therefore said, "Hereafter I will not talk much with you: for the prince of this world cometh, and hath nothing in me" (verse 30). The prince of this world is sin, to be "cast out" in the "lifting up" of Jesus, as he had said (12:31). For the moment "the prince of this world" was represented by the Roman and Jewish authorities. Were the rulers then deciding to gather their officers and servants to arrest Jesus? It would give a vivid meaning to the words of Jesus if, as he spoke, Caiaphas was on the way to interview Pilate to arrange for the unusual trial at such an irregular time.

The prince of this world had nothing in Jesus—there was no ground for condemnation. Neither Jew nor Roman could formulate a charge that could justly condemn him. On a higher plane Sin could not arraign him, for he had done no sin. In the words of Daniel's prophecy of the Seventy Weeks, "Messiah shall be cut off, and shall have nothing"; and the language of Jesus is like an echo of these words.

Sin and the authorities would find no fault in Jesus: yet in blind envy and human weakness would crucify him. There is a time coming when the world that crucified Jesus will realize its folly. With no real interest in Jesus or the work he came to do, they found no point of contact or sympathy with the Son of God. Yet the circumstances were such as left them without excuse; and very solemnly Jesus says that his course was set that the world might ultimately be convicted of its wrong. "But that the world may know that I love the Father, and as the Father gave me commandment, even so I do." The world of his day did not know it. But the words of Jesus indicate a day of judgment when too late it will be realized. As one writer has said:

"The words of Jesus in short express, though more pointedly than elsewhere, the great truth so often stated in Scripture, that those who reject the salvation shall meet the judgment of Jesus, and that, when they meet it, they shall acknowledge it as just. Blind now, they shall not always be blind; their eyes shall be opened; and to their shame they shall confess that he whom they rejected was the Beloved of the Father, and that his work was the doing of the Father's will."

The corollary of an offer of life is responsibility. It cannot be evaded. To reject is to accept the responsibility of refusing.

Only when the issues are not presented is there freedom from this. But the issues must come to some for decision, for divine intervention in the person of His Son in human life is God's challenge to sin, and its overthrow. "Arise, let us go hence"— to meet the foe that is already coming, to engage in the conflict that may bring my death, but, which will ensure life because of my love and obedience to the Father.

THE ALLEGORY OF THE VINE (15:1–11)

THERE are two notes of movement in the discourse of Jesus to his disciples: first, the closing words of chapter 14, where he says to his disciples in the upper room, "Arise, let us go hence"; then the opening words of chapter 18, following the prayer of Jesus, "When Jesus had spoken these words he went forth with his disciples over the brook Cedron".

From what place did Jesus go forth? From the upper room? If so, we must think of chapters 15–17 as spoken while Jesus and the eleven stood together before they left the room where they had the last supper. Some have thought it possible that Jesus and the eleven entered the temple courts on the way to Gethsemane. At midnight when the Paschal Supper ended, the temple courts were opened: and in the deserted courts Jesus would find a safe haven for the closing words to his apostles.

On this view the golden vine with clusters a man's stature in length, wrought over the gateway, suggested the figure of the vine which Jesus uses as an allegory. It is impossible to say with certainty, and it may not be necessary to find any external suggestion for the figure beyond the cup upon the supper table, and the Lord's own allusion to the fruit of the vine of which he would no more partake until he partook anew in the Kingdom of God.

There is, of course, also an Old Testament background. Isaiah had sung his "song of the vineyard", in which he described how God had planted a choicest vine in his vineyard, taking every care of it that it might bring forth fruit, only to find a crop of wild grapes. Therefore, God would lay waste His vineyard, the house of Israel, and His "pleasant plant", the men of Judah.

Jeremiah, too, at the time when this wasting and destruction came to pass, bewailed the degeneration of Israel:

"Yet I had planted thee a noble vine, wholly a right seed;
how then art thou turned into the degenerate plant of a
strange vine unto me?"   (2:21)

The Psalmist has a touching reference to the lot of God's
people when He fed them with "the bread of tears", and "gave
them tears to drink in great measure". The writer looks back
on the history of the nation's founding, and forward to a
future when the Son of man would save them.

"Thou hast brought a vine out of Egypt:
Thou hast cast out the heathen and planted it.
Thou preparedst room before it,
And didst cause it to take deep root,
And it filled the land.

"Why hast thou then broken down her hedges,
So that all they which pass by the way do pluck her?
The boar out of the wood doth waste it,
And the wild beast of the field doth devour it.

"Return we beseech thee, O God of hosts,
Look down from heaven, and behold,
And visit this vine;
And the vineyard which thy right hand hath planted,
And the branch that thou madest strong for thyself.

"Let thy hand be upon the man of thy right hand,
Upon the son of man whom thou madest strong for
thyself."

This eightieth Psalm, as J. W. Thirtle showed in *The Titles
of the Psalms*, was marked out for use at the feast of
Tabernacles by the note of the Chief Musician "Upon Gittith".
This word means "winepress", and with reference to this
Psalm not only linked its use with a particular season, but
also denoted the judgment of God, which had come upon the
nation, of which the winepress was only too apt a figure.

Jesus was by birth a branch of the vine of Israel. In a
spiritual sense he was "the true vine"; *true* in that he fulfilled
all the lessons and significances of the noble plant. But Jesus
is not thinking of himself alone when he uses the figure: he

adds, "Ye are the branches". He does not say, "I am the stem, ye are the branches"; the "I" includes stem and branches: the branches are one with him.

With this thought we might compare Paul's use of the figure of "the body of Christ", "the full grown man—the measure of the stature of the fulness of Christ" (Ephesians 4:12,13). Of this body Jesus is the head, and the whole body is fitly joined together and compacted by that which every joint supplieth, and by the effectual working of every part maketh increase of the body unto the building up of itself in love (verse 16).

Even more explicitly in the first letter to the Corinthians he says: "As the body is one, and hath many members, and all the members of that one body, being many, are one body; *so also is Christ*" (12:12). A similar thought underlies Paul's words that in his sufferings for the saints he was "filling up that which is behind of the afflictions of Christ for his body's sake, which is the church" (Colossians 1:24). The church is "his body, the fulness of him that filleth all in all" (Ephesians 1:23).

In considering the allegory we must keep in mind the Christ body—Jesus and the believers united together and forming one vine, the planting of the Lord that He might be glorified. The Lord is the husbandman, the owner of the soil, who tends the plant, whether the national or the spiritual Israel, that it may bring forth fruit.

The husbandman's work as mentioned by Jesus, is twofold. The branch that is found to be unfruitful is removed. Perhaps there is present in the thought of Jesus the man who had gone away to do his traitor's work, who for long time had shown that he was not a fruit-bearing branch, and who fulfilling his course was being removed from association with the source of life.

But it is by no means limited to Judas. To "every branch"— in that age and every succeeding age—the words apply. There were many severed from the Christ body before the first century ended, and John, near its close, says:

"They went out from us, but they were not of us; for if they had been of us, they would no doubt have continued with us; but they went out, that they might be made manifest that they were not all of us."   (1 John 2:19)

The fruit-bearing branch is pruned, or cleansed as Jesus describes it, using a word which carries a deeper meaning than simply pruning. The cleansing involves the cutting away of useless twigs and foliage, and excrescences which drain the strength of the tree. Could the vine speak it might ask why it should be subjected to hard treatment and the removal of much fair foliage, all seemingly so natural and in order. And the answer would be that the husbandman deals wisely with the plant in his care, knowing that the restriction of energy which results from the use of his knife leads to finer fruit. Leaves are necessary to the plant's life, but the vine exists in the purpose of the husbandman for fruit. While the fruitless branch is cut away, the fruit-bearing branch is encouraged to increase gradually the amount and the quality of the fruit produced.

The counterpart of this in the life of Christ and his disciples is to be found in the discipline which a wise Father brings to bear. The Son learned obedience by the things that he suffered, and he is the captain of salvation to all who obey him.

"Now no chastening (discipline) for the present seemeth to be joyous, but grievous: nevertheless afterward it yieldeth the peaceable fruit of righteousness unto them which are exercised thereby."   (Hebrews 12:11)

The fruit produced is twofold. There is individual fruit, called by Paul "the fruit of the Spirit". But the labour of disciples brings others to Christ and fruit abounds to him in the increase of disciples. To this Jesus refers in verse 16: "I have ordained you that ye should go and bring forth fruit".

The apostles were first in this work, being "fruit" from the Lord's own ministry. They had been instructed by Jesus, and had entered into his trials. He could therefore say to them (verse 3): "Already *ye* are clean because of the word which I have spoken unto you". The word in them was purifying them, and they were fitted to carry to others the message which would cleanse others and make them fruit-bearers to Christ.

But one essential above all others must be kept in mind. They must abide in him. This action conditions not only their relationship to Jesus but also his relationship to them. Jesus said, "Abide in me, and I in you". The command had two sides. The action, which will have two effects, must come from them. The human will decides to abide in Christ, and so doing decides that Christ abides in them. It could not be otherwise if man is free to choose. Any man can cut himself off, as Judas had already done: and Christ cannot abide in a man who breaks away. But a man who does that takes the action which destroys all hope of producing fruit. A branch separated from the stem, dies. A man separated from Christ dies spiritually. There is reciprocal action between branch and tree—each serving its purpose. So with the Christ-vine: every branch may contribute to the good of the whole, helping while being dependent upon the tree. Only in vital union is this accomplished. Jesus adds as the reason why they must abide in him and he in them, that "as the branch cannot bear fruit of itself, except it abide in the vine; so neither can ye, except ye abide in me" (verse 4).

In verse 5, Jesus makes the application of the figure which had been implied in the preceding verses, of the branches of the vine. He was the vine; they were the branches; only by union with each other could fruit be produced.

Not all would abide, as Jesus knew; and he continually keeps the solemn thought of the effects of refusal of his teaching before his hearers, whether friends or foes, rejecters of his message or disciple. In the cultivation of the vine, the branch broken away withers, and is gathered and burned. At the time he spoke many fires burning the spring prunings would be smouldering, bearing immediate witness to the lesson of his words. Reduced to ashes, the branch was utterly destroyed. Its end was irrevocable. With a similar thought, Paul speaks of the thorns and briers being rejected, "whose end is to be burned" (Hebrews 6:8). The figure of burning for complete destruction is very apt; it is universally known, and should not be mistaken. The doctrine of the immortality of the soul has led to a literal application being given to the fire which is the end of the wicked, producing the horrible doctrine of endless torments, a doctrine at once immoral and dishonouring to God.

The moderns may quietly try to forget the doctrine, but it seems to be an inevitable corollary of the doctrine of the immortality of the soul. Alternatively, men must accept universalism, which also violates moral principles.

With the true doctrine of man's mortality, of the universal reign of death, because of sin both at the beginning of the race and in every individual of all generations, with the one exception of the man God made strong for Himself, all difficulty vanishes. Sin, which is rebellion, brings destruction to the sinner. This is right. It is endorsed on page after page of the gospels in which the severer side of the teaching of Jesus is set forth.

With the passing reference in this place Jesus returns to the subject of fruit-bearing, upon which he wishes attention at that time to be focussed. The conditions necessary for yielding fruit must be understood. If "abiding not" brings destruction, abiding in him produces fruit. This is related to other conditions (verse 7), which are connected with knowledge of his sayings and with prayer to the Father. The "words" are the "word" of verse 3, which cleansed; collectively, they are the word of God; in detail they include all His words. The knowledge of the teaching of Jesus is a governing condition of the apparently unlimited blessing and power involved in the words, "Ye shall ask what ye will, and it shall be done unto you". An ignorant person might ask many things which could not be granted, and then complain that the promise had failed. But as in 14:13 a similar statement had its qualification and its limitation in the phrase "in my name", so the "asking" which brings such a complete response is one that is based on knowledge of God's will, and asked subject to His will. What disasters might follow the answering of prayer uttered without such restraints! The saying does indicate a prayerful attitude, a desire to be in harmony with God, a willingness to serve God, and a close communion with the Father.

In such conditions God was glorified: "Herein was my Father glorified" (verse 8, RV margin); and the consequences are twofold: "that ye bear much fruit; and so shall ye be my disciples".

The fellowship involved in these thoughts is re-expressed in terms of love. "As the Father hath loved me, so have I loved you: continue ye in my love." The source of this all-embracing love is with the Father: He first loved, He gave the Son who always pleased Him, who so loved that he gave his life for his friends. But, love must be known and reciprocated; communion is based on oneness of purpose and thought. It is not sentiment of which Jesus speaks: it is feeling expressed in action. The action of the Father and the work of the Son exhibit their love—the Son's love being exhibited in his keeping God's commandments. The way he showed his love is the pattern for his brethren and servants. There is no other way. "If ye keep my commandments, ye shall abide in my love." This provides a test for all religious professions of loyalty to Jesus. His word is accepted as authoritative, his commands are followed as the rules of life by those who love him. Where the test fails, all professions are in vain.

Thus tested, the religious world is found wanting by its complete disregard of baptism. All piety, and claims that Jesus is Lord, in the absence of obedience will bring at last the devastating words: "Why call ye me Lord, and do not the things that I say?"

The test is not to be limited to the religious world at large. All who know the truth, who think seriously of the words of Jesus, must experience heart-searching to see whether the condition exists to which Jesus will respond in love.

But he aims at instructing them, not that they might be distressed, but that they might know the secret of his life in the orbit of God's love. Amidst all that appeared to contradict it, because of that secret Jesus knew joy. At that moment it seemed paradoxical to speak of joy—but the joy of Jesus could be theirs in fulness even in similar circumstances. The keeping of God's commandments, and the assurance of God's love, combine to produce joy amidst physical pain and mental stress, amidst peril and persecution, and all the other circumstances which have beset in some measure those who are followers of the Man of Sorrows who yet knew joy.

THE DISCIPLES' UNION IN CHRIST (15:12–17)

SPEAKING on behalf of the Pharisees during the day of disputes two days before the Passover, a lawyer asked Jesus the question, "Which is the great commandment in the law?" And Jesus answered,

"Thou shalt love the Lord thy God with all thy heart, and with all thy soul, and with all thy mind. This is the first and great commandment. And the second is like unto it, Thou shalt love thy neighbour as thyself. On these two commandments hang all the law and the prophets."

(Matthew 22:35–40)

The second is involved in the first, for

"if a man say, I love God, and hateth his brother, he is a liar; for he that loveth not his brother whom he hath seen, how can he love God whom he hath not seen? And this commandment have we from him, That he who loveth God love his brother also." (1 John 4:20,21)

When the love of God was revealed in the gift of His Son "to be the propitiation for our sins", man was provided with the example and also the inducement to love. But the love of God is known by its expression in Jesus himself. He loved as God loved, and gave himself according to the Father's will. This was in his mind continually as the day drew nearer for his great offering. The disciples knew the warmth of his friendship and his kindness to them, his splendid qualities of leadership; but they did not know at that time the extent of his love. The words he spake had an increasing value when time had interpreted their full significance. He doubtless knew this as he said:

"This is my commandment, That ye love one another, as I have loved you. Greater love hath no man than this, that a man lay down his life for his friends. Ye are my friends, if ye do whatsoever I command you." (verses 12–14)

There is an indication that friendship with Jesus can only be enjoyed when right conditions exist. His love for the Father required a sacrifice that might embrace all, but because so many will not respond to the love of God it is impossible for them to share the fruits of that love. Those only know the friendship that is founded on God's work in Jesus Christ who reciprocate the love in obedience to his commands. In a particular and emphatic sense those twelve, his intimates for three years, were his friends, and Jesus was probably thinking immediately of them to whom he was then speaking.

Earlier in the evening he had described them as servants (13:16). Then he was emphasizing the need of humility and showing them through their Master, by his own example, how they should act. But there were many sides to their relationship. He was Master and Lord, they were servants; he was the Saviour, they the redeemed. He was the Son of God, they sons by adoption, the "many sons" brought to glory through his sufferings. Some things they shared in common—the physical nature of Adam's children, the woes of life, its common joys, its friendships and companionships. Some of these things were lifted to a higher level, and purified and ennobled. Such was the bond of friendship between them. Hitherto he had stressed the need for obedience as servants, now he draws them closer to him—he gives them the confidence that belongs to friendship. "Henceforth I call you not servants; for the servant knoweth not what his lord doeth; but I have called you friends; for all things that I have heard of my Father have I made known unto you." They did not cease to be servants, but rather the very friendship intensified the willingness to serve.

The initiative was his in this service. He had acted with a purpose in view, for the work he had begun would continue and expand in the labours of others. Much of his work during his ministry, more in fact than is sometimes realized, consisted of training and preparing the Twelve for work when he was no longer with them. We have only to think of the revolution wrought in the Roman world in a very short time through the spreading of the gospel to realize the need for such a preparation. They had not chosen him; he had appointed (RV) them, assigning them apostolic duties, that they should go away—as he afterwards explained more fully, carrying his message from Jerusalem to Samaria and then to the uttermost parts of the earth. So labouring they would themselves bear fruit, but also others would be brought as fruit to the glory of God.

As a consequence of this labour and also as a means of its effectual operation the promise, made for the third time, is added, "that whatsoever ye shall ask of the Father in my name, he may give it you" (verse 16); (compare 14:13, and 15:7). The promise is associated with the work to be undertaken. The treasuries of Heaven were available, in connection with that mission. They would have discouragement, opposition, persecution. Their difficulties might seem to be insurmountable: the trials greater than they could bear; the opposition apparently overwhelming. But if they remembered the resources on their side, and so laboured that all they did was "in his name", they would be blessed with the necessary strength and endurance to accomplish the Father's purpose.

If they recognized they were co-workers in such a high calling, friends of the Son of God, they would then love one another (verse 17). It would cause them to close their ranks to meet a common foe—in mutual love finding the means of successfully resisting the hatred that would be their lot as they went out on their mission. The love they had for each other would be the more marked because of the hatred of the world to them.

WORLD HATRED OF JESUS AND HIS DISCIPLES (15:18–27)
JESUS had spoken of the love which was the bond of union between the Father and the Son, and the disciples (verses 9–14). But the attitude of the world would contrast sharply with the spirit known among themselves. They would meet hatred and all the actions that spring from hatred.

It might be thought that an appeal based upon such love as God "commends" to us in the giving of His Son would meet a ready response. It is not so. A few, who prove to be the remnant according to the election of grace, are responsive to the word of grace. But the majority of mankind refuse all divine approaches.

Jesus had no illusions about this. He repeatedly warned his hearers of the urgency of his call and the need for personal effort. The crowd goes its own way. The "many" enter the wide gate and travel the broad way only to meet destruction at the end. The "few" enter through the strait gate, tread the narrow way, but find life. Universalism, however pleasing to generous souls, is based on a desire that is not in harmony with the facts of experience in every generation. The whole history of the race as recorded in the Scriptures—and these are the only source of evidence that matters—is a witness that the majority follow their own devices rather than the counsel of God.

But the attitude of the world is not one of indifference. Where the claims of God's truth are actively and forcefully put forward, opposition is provoked. The silent witness of a righteous life induces the scorn and hatred of the unrighteous. "Blessed are they", said Jesus, "who are persecuted for righteousness' sake; for theirs is the kingdom of heaven. Blessed are ye when men shall revile you, and persecute you, and shall say all manner of evil against you falsely, for my sake. Rejoice, and be exceeding glad: for great is your reward in heaven: for so persecuted they the prophets which were before you" (Matthew 5: 10–12).

If God had not raised up the witnesses for truth, error would hold undisputed sway. Divine truth is productive of righteousness. In the figure used by Jesus and John, light and darkness are opposed as truth and error, righteousness and sin. The purpose of God requires the maintenance of the witness, and in each age the conflict has been continued. From the very beginning this was indicated:

"I will put enmity between thee and the woman, and between thy seed and her seed; it shall bruise thy head, and thou shalt bruise his heel."   (Genesis 3:15)

In these words God decreed that the world should be the arena of conflict, but that at last His truth would prevail.

The apostles had "to go" into the world (verse 16), carrying the message of their Master. He therefore warns them:

"If the world hate you, ye know that it hated me before it hated you. If ye were of the world, the world would love his own: but because ye are not of the world therefore the world hateth you. Remember the word that I said unto you, The servant is not greater than his lord. If they have persecuted me, they will also persecute you; if they have kept my saying, they will keep yours also. But all these things will they do unto you for my name's sake, because they know not him that sent me." (verses 18–21)

How often must the men who heard these words have recalled them in later days! The testimony of the apostles had a tormenting effect upon paganism, as in later days that of their successors had upon catholicism. In both cases fires of persecution were kindled and many followed the steps of their Lord to martyrdom and death. The example of Jesus was a warning and an encouragement.

The world loves its own: as Jesus told his own brethren, "the world cannot hate you; but me it hateth, because I testify of it, that the works thereof are evil" (7:7). They then showed the same unbelief as the Jewish world, and the world was not rebuked by what it saw in them. The disciple is not "of" the world, having been begotten from above to the living hope of sharing the life of the age to come: such are "chosen out of the world". The truth separates men from the world.

It deserves notice that Jesus places the word of the disciples on the same level of authority as his. They would experience the same rejection of their testimony as he had done.

The root of the whole opposition is traced to ignorance of God: "they know not him that sent me". Ignorance of God is the cause of hatred of God's children. Ignorance is blighting in its moral effects upon those enshrouded by it.

There is a culpable ignorance. Jesus had given to them the counsel of God: he had shed the light of the knowledge of God in the darkness. The light exposed the sin and ignorance and folly of man: but they did not forsake the darkness and follow the light. Yet the fact that it had shone across their path made an ineffaceable difference to them: the consequences they could not avoid. They might follow or forsake the light, but the responsibility remained. They had not had sin if Jesus had not come and spoken; but sin had no excuse when he had spoken (verse 22, RV).

The hatred of Jesus involved hatred of God. "He that hateth me hateth my Father also." The teaching of Jesus had been plain, but they had derided the claim that he was the Son of God. Since the claim was true, to reject Jesus was rejection of God, and hatred of the Son was also hatred of his Father. The two are inseparable in their relationship to men, and men can judge their attitude to God by their treatment of the Son.

The teaching of Jesus brought responsibility to the hearers (verse 22). His works partook of the same character as his words. Both were distinct from anything that other men had done; both showed that Jesus was true, that his words and works were divine. The rejection of his message, and refusal to accept the evidence of his works, were equally grounds of condemnation. "If I had not done among them the works which none other man did, they had not had sin; but now have they both seen and hated both me and my Father" (verse 24).

Their hatred was further inexcusable in that it fulfilled the prophecies in the very Scriptures they claimed to know and reverence. The Scripture must be fulfilled; but their responsibility for its fulfilment was increased by their professed respect for what was written. "This cometh to pass", said Jesus of their hatred, "that the word might be fulfilled that is written in their law, They hated me without a cause."

The place where it is written is in the Psalms, whether the source of the quotation be found in 35:19 or 69:4. The general Messianic character of Psalm 35 is evident. It was written by David, probably during the dark days of Absalom's revolt, when the King left his city and trod the same valley as did his greater Son many centuries later, rejected for the time by his people. The calamity was indeed the out-working of sin—a bearing of the effects of sin. David's life at its close was overshadowed by the clouds that gathered from his own wrongdoing. The sword did not depart from his own house. But the defection of his people was a hard blow, as was the betrayal of his friend and counsellor: and both were unjustified on personal grounds. David can therefore pray: "Let not them that are mine enemies wrongfully rejoice over me: neither let them wink with the eye that hate without a cause".

The sixty-ninth Psalm is a detailed foreshadowing of the sufferings of Christ, foretelling the lack of understanding of his mother's children (a remarkable hint of the virgin birth of Jesus), his zeal for God's house, his bearing reproach, his anguish of soul at the flood of evil opposition at which he cries:

"They that hate me without a cause are more than the hairs of mine head: they that would destroy me, being mine enemies wrongfully, are mighty: then I restored that which I took not away."   (verse 4)

187

The Psalms have all the binding force of "law". The word is not to be limited to the enactments of the first five books. All parts of the Old Testament are by virtue of their divine authority to be regarded as "law". Jesus spoke of it as *their law*" to emphasize that it was the law they acknowledged and studied: but no attitude on their part, favourable or unfavourable, could affect its authority.

Jesus adds a further ground for confidence and assurance on the part of the disciples. Not only would they be strengthened to meet the hatred of men, but they would have divine help to discharge their work. "But when the Comforter is come, whom I will send unto you from the Father, even the Spirit of truth, which proceedeth from the Father, he shall testify of me: and ye also shall bear witness, because ye have been with me from the beginning." He is speaking of the gift of the Spirit which after Pentecost guided them in their testimony, whether spoken or written. The description of the Spirit as "the Spirit of truth" gives emphasis to the accuracy of the witness made by the apostles under its guidance, and is another confirmation that the writings of the New Testament are equally with the Old Testament, the inspired word of God.

The witness of the apostles was not an unwilling service; there was co-operation on their part; the Spirit did not destroy their freedom or remove their responsibility. But their very association with Jesus from the beginning proved to be the qualification and the energizing power that led them to "bear witness" in faithful testimony, which has borne its fruit in every generation by means of the writings to which their message was committed.

COMFORT IN THE COMING OF THE ADVOCATE (16:1–15)

IT is evident to the most casual reader that the chapter divisions of our Bible have the unfortunate effect on many occasions of breaking up an address or separating important parts of a narrative. It should be kept in mind continually that chapters 13–17 are all parts of the conversation of Jesus while with his disciples before going to Gethsemane.

It had been written before, that when the Lord of Hosts should be for a sanctuary in Israel, when the Word made flesh tabernacled amidst them, then He would also be a stone of stumbling and a rock of offence, resulting in many stumbling thereon (Isaiah 8:14). The rulers and people of Israel generally, fulfilled this prophecy. But Jesus was careful that such a calamity should not befall his disciples. This was one of the objects in his mind when he gave them his final words at and after the Supper. This he explains to them: "These things have I spoken unto you that ye should not be made to stumble" (verse 1). "These things" included the announcement of his sufferings according to what was written, the hatred they would receive in the world, and the comfort they would find in the Spirit to be bestowed (15:18–27). To be forewarned prevented any dismay and panic when the fires of hatred shone upon them.

The prospect was bleak enough: excommunication from the synagogue, a serious experience for a Jew, and persecution unto death in the supposed service of God (verse 2). It was a paradoxical position. Their enemies would stir up a religious persecution, convinced that they were serving God, and yet the real root of their actions arose from ignorance of God and of Jesus (verse 3). The Jews had a maxim, "Everyone who sheds the blood of the impious is as if he offered a sacrifice". Guided by such teaching we can understand how the bitter opposition to the early believers grew to the persecution led by Paul. But he came to recognize that he had done it ignorantly in unbelief, even as Jesus here declares.

Jesus said "the hour cometh" (verse 2, RV); and again in verse 4, "These things have I told you, that when their hour is come ye may remember that I told you of them". The language suggests a parallel between his experience and theirs, which would arise from the same cause. "This is your hour, and the power of darkness", said Jesus, when on trial before the high priest, as Luke records. It is phrased in the style of John's gospel and shows that the fourth gospel is not so singular in its form as some would have us believe. It is a phrase full of sombre meaning: the forces of darkness were arrayed against the light of the world and allowed a temporary triumph. Sin, opposed to righteousness, was to bruise the woman's seed in the heel. And since the disciples were part of that seed multitudinous they would know a horror of darkness when the "hour" of the enemy came in their lives.

There is a time to speak and a time to refrain from speaking. As a wise teacher, Jesus gave instruction as the disciples were able to receive it, and as occasion called for it. Hitherto his presence had made it unnecessary for him to tell them of many matters, but his impending separation made it now essential. They had to take his place and must be prepared for the work. Yet even now they had misunderstood him. In what seems, as a matter of words, to be contrary to fact, he said to them, "Now I go my way to him that sent me; and none of you asketh me, Whither goest thou?" (verse 5). Only a little while before Peter had actually used the words (13:36). But the emphasis then was wrong; Peter was thinking of the *going*, and not of *where* he was going; and now the effect of his words was not what it should have been. Had they emphasized the *whither*, they would not have been so downcast and so sad.

A consideration of *whither* he was going would have led to other feelings altogether. His departure to the Father was an exaltation surpassing that which might come to any other man. It remained for Paul in such passages as Ephesians 1:19–23, Philippians 2:8–11, and Colossians 1:18,19 to open out the glory that belonged to their exalted Lord.

For reasons that affected them it as necessary that he should go away. "Nevertheless I tell you the truth: it is expedient for you that I go away; for if I go not away the Comforter will not come unto you; but if I depart, I will send him unto you" (verse 7). His absence from them was not only necessary for his exaltation but for the work still to be done by them. The extension of their preaching to the Gentiles, and the unfolding of the place of that preaching in the plan of God, needed the guidance of the Spirit, which is again promised unto them.

"When the Spirit of truth is come, it shall bear witness of me", Jesus had said (15:26). The nature of that witness is now made known. By it the world would be convicted of sin, righteousness and judgment. The conviction would not necessarily lead to acceptance of the teaching of the apostles: but their testimony would be unanswerable, unless indeed the blows of silenced disputers be considered as answers.

The points of conviction are particularized. They are all related to the work of Jesus and his controversy with men in word and act. It would be shown that Jesus was true, that he was the one in whom God's righteousness was exhibited, and sin condemned.

The world would be convicted "of sin, because they believe not on me". Jesus had been accused of sin in his attitude towards the sabbath, and other actions in which he set aside their ceremonial distinctions. But he was free from sin, while the root of sin was exhibited by them. They had refused to believe in him. This really showed them to be opposed to divine righteousness. Men think belief to be a matter of little moment, whereas in fact it shows the true sympathy and loyalty of every individual. By their wrong estimate of Jesus they were shown to be on the side of sin.

The world would be convicted of "righteousness"—that is, of the righteousness shown forth by Jesus in his life. As far as this concerned the Jewish world there is indicated a sharp contrast between their self-righteousness, sought by the keeping of law and made a ground of boasting and self-satisfaction, and the righteousness of God revealed in Jesus. This was positively shown in the manifestation of the spirit of God in all the ways of Jesus, and negatively in the condemnation of sin, both in his life and by his baptism and his crucifixion. The ascent to the Father was a final vindication of Jesus and of the righteousness of God, as against the world's attitude to him.

Lastly, the world would be convicted of "judgment", which Jesus explained, "because the prince of this world is judged". Here again would be brought home to the world that its judgment of Jesus was wrong. The world had condemned Jesus as unfit to live, when he was the only one worthy of life. The rulers thought that they were condemning Jesus, when Jesus by his action in submitting to crucifixion was working with God in the condemnation of sin. For the law could not condemn sin, but God, sending His own Son in the likeness of sinful flesh, condemned sin. The judgment then was by God, and as such was a condemnation of those who crucified Jesus, and also of all who followed the desires of the flesh, and of the world.

In the words of Dr. Thomas in *Elpis Israel*:

"The judgment of the Prince of the World by God, was exhibited in the contest between Jesus and the civil and spiritual power of Judea. Its poison was like the poison of a serpent, when the iniquity of his heels encompassed him about. The battle was against him for a time. They bruised him in the heel. The enemy smote his life down to the ground; and made him to dwell in darkness, as those that had long been dead.

But here the serpent-power of sin ended. It had stung him to death by the strength of the law, which cursed every one that was hanged upon a tree: Jesus being cursed upon this ground, God condemned sin in the flesh, through him. Thus was sin, the Prince of the World, condemned, and the world with him according to the existing course of it. But Jesus rose again, leading captivity captive; and so giving to the world an earnest, that the time would come when death should be abolished and sin, the power of death, destroyed. Sinful flesh was laid upon him, that through death, he might destroy him that had the power of death, that is, the devil, or sin in the flesh: for, for this purpose the Son of God was manifested, that he might destroy the works of the Devil."

The words of Jesus probably sounded strange—their import not fully discerned, they would seem far removed from the work of ruling the disciples had cherished in connection with Jesus. Perhaps their faces showed their perplexity, leading Jesus to add: "I have yet many things to say unto you, but ye cannot bear them now" (verse 12). They must wait patiently—enough had been said; and the experiences that were so near, but unknown then to them, made further disclosure difficult. But he told them that shortly their difficulties would be resolved in the enlightenment that the Spirit would give. "Howbeit when he, the Spirit of truth, is come, he will guide you into all the truth: for he shall not speak of himself; but whatsoever he shall hear, that shall he speak: and he shall show you things to come" (verse 13).

When Jesus spoke of the spirit as *he* who should come, he was using the language of personification. The Spirit is the power of God, and the agent of God in revelation. "Holy men of God spake as they were moved by the Holy Spirit." The apostles were to be the instruments of further communications. These would be true—"all the truth"; and the revelation of "things to come" is the way of divine endorsement of God's messengers. It is a strange disregard of the words of Jesus that has allowed men who even claim to be in the line of apostolic succession, and themselves the possessors of the same Spirit that Jesus promised, to discredit the truth of the gospels written by the apostles. The modern treatment of the gospel records is opposed to the promise of Jesus and an outrage on sound criticism. The Apocalypse, which more than any other book of the New Testament deals with things to come, is regarded as a pictorial representation of a conflict then proceeding when John wrote, and designed to encourage the martyrs for the faith. But to treat it as a divinely written outline of history to be fulfilled in the divine control of human affairs is regarded as evidence of religious aberration. The very witness of fulfilled prophecy which God cites as confirming the words of His messengers is treated as impossible.

The work of the Spirit would lead to the glorification of Jesus (verse 14). This is seen in the apostolic writings, which unfold the greatness of Jesus in relation to the Father, to the redeemed, and to the whole creation, and the age to come.

Paul has even been called the creator of the Christ of the Creeds. But in truth the Jesus set forth in the epistles is the Jesus of the gospels glorified according to this promise. The nature of the glory is hinted at in the explanation Jesus gives. The Spirit "shall take of mine, and declare it unto you"; and that "mine" denotes nothing less than "whatsoever things the Father hath", all of which Jesus says he shares. In declaring the Father, the work of the Son must be included. In setting forth the glory of the Father, His love, His righteousness, His holiness, the same must be shown of the Son: "for in him dwelleth all the fulness of the godhead bodily", and he "is the image of the invisible God" (Colossians 2:9; 1:15).

Sorrow Turned into Joy (16:16–24)

JESUS resumes the thought, already mentioned in verse 10, of his going to the Father. "A little while, and ye shall behold me no more; and again a little while, and ye shall see me, because I go to the Father" (verse 16). Here are two "little whiles" connected with seeing him no more, and yet seeing him, and the second seeing made possible because he was going away.

It is small wonder that the disciples were perplexed. We can picture them, eleven men with Jesus, standing loosely around him, questioning each other as they sought the meaning of his words, and reaching the conclusion, "We know not what he saith" (verses 17,18).

The answer is found in the events which shortly came to pass. "A little while"—but a few hours, and they beheld him no more; his death brought to an end the close personal contact with him as they journeyed from place to place, and discussed with him the meaning of his teaching. His death closed that experience of him enjoyed "in the days of his flesh". Then came a little while, reaching to "the third day", and he was raised from the dead and a new experience of him became theirs. At first there was close physical contact, they handled him, ate with him, talked with him; but he was changed, no longer limited by the conditions of mortal life. Then after forty days he left them, going to the Father, but the eye of faith was never darkened henceforth, for by it they continued to "see" him, raised and glorified, exalted to the heavens.

All this being known to Jesus, he could explain to them: "Verily, verily, I say unto you, that ye shall weep and lament, but the world shall rejoice; ye shall be sorrowful, but your sorrow shall be turned into joy" (verse 20). There are two contrasts: at the death of Jesus the world rejoiced and they sorrowed; but at his resurrection their sorrow passed in a new-found joy. Their sorrow endured during the first "little while"; when the second interval passed they became radiant with a knowledge that made it even possible to be "joyful in tribulation".

Jesus turns to a figure from the very heart of home life, made familiar to all by its use in the prophets. The sentence at the beginning, "In sorrow shalt thou bring forth children", had made the time of birth, while a natural process, a time of labour and travail. When "her hour was come" the mother had her taste of sorrow and pain, but it was quickly forgotten in the joy of motherhood. In many ways the figure is used. Jesus, upon whom met all the curses that came by sin, knew "*travail* of soul". "He shall see and be satisfied with the travail of his soul" for as the result of it he should see "his seed". It is remarkable that this figure should be used of his soul's agony, but he was to be tried in all points, and this experience did not pass him by. Very shortly it was "his hour", and he felt the pangs which presently became so acute that they produced the sweat of blood as he knelt in Gethsemane.

It was "an hour of travail" for the disciples too. New ideas had been forming in their minds, and out of the anguish now upon them a new faith would be born. And the Church, which is his body, was built up from the riven side and the sleep of death of the second Adam. The woman was "of the man", whether we think of Adam and Eve, or of Christ and the Church.

It deserves notice, that Jesus did not say "a child is born" (verse 21) but a *man* is born . It may be thought that the language is being pressed too far, but out of that night of sorrow a new man came, and he is the head of all the redeemed which form his body, the whole forming "one new man".

Closely connected with these ideas is the figure of Zion as a mother, which is frequent in the prophets. The allegory in Abraham's domestic life is explained by Paul as being a fore-shadowing of Jerusalem in the past under the law, and Jerusalem of the future, the mother of all children of promise, under the new covenant (Galatians 4). Jerusalem was described by Isaiah as widowed and bereaved of children, and also as finding a new family brought to her, to her great surprise. "These—where had they been? Who hath brought up these?" she exclaims. The answer is that many Gentiles had become adopted children of Zion because of "the man" brought forth in Jerusalem nineteen hundred years ago. They will have been "brought up" from death where so many sleep. Isaiah links together the birth of the man-child, and the birth of a nation from the dust long afterwards. "Before Zion travailed", he says, "she brought forth; before her pain came, she was delivered of a man child. Who hath heard such a thing? Who hath seen such things? Shall the earth be made to bring forth in one day? Or shall a nation be born at once? for as soon as Zion travailed, she brought forth her children" (66:6–8).

Jesus at once applies the figure to the disciples. "And ye therefore now have sorrow: but I will see you again, and your heart shall rejoice, and your joy no man taketh from you." "I will see you"; before he had said " ye shall see me", which we saw was with the eye of faith (verses 22,16). And so in his seeing—no bodily presence is involved; he is away from the earth but he knows all who are followers of him.

They had many times in the ministry plied him with questions, and the last hour had been one of earnest seeking for answers to their misgivings and problems. That would end with his departure: but they would not be without guidance. If they asked anything of the Father, He would give it to them. Their approach would be in a new channel henceforth: "Hitherto have ye asked nothing in my name: ask, and ye shall receive, that your joy may be full". In the light of the context it is evident that Jesus had in mind the operations of the Holy Spirit in illuminating their minds with the fuller understanding of him; and their prayers thus guided, offered through his priestly activity, would bring a rich answer in fulness of joy.

CONCLUSION (16:25–33)

CONCLUDING the conversation, Jesus told them that he had spoken in parables or proverbs—in sayings the meaning of which was hidden. An hour was coming (verse 25, RV), called "that day" in verse 26, when he would speak plainly. This again must refer to subsequent revelations made through them by inspiration. It gives the writings of the apostles the same authority as the spoken words of the Lord.

They would ask in his name, but for two things his intercession would not be necessary: the advocate-spirit would be with them, guiding them; and "praying in his name" they were assured of the love of the Father. The ground of assurance was their love of him and their belief that he came from God. "I came forth from the Father, and I am come into the world; again, I leave the world, and go to the Father." This saying of Jesus epitomizes the very message of John's gospel. It shows the source and end of salvation illustrated and embodied in the man who is the Saviour.

The words spoken by the disciples in reply are evidently hasty, and show they have not grasped his meaning. Only a minute before they had been in doubt; he had told them clear understanding was reserved for the future; yet now they say they know, that his words are plain. They evidently were putting a very limited construction on his words. Such a view harmonizes the contexts before and after. For Jesus adds: "Do ye now believe?"—so quickly? And he tells them that they will soon be scattered, having left him alone—alone in that human companionship was wanting, but not alone in that God was with him (verse 32).

He then in a final word explains that he had spoken all this last discourse that they might find peace in him. They would find tribulation in the world, but they need not despair, he had overcome. And if he had overcome their victory was assured. Amazing words of confidence from a man going out to certain arrest and crucifixion!

The Closing Prayer (Chapter 17)

"THIS chapter", says an old writer, "of all chapters in Scripture, is the easiest in regard to the words, the most profound in regard to the ideas meant." This might be expected, for in this prayer we are for a brief period overhearing the communion of the Son of God with his Father.

It has many times been called the High Priestly Prayer, but without good reason. His office of intercessor began with the ratification of the new covenant, when he approached, as a high priest of good things to come, to the throne in heaven through his own blood (Hebrews 9:11,12).

The prayer breathes the spirit which in the preceding conversation he had counselled his disciples to maintain. He had said, "Be of good cheer; I have overcome the world". Now the note of cheer and confidence of victory pervades his spoken approaches to the Father. It was spoken intentionally in the hearing of the disciples, and therefore we may conclude for their benefit as well as for himself. Its preservation here is for others also, and all who have faith and understanding of the apostolic teaching in this day may stand with the eleven apostles and feel the touching appeal of the Saviour for them.

PRAYER FOR HIMSELF (17:1–5)

"THESE things (chapters 14–16) spake Jesus"; thus John connects the prayer with what had gone before, and points to it as the climax of the hour's communion of Jesus and his little band. "And lifting up his eyes to heaven, he said ...": thus with uplifted face he leads them in his thought, lifting hearts in devotion to God.

"Father"—he begins with the simple address; how out of place would any other terms have been! He does not say "Our Father", for while the eleven listen it is his prayer, and he never joins himself and them in the one term of address. "When ye pray, say, Our Father", he had taught them. It was not by virtue of any exclusive sonship that any one of them could use such a term of relationship to the Creator. They were all of the "many sons" whom God was bringing to glory, through the captain of their salvation made perfect through suffering. In using the plural pronoun "Our", this fact is constantly in view. What could give any son of Adam the title to come to the Eternal with "My Father" on his lips! But as one of a redeemed family his relationship is beautifully and comfortingly indicated, both privilege and responsibility being in view, in "Our Father".

Jesus, however, could and did use "My Father", for he was Son of God in the strict sense, the "only begotten". But the use of the simple "Father" in this prayer is at the same time fitting to the occasion when others were present for whom the prayer was in part offered.

"The hour is come"—until that hour his enemies could not touch him. He was hid in the shadow of his Father's hand. Now his enemies were to triumph and to suffer defeat; while he was to be both dishonoured and glorified. The essence of the events before him—the inner reality—is his exaltation; the hour had come for that. Because the inner significance was so clearly before him, the outward shame and the physical pain were lost to view, and the spirit exalted in

197

strength. Hence the petition "Glorify thy Son that thy Son also may glorify thee".

The word "glory" enfolds a very comprehensive idea of the purpose of God. The Son's glorifying the Father which follows the Father's glorifying the Son, excludes any restricted view. The earth will yet be full of God's glory (Numbers 14:21). When the time for that comes, the saints will join in a thrice-expressed ascription of holiness to God (Isaiah 6:3). The exaltation of Jesus, and the bowing of every knee to him, is "to the glory of God the Father", as Paul says (Philippians 2:9–11). The physical phase of glory seen in the shining face of Moses was typical of something deeper and more lasting. For the glory on his face passed; but the glory of the new covenant, says Paul, abides (2 Corinthians 3:11). Because this glory is embodied in the Lord, and when beheld has transforming power, upon all who look, into his image from glory to glory (2 Corinthians 3:18), the gospel is therefore "the gospel of the glory of Christ, the image of God" (4:4, RV), and the light of that gospel has the same divine energy to dispel moral darkness as the original fiat "Let there be light" had to scatter the primeval darkness. Hence the glory is a thing much more than physical, although it embraces at last the physical in bringing about the change of the body of our humiliation to likeness to the body of his glory.

"Glorify thy Son": who is sufficient for adequate exposition of all that is involved—the exhibition of the moral excellence of Jesus, his resurrection and exaltation, his victory over sin? And this is a glorifying of the Father (to whom ultimately all glory belongs) for sending the Son, and in and through him working out that purpose among the sons of men, according to the counsel of his own will, that leads "to the praise of his glory" (Ephesians 1:12,14); or in the ampler terms of verse 6, "to the praise of the glory of his grace".

Jesus passes to the means by which the Father and Son will be glorified: "Even as thou gavest him authority over all flesh, that whatsoever thou hast given him, to them he should give eternal life. And this is life eternal, that they should know thee, the only true God, and him whom thou didst send, even Jesus Christ" (verses 3,4, RV).

"All flesh" is all mankind, described in this way to emphasize the mortality that belongs to flesh, and the weakness which inheres in it, which disables it from reaching by its own effort the glory of God. Because Jesus is the Saviour, the authority over all men is his: and since it is over all, Jewish exclusiveness is set aside. The need is universal, and the remedy extends to the need. In its outworking it is narrower than the whole race, but this is not due to limit in the remedy. The limit is imposed by God; and is expressed in the phrase "as many as thou hast given him (Jesus)". The Father's giving is conditioned by human response, only the co-operation of man can bring any one within the blessings of the grace of God.

The thought re-echoes the idea of 6:37: "All that which the Father giveth me shall come unto me; and him that cometh to me I will in no wise cast out". The giving is dependent in human life upon the coming, although those who come may "have been chosen in him before the foundation of the world" (Ephesians 1:4), because the Father knows the end from the beginning, and He can therefore give them to Christ antecedently to their choice to come.

The "eternal life" given must be closely associated with the glorifying of Father and Son of verse 1. In the giving of this life the Father is glorified, because those who receive it have first received of His grace, and have then manifested that manner of life for which the Father chose them: "that we should be holy and without blame before him in love" (Ephesians 1:4).

The emphasis is upon the moral rather than the physical. "Eternal life" truly involves physical change, but it also involves a permanent moral life that belongs of necessity to eternal things. Jesus therefore defines the eternal life as "knowing God". He is not speaking of the condition whereby it may be attained, although to know God must be a prerequisite. But eternal life in its moral bearings consists in this, that all who attain that life "know God" and his Son.

What is it "to know God"? Surely it is the completion of that process which begins now in knowledge of God.

"Grace and peace be multiplied unto you through the knowledge of God, and of Jesus our Lord, according as his divine power hath given unto us all things that pertain unto life and godliness, through the knowledge of him that hath called us to glory and virtue."   (2 Peter 1:2,3)

Peter is thinking of *our* knowledge of God, and he includes knowledge in the list of things to be "supplied" (verse 5) as a condition of the entrance into the kingdom being "supplied" to them (verse 11, RV). Here the relationship between the present and the future is shown: the future continues the present and brings it to completion. We "supply" the qualities which have an abiding value in God's sight, and "these things", faith, virtue, knowledge, temperance, patience, godliness, being "in you", says Peter, "ye shall never fall", but God will "supply" the entrance. Peter distinguishes between what man does and God's part by the word "richly" (RV). God richly supplies. Is not the abundance an expanding to the full development of the graces striven after?

"The only true God" is the description of the Father which Jesus uses. The One who has sent Jesus into the world is the only God, for God is One: but He is the true God, in that all subsist in Him, and all reality resides in Him. To know Him is to partake of this reality, to be assimilated to the divine; or as John expresses it in his first epistle:

"We know that the Son of God is come, and hath given us an understanding, that we may know him that is true; and we are in him that is true, even in his Son Jesus Christ. This is the true God, and eternal life." (1 John 5:20)

The exultant triumph shines out in the confident note, "I have glorified thee on the earth; I have finished the work which thou gavest me to do", even although the closing events were yet future. " It is finished", he said on the cross: but it was finished before, so far as the decision of Jesus was concerned. Therefore he petitions: "And now, Father, glorify thou me with thine own self with the glory which I had with thee before the world was". His work of glorifying God had been *on earth*—the glory he was to receive was with God; in His presence, beside God; and it was a glory contemplated in the eternal counsel before the world was.

PRAYER FOR DISCIPLES (17:6–19)

AFTER Jesus had spoken of his work in relationship to the Father he turns to what he had done on behalf of the disciples. His work (in that phase of it) was closing—theirs was about to begin; but he had prepared them for it. Continuing his labours, they would meet a like opposition to that which he had endured, and he would have them meet trial and difficulty in the same spirit as he had shown.

"I have manifested thy name unto the men which thou gavest me out of the world: thine they were, and thou gavest them to me; and they have kept thy word" (verse 6). The name of God in Scripture usage is expressive of all that God is and all that He has revealed of His purpose. By His revelation He is known—and that by which He is known is

His name. It is much more than a name which distinguishes the God of Israel from the gods of other nations.

Yet in the name which God gave Himself at the bush there is embodied a memorial of His purpose in the highest sense, and to know His name in that sense is to know what He has revealed. It is evident that Jesus is practically using a synonym for name when he says they have kept God's *word*: for by the word the name is known.

In a personal sense Jesus had revealed the name of God, for he had shown by word and act the character of God; and by revealing himself as the Son of God had made known the steps by which God would fulfil the significance of the name "He-who-shall-be". In that purpose of "becoming" God sent forth His only begotten Son, to prepare the way for many sons to be brought into the name. The apostles set forth the way for sharing the sonship when they declared that there was "no other name under heaven by which men might be saved". All who respond to the message are "taken out of the Gentiles as a people for God's name".

God "did visit the Gentiles" to take out this people. It was a divine work, although performed by human instruments, for the phrase "did visit" is used in Luke's gospel of the *visit* of the dayspring from on high. In the birth of Jesus and in the taking out of the Gentiles of his brethren, we have God's approach for the salvation of men. Those who respond are foreknown to Him: they were His, as Jesus said, and were given to Jesus. This giving was by means of the instruction which Jesus gave to them; and in a particular sense they were given to Jesus to carry on his work.

By his teaching the disciples had perceived the divine source of Jesus and of all that Jesus had. His words—the individual words which together form "the word" of verse 6— were of God, just as he was from God. What better ground could there be for intercession! "I pray for them." The world had rejected the light shining forth in Jesus, preferring the darkness. How could prayer be offered on their behalf in this connection? "I pray not for the world, but for them which thou hast given me, for they are thine." The world opposed Jesus and then his apostles; but the apostles were continuing the divine work, enjoying the closest fellowship with Father and Son. Between them there was the closest unity—"mine are thine, and thine are mine"—and in them the Son was glorified.

Jesus has this thought upon their needs when he would no longer be with them. He addresses the Father, in this instance only, as "Holy Father" (verse 11). Why *"Holy Father"*? Holiness is an inseparable element of God's character and name. The disciples had been separated from the world: to preserve the unity of which Jesus had spoken they must be kept holy—separate from the world's evil. "Keep in thine own name those whom thou hast given me, that they may be one, even as we are."

This had been throughout the aim of Jesus. He had *kept* them—and then changing the word, for the keeping was contingent upon their willingness—he says, "And I guarded them, and not one of them perished, but the son of perdition; that the scripture might be fulfilled". The guardian cannot compel against the wishes of the men invited. Judas had made his choice; he was "son of"—a Hebraism involving a moral choice. He was "son of perdition"— for his choice led to destruction.

Jesus felt keenly the withdrawal of his personal contact with the disciples, and his prayer was spoken in their hearing so that the memory of his words might remain to give them joy (verse 13).

The giving of the word has a twofold effect: in those who receive it is produced faith (verse 8): in those who refuse it hatred springs up towards those who have faith (verse 14). They would, therefore, as the result of his work find faith and know persecution; the world would hate them, because it would be seen they were not of it. But to withdraw them from the world would frustrate the very purpose God had in giving them the word. They cannot be taken out of it: Jesus does not pray that they shall; but he petitions that they may be kept from the evil of the world.

The ground of the world's hatred (verse 14) is also the reason for their sanctification. They have been separated from the world: they are not of it. They must then be consecrate or dedicate to holiness, as the Father is holy. In one environment only is this possible. "Sanctify them *in* the truth" (RV). And in one way only is that truth known—"Thy word is truth".

The need for consecration was emphasized by the work before them (verse 18). They could not call the world to holiness and follow the unholiness in the world. But they had the best of examples. "For their sakes" Jesus had "sanctified himself" that "in the truth" they might be sanctified. He was sanctified in his whole devotion to God, with an unfailing obedience: they were sanctified because cleansed from sin for his sake. "Ye are washed, ye are sanctified", and they were therefore called upon "to perfect holiness in the fear of God" (1 Corinthians 6:11; 2 Corinthians 7:1). And as Paul says, Christ "gave himself for the church, that he might sanctify and cleanse it with the washing of water by the word" (Ephesians 5:26).

PRAYER FOR ALL BELIEVERS (17:20–26)

WHEN Jesus had drawn from Peter the confession at Caesarea Philippi that he was "the Christ, the son of the living God", Jesus pronounced him blessed, and told him that upon that rock he would build his Church, against which the gates of hell would not prevail (Matthew 16:16–18). "My church"—"my ecclesia": the words show how clearly Jesus saw the future course of events in the extension of his own work through the labours of the apostles. By them Jesus would gather out of the nations a people for the name of God. This separated people would be his "called out"—his saints. On their behalf Jesus would unlock the doors of the grave, and give them the victory over death.

It is beautifully fitting that in the closing prayer of Jesus before he suffered, he should petition first for himself in view of the now accomplished work; then for the apostles with whom so much of the ministry had been spent, and for whose instruction he had so laboured; and lastly for that larger number who would believe through their being "sent into the world". "Neither pray I for these alone", said Jesus, "but for them also which shall believe on me through their word" (verse 20).

We must not limit the apostolic ministry to the labours of their lifetime. A phase of their work more permanent than the oral preaching has been the writing under the Spirit's guidance the books which form the New Testament. The needs of the church of Christ during the first century led to the writing of the gospels and the epistles either by the apostles or their associates, and by these books the ministry of reconciliation has gone on. The writers, while dead, yet speak, "We therefore beseech you in Christ's stead, Be ye reconciled to God". All the reconciled of every age out of every kindred and tribe and nation and tongue will have had in common "the word of faith" which, said Paul, "we preach".

The prayer of Jesus for them was "that they all may be one; as thou, Father, art in me, and I in thee, that they also may be one in us: that the world may believe that thou hast sent me" (verse 21).

We need not labour to disprove any implication of such a unity as the Trinitarians seek in this and similar passages. The "oneness" of the Father and Son embraces all the believers—they are part of the unity, and this excludes the Trinitarian interpretation.

But what is the "oneness" for which Jesus prays?

It is a fundamental feature of divine revelation that God is One. "Hear, O Israel, the LORD our God is one Lord", Moses proclaimed; and Israel have *heard* in all their generations and still hold fast to the doctrine of the unity of God. God is the LORD—He is the LORD our God. As the Psalmist said:

"Know ye that the LORD, he is God; it is he that hath made us, and not we ourselves; we are his people, the sheep of his pasture." (100:3)

There were lords many and gods many in the Gentile world—gods that they had made for themselves, whose characters were but projections of their own base passions, and whose worship gave a securer hold to the habits represented by the gods. "To us", says Paul to the Corinthians, "there is but one God, the Father, of whom are all things, and we unto him; and one Lord Jesus Christ, through whom are all things, and we through him" (1 Corinthians 8:6). That one God is the source of all; and only by man's being quickened by the divine energy, and receiving the divine nature, will he survive. Therefore the object of the preaching is to turn men "unto him", that the direction thus given to their lives may at the appointed time bring them into full oneness.

If God is One, the God of the Jews must also be the God of the Gentiles; so Paul reasons in Romans 3:29. And from that basic fact of the unity of God he deduces that by one fundamental method, by faith, Jew and Gentile will be saved. And that oneness of God also carries with it that at last only those who are one with God will survive, when all that are opposed will be destroyed.

Paul speaks of "unto God" "through Christ". Jesus also points out the same means in the establishing of unity out of the disharmony caused by sin. "Thou in me"—the impulse for restoration has its source in God; "God was in Christ reconciling". "I in thee"—there was a never-failing God-ward-ness of the thoughts of Jesus; a perfect harmony in will: "not my will, but thine be done". Then as the consequence, "they may be one in us".

This is even now established: for Paul speaks of the Thessalonians as "in God the Father and the Lord Jesus Christ" (1 Thessalonians 1:1). This present phase is in the mind of Jesus, for he says that as the outcome of the unity established "the world may believe that thou hast sent me". The change in the lives of the pagans who accepted the gospel was evidence of a new force that had entered the Gentile world, with life-giving power. They became lights which shone in the world, and examining the light men found it was lit by a greater light that had shone in Judea. "Have your behaviour seemly among the Gentiles", wrote Peter, "that wherein they speak against you as evil-doers (that is, as Christians), they may by your good works, which they shall behold, glorify God in the day of visitation" (1 Peter 2:12).

In that day of inspection, as Dr. Thomas translated the word, they would not only glorify God, but be partakers of the glory to be revealed (1 Peter 5:1; 4:13). The One Man, the Perfect Man, of apostolic and prophetic allusion, will be revealed as a Redeemed One Body (Daniel 10:5; Ephesians 4:13; Romans 8:23), fulfilling the words of Jesus: "I in them, and thou in me, that they may be made perfect in one; and that the world may know that thou hast sent me, and hast loved them, as thou hast loved me".

There is here, as we have noticed on other occasions, an ominous note. When the "perfect man" is revealed the world will know the purpose of love in Christ, and in many cases know it in shame.

The closing words express the desire for the consummation of the union of the redeemed in spirit-nature; to be with Christ, to behold the glory given him by God. It is a completion of the fellowship begun now in the knowledge of God. That knowledge is more than an acquaintance with first principles of revelation, while including them. To know God is to love Him, to serve Him, to enjoy communion with Him. The world knew not God; but Jesus, who revealed Him, knew Him; and the disciples knew that God had sent Jesus. With the knowledge that Jesus was sent of God, they had the necessary preparation for the reception of further revelation. This Jesus had given them: "I have made known unto them thy name, and will make it known"; and the purpose of that sharing of knowledge is the perfect fellowship in the love of God: "that the love wherewith thou lovedst me may be in them, and I in them".

THE GOSPEL OF JOHN

SECTION 6

THE CRUCIFIXION
THE BETRAYAL (18:1–11)

WE have noticed before that John uses language which carries a suggestion of a hidden meaning—his words are to be understood literally, but there is an emphasis which gives an added sense. It is so in this record of the betrayal of Jesus.

The last discourse had been spoken, and the prayer recorded in chapter 17 had been offered. And "when Jesus had spoken these words he went forth with his disciples over the brook Cedron, where was a garden, into which he entered, and his disciples". He "went forth" from the city; the action was voluntary, and he knew it was going forth to initiate the last moves in the conflict which must end with his death. It was an initial fulfilment of the type of the burning of the sin-offering without the camp, which Paul connects with Jesus.

"The bodies of those beasts, whose blood is brought into the sanctuary by the high priest for sin, are burned without the camp. Wherefore Jesus also, that he might sanctify the people with his own blood, suffered without the gate."   (Hebrews 13:11,12)

Very shortly the authorities would take him outside the city; his willing compliance with the Father's will, that thus it should be, was shown by this going forth to Gethsemane.

There was an episode in David's life which bore a close resemblance to this incident in the life of Jesus. The great sin of David brought a series of troubles in his own house, which reached their climax in the rebellion of Absalom. David then left the city of Jerusalem and travelled the way his greater Son was now taking across the Cedron valley. The Psalms written by David at this time are prophetic of the experiences of Jesus. Both were betrayed by a "friend" with whom sweet counsel had been taken; and each had gone with the "friend" to the courts of the Lord. The same phrase in the Greek Old Testament and the New Testament describes what befell the "friend"—he went and hanged himself. But David returned, and if Jesus thought of his ancestor, as the Psalms he quoted suggest he did, he would find assurance that beyond the night of sorrow was the day of return.

There has been speculation concerning the word Cedron, some translating it "the Cedars" with reference to the dark-foliaged, black-green tree of that name. The RV gives us "the winter-torrent Kidron". Once before, John had pointedly drawn attention to the season of the year to draw out its significance: "and it was winter" (10:22)—the time of shortening days when darkness asserts its power. Does John hint that the time in the life of Jesus was like the Cedron in its winter flow through the ravine so full of shadows? The floods are significant of trouble and affliction. "The sorrows of death compassed me, and the floods of ungodly men made me afraid", says the Psalmist (18:4).

In another place (124:1–4) David says that if God had not been on his side when men rose up against them, "then the waters had overwhelmed us, the stream had gone over our soul; then the proud waters had gone over our soul".

The word Kidron means black, with its associations of mourning and distress. The garden which John mentions was Gethsemane: more properly an orchard, and since the name means "oil-press", it would be an orchard of olives. Putting together these significant underlying meanings, it is evident that John is leading his readers to a deeper understanding of the sorrow of soul to which his Master "went forth". He had indeed companions—but they slept while he suffered. They travelled down the hill together—but how different the experience. The RV brings out that the experience was not the same for all, "he entered, *himself* and his disciples".

While they were picking their way down the slope to the valley, the absent disciple had entered the valley of decision too. Judas also, who was betraying him, knew the place: for Jesus ofttimes resorted thither with his disciples (verse 2). In what did the betrayal consist? Jesus had been openly preaching for over three years. His whereabouts were never secret— the betrayal then did not consist in simply revealing where he might be found. It is an interesting suggestion put forward in *Who Moved the Stone?* that Judas recognized that Jesus was thinking of death, and hurried off to the rulers, with whom he had had previous contact, to tell them that acting at once they would find no resistance from Jesus. Judas knew where Jesus was going, and guided the cohort of soldiers and the officers of the Temple to the place. Jesus was really the master of the situation: he had told Judas to proceed with his evil deed; he tarried in the garden when escape would have been easy. He maintained a shepherd's care for his flock to the end. He did it, John says, "knowing all things that should come upon him". In every detail the same calm, courageous facing of the issue before him is revealed. He "went forth" to meet them.

"Whom seek ye?" he asked, now that the hour was come, directing their attention to himself, and thus ensuring that his disciples were not the subject of a sudden attack. They answered him, "Jesus of Nazareth". Briefly he replied, " I am he". Before telling the effect of the approach and answer of Jesus, John notes the presence of the betrayer. It marks his debasement that he should join the Lord's enemies. The "son of perdition" was a symbol, as it were, of that power of darkness of which Jesus had spoken. The effect of the words of Jesus was almost symbolic also. Judas and his associates fell prostrate at the feet of Jesus. His innocence and majesty had even then a disabling power: but there was no effort to take advantage of it.

He again asks them, "Whom seek ye?" and receiving the same reply, he says, "I told you that I am he; if therefore ye seek me, let these go their way".

John then adds a remarkable comment. The action and words of Jesus were done, he says, "that the saying might be fulfilled which he spake, Of them which thou hast given me have I lost none". The saying had been spoken but a few hours earlier, but the words have the same divine imperative as the Scriptures. They must be fulfilled. It is true that the fulfilment was not complete; the saying refers to an eternal loss in the last day; but even in a partial sense they hold good, and the partial is related to the perfect, for had they been arrested they might have succumbed under the trial. Their faith and strength were not yet equal to that; the Shepherd's care continues so long as he is with them.

The impetuousness of Peter again revealed itself. He had a sword—one of the two which they had shown to Jesus the same evening when he had told them to sell their cloak and buy a sword. A servant of the high priest was possibly at the front of the company; perhaps he was the first to touch Jesus. Peter was not lacking in physical courage, and he quickly drew his sword and cut off the ear of the servant. His name was Malchus, John adds, revealing an intimate knowledge of the household of the high priest.

The answer of Jesus is a corrective to those who take literally the words of Jesus to buy a sword. "Put up thy sword into the sheath", Jesus bade Peter. To fight then was not in the purpose of God. The mission of Jesus then was far removed from a throne. It was to drink deeply the cup of suffering the Father had given him. The cup was also a cup of death. It was a cup to be drunk alone.

John does not record the agony in the garden, but the figure Jesus uses is that employed in his anguished cry during the agony, as recorded by Matthew. "O my Father, if it be possible, let this cup pass from me; nevertheless, not as I will, but as thou wilt." The two gospels complement each other. The figure appears to have been often on the lips of Jesus. It was a cup others must share in measure, as he told the sons of Zebedee, "Ye shall drink indeed of my cup, and be baptized with the baptism that I am baptized with". To the extent to which men and women enter into the fellowship of his sufferings they drink of the cup which the Father gave him, and fill up that which is behind of the sufferings of the Anointed.

THE JEWISH TRIAL (18:12–27)

THE space which the gospel writers give to the trials of Jesus shows the subject's importance. The trials were twofold, Jewish and Roman, and they bring out clearly the two most important elements in the teaching and claims of Jesus. "These things are written", John tells us, "that ye might believe that Jesus is the Christ, the Son of God." The Jewish authorities condemned Jesus because he affirmed that he was the Son of God, while the confession that he was a king led to sentence of death by Pilate. Because both claims were true, the trials by which men showed their rejection of Jesus were really a judgment of men.

"Now is the judgment of this world: now shall the prince of this world be cast out", Jesus had told the disciples, adding by way of explanation, "and I, if I be lifted up from the earth, will draw all men unto me" (12:31). Again he said, "The prince of this world cometh, and hath nothing in me" (14:30). "The prince of this world is judged" (16:11). The outward acts of men revealed spiritual forces: the judges and the prisoner were representative; sin and righteousness faced each other, with sin on the throne condemning righteousness to the scaffold, but in the very act being itself condemned, to be afterwards entirely destroyed.

The twofold character of the trial of Jesus arose from the political situation of the time, yet because of it both Jew and

Gentile were compelled to take part and express themselves. Had it been otherwise the Gentiles might have reproached the Jews with the most outrageous decision ever passed in a court of law; but as it is, Gentile and Jew joined in condemning the innocent. The early disciples saw in it a preliminary fulfilment of that opposition to the Lord's Anointed predicted by David in the second Psalm. The kings of the earth and the rulers gathered together—they joined in the arraignment;

"for of a truth against thy holy Servant Jesus, whom thou hast anointed, both Herod and Pontius Pilate, with the Gentiles, and the people of Israel, were gathered together, for to do whatsoever thy hand and thy counsel determined to be done." (Acts 4:27,28)

The times of the Gentiles had begun, and Israel had lost much of her independence. The Romans had curtailed the powers of the Jewish rulers and required that the sanction of the Roman governor must be obtained before sentence of death could be executed—otherwise a trial before the Sanhedrin would have been sufficient. It was therefore necessary that Jesus should be first brought before the Sanhedrin and a charge formulated; and then brought before Pilate for sentence.

The situation was peculiar. For a long time the death of Jesus had been determined upon; but in the effort to veneer with a form of legal sanction the evil purposes of their envious hearts, the Jews must find some grounds upon which to condemn Jesus. The law must be violated by a man before he can be righteously condemned; in what a predicament were these rulers of Israel when the man who always magnified God's law and made it honourable stood before them! They met the difficulty by themselves breaking every rule that had been devised to hedge about the procedure of capital trials so that justice should not miscarry.

The president of the Sanhedrin was the high priest, who held the position by virtue of his office. Caiaphas was high priest that year, and he had before given counsel that it was expedient that one should die rather than the nation should perish (11:50–52). John recalls this (verse 14), marking out thereby the man who was giving effect to the prophecy he had unwittingly expressed, and also showing that with such prejudgment the issue could only take one form. Caiaphas was son-in-law to Annas, who had been high priest from AD 6 to 15, when he was deposed by the governor Valerius Gratus. But the office remained in his family, for four sons and a son-in-law were high priests in turn. Such good

THE GOSPEL OF JOHN

fortune, Josephus says, "has fallen to the lot of no other of our high priests". It was neither to the credit of Annas nor to the good fortune of the nation. The office was at the disposal of the Roman governors and the Herodian princes, and went commonly to the highest bidder. The price paid by the house of Annas was abundantly regained in the extortion they imposed upon the people. The Talmud says:

"Woe to the house of Annas! Woe to their serpent's hiss! They are high priests; their sons are keepers of the Treasury; their sons-in-law are guardians of the Temple; and their servants beat the people with staves".

Well might the woe be recorded, for they had made the courts of the Lord a den of thieves, and the office was exploited on every hand for gain.

Since a high priest retained his prestige after he had vacated his office, and particularly in view of the dominant influence exercised by so astute a man as Annas, Jesus was taken first before him. This trial was doubly wrong: it was a private sitting and it was still night; it was arranged to elicit from Jesus something by which they could condemn him, although the law enjoined that a charge must be laid by witnesses, and a meeting for a trial could only be held between sunrise and sunset.

Before describing the investigation by Annas, John interposes the record of what was happening to Peter at this time. Peter and John had followed Jesus, probably slipping through the gate of the city with the crowd who had arrested Jesus. The other disciples would be outside the city, and it is interesting to conjecture what happened to them, and their probable ignorance of what happened to Jesus until he was crucified. John was known to the high priest; it may well be that the fishing firm of which he was partner had business connections with the house of the high priest; because of this acquaintance John entered the palace unquestioned by the portress, while Peter remained outside. John then secured the admission of Peter. There was a certain reckless courage in Peter's following Jesus and entering the palace with John. He was in danger of reprisal for his attack on the servant of the high priest, and was indeed challenged by a relative of Malchus.

But his over-confidence did not stand the test. The portress on letting him through asked if he were not a disciple of the prisoner. Had Peter acknowledged it, all might have been well, and the affair gone no further. But Peter denied. There was a fire in the courtyard, and Peter joined

212

the company around it. "It was cold", John says. It is a simple historical fact: the spring nights are cold, and to provide a fire was quite a natural thing for the servants to do. But what has Peter to do with the officers and men who had just brought in Jesus? He was "with them", warming himself. If he did it to try to appear at ease, it was courting danger. But he had already denied association with Jesus and must act the part.

While Peter stood with the servants, Jesus stood before Annas. "The high priest therefore asked Jesus of his disciples and of his doctrine." Jesus answered, "I have spoken openly to the world: I ever taught in synagogues, and in the temple, whither the Jews always resort; and in secret have I said nothing. *Why askest thou me? Ask them that have heard me,* what I have said unto them: behold they know what I said."

A. Taylor Innes has said of this answer:

"It was in every word the voice of pure Hebrew justice, founding upon the broad principle of their judicial procedure, and recalling an unjust judge to the first duty of his great office. But as one who studied that nation in older times observed, 'When a vile man is exalted the wicked walk on every side' around him; and when the accused had thus claimed his rights, one of the officers of court—a class usually specially alive to the observance of form, and of that alone—'struck Jesus with the palm of his hand, saying, Answerest thou the High Priest so?' The reply of Jesus is exceedingly striking. In it he again resolutely took his stand on the platform of the legal rights of a Hebrew—a ground from which he afterwards rose to a higher, but which he certainly never abandoned: 'If I have spoken evil, bear witness of the evil: but if well, why smitest thou me?'

"The words are, no doubt, a protest for freedom of speech and liberty to the accused. But they appeal again to the same principle of the Hebrew law—that by which witnesses took upon themselves the whole burden and responsibility, and especially the whole initiative, of every accusation, even as they were obliged to appear at the close, and with their own hands to hurl the stones. And the renewed protest was so far effectual. For now the witnesses came forward, or, at least, they were summoned to bear their testimony; and only when they came forward could a formal trial, according to Hebrew law, be said to have commenced."

On the answer of Jesus, Innes further remarks:

213

"The last words of Jesus were his demand for open accusation and trial: 'Why askest thou me? ask them which heard me'. And we hear no further utterance until the close. For when this demand for public justice was met by a nocturnal trial, the accused declined to take part in it. Meantime much was going on. The members of the Council present sought for witness against Jesus. Matthew says they sought for false witnesses. But even the former was scandalous indecorum. Hebrew judges, as we have seen, were eminently counsel for the accused. And one of the strangest sights the world has ever seen must have been the adjuration or solemn address to the witnesses who came to speak against the life of Jesus, by the magistrate who had—no doubt with perfect sincerity—held it expedient that one man should die for the people. In our courts an oath means a solemn undertaking by the witness, in the presence of God and the magistrate, to tell the truth. In the Hebrew Courts it was an adjuration by the magistrate of the witness as standing in God's presence. That form of adjuration or solemn appeal still exists in the body of the law. It was the duty of the high priest to pronounce it to each witness in a capital case, and so to put them on oath. Who can measure the force of its utterance on this occasion by the sacred Judge of Israel upon the men who, while words such as these were uttered, were forced to gaze into the face of him whose life it guarded?"

John does not record the interview with Caiaphas and the trial before the Council. After giving the answer of Jesus he merely tells that "Annas therefore sent him bound unto Caiaphas the high priest" (verse 24). From the other gospels it is evident that Jesus was questioned by Caiaphas, and then taken at dawn before the Sanhedrin and condemned for affirming the truth that he was the Son of God.

After telling of the removal of Jesus, John returns to what happened to Peter, and records a second time that Peter was warming himself (verses 18,25). By this repetition, is John pointing the lesson that Peter had put himself in danger by associating with the servants? It certainly led to further denials, first to the crowd, and then particularly to the kinsman of the servant whose ear Peter had cut off. One denial was followed by another; and then the cock crew, as Jesus had said.

THE ROMAN TRIAL (18:28—19:16)

BOTH the ecclesiastical and the civil trials of Jesus assumed a threefold form. The first consisted of the trial before Annas, then before Caiaphas, and lastly, the formal condemnation by the Sanhedrin at sunrise. The civil trial had two phases before Pilate, between which there was the form of trial before Herod.

It has been suggested that in the interval between the visit of Judas to the authorities and the arrest of Jesus a hurried meeting of the rulers was held, and a visit paid to Pilate, probably by Caiaphas, to secure from Pilate a promise that he would hold a court to sentence a prisoner whom they wished to bring before him. The trial was held at an unusual time, and special arrangements would have to be made. It may be that the rulers thought Pilate would be willing to give a formal sentence without exercising his right of review of all cases brought to him for confirmation of sentence.

If the Jews expected this, the first words of Pilate brought disillusionmnent, and showed Pilate intended to conduct an examination. He asked, "What accusation bring ye against this man?"

The time was very early—probably between 3 and 4 in the morning—when they led Jesus to the hall of judgment. They avoided entering themselves for fear of defilement; for while the Paschal meal had been eaten the evening before, the feast following, which was also called the Passover, required ceremonial purity of all who partook. How little they thought of the sins of envy and hatred, of the crime of striving to encompass the death of an innocent man, as they with punctilious care halted at the entrance and required that Pilate should come out to them. Regard for outward form with marked indifference to holiness stamped the nation as at once religious and godless.

The answer of the Jews to Pilate, says Innes, was "an insolent evasion", which was not likely to propitiate Pilate, who instantly put the matter on its true footing by the calm but somewhat contemptuous reply, "Take ye him, and judge him according to your law".

The Jews met this rejoinder that if there was no charge there would be no trial, with the degrading admission that they had not the power to inflict the capital punishment. The royal people were a subject race, and in their high pretensions in condemning the Son of God they must confess their servile state. The confession also indicated that the charge against the prisoner was one involving life and death.

John interposes a comment (18:32) that this reply of Israel's leaders, that Jesus must be handed over to the Romans to be put to death, was required in order that "the word of Jesus might be fulfilled, which he spake, signifying by what death he should die". Jesus had spoken of "being lifted up" (3:14; 12:32); or more plainly, as recorded in the other gospels, he must be crucified. This was the Roman method of inflicting death, the Jews practising stoning.

Through the Jews having to surrender Jesus to the Romans, his death came in the way he had said. It should be noted once more that the words of Jesus have all the authority of a divine prophecy, and equally with the OT predictions must "be fulfilled".

The next statement of Pilate recorded by John (verse 33) presupposes that the accusation which is recorded by Luke is known to the reader: "And they began to accuse him, saying, We found this fellow perverting the nation, and forbidding to give tribute to Caesar, saying that he himself is Christ a king" (Luke 23:2). The accusation was not the same as that upon which *they* had condemned Jesus. Had they said at once what they passionately declared at a later stage of the trial, that "by our law he ought to die, because he made himself the Son of God", the course taken by Pilate might have been different. They must make charges that had reference to Roman law, which they did by a mixture of ambiguity, falsehood, and truth.

Pilate must have had some knowledge of the activities of Jesus: reports of the crowds that had followed him and of his teaching would have come before him. He had the difficult task, which his own imperious methods had made harder, of keeping order in this province. He must have been kept informed of all the movements which might lead to trouble. He knew the character of the men with whom he had to deal, and resented the success with which they had resisted some of the things he had done. He knew that envy was the moving impulse in their opposition to Jesus.

Pilate returned to the prisoner within the Hall, to examine him. He at once put his finger on the essential point. All the gospels record his question: "Art *thou* the King of the Jews?" There is an emphasis on the pronoun—"You, are you the King of the Jews?" The appearance and humble, yet not servile, bearing of Jesus appeared to belie the charge. A quiet dignity was there, but otherwise the adjuncts of royalty were missing.

The reply of Jesus, "Sayest thou this thing of thyself, or did others tell it thee of me?" goes deeper than a mere enquiry whether that was the charge made by his accusers outside. It was a question which fixed the blame in the right quarter for the events proceeding. It was not in the first place a Roman charge, but a Jewish one—"Thine own nation", as Pilate said, "delivered thee unto me: what hast thou done?"

This threw back upon Jesus the burden of explanation. He at once accepted it. He had kept silence before the Jewish rulers when assembled in illegal session, but now he entered upon an explanation of his kingdom as it affected Roman law. So far from being guilty of the treason implied in the charge, the origin and nature of his kingdom disproved it. His kingdom was not of this world-order; it was not "out of" this world, deriving its power and title by human prowess. Had it been so, even then his servants would be fighting for his release. But "now"—as it is—his kingdom is not from hence. It was of divine origin, and divine title, and would be established by divine power. Then he and his servants would all engage in its establishment. At this time there was no conflict with Rome; he advanced then no rival claim to Caesar; it was not a human kingdom of which he would be king.

The change in emphasis in Pilate's next question reveals a growing scornfulness for the prisoner. Pilate's incredulity was shown in the tone not free from mockery, as he answered "Art thou a *king* then?" (verse 37). He really claimed to be king after all; but what sort of kingship was it? Pilate could not follow the idea of a divine rule on earth through such a man as the prisoner.

The answer of Jesus was clear and definite, says Innes:

"And as before, to the adjuration of God's high priest, so now, to the representative of all the greatness of earth, the answer came back, making a crisis in the world's history. 'Thou sayest it: I am a king.' He who so spoke to a Roman governor knew that he was offering himself to the cross, and that the next few hours might close that fateful life. And the thought was in his mind when he deliberately added, 'To this end was I born, and to this end came I into the world, that I might bear witness unto the truth'".

Jesus had already told the high priest that he had spoken openly to the world. He had confessed before his Jewish judges that he was the Son of God and the Messiah of Israel, although the confession provided them with the grounds for putting him to death. Now before Pontius Pilate he witnesses "the good confession" (1 Timothy 6:13). It was written of the Messiah: "Behold, I have given him for a witness to the people, for a leader and commander to the people" (Isaiah 55:4). How essential a part of his work was this witnessing appears from the later references: "Jesus Christ, who is the faithful witness, the firstborn of the dead, the ruler of the kings of the earth", "The Amen, the faithful and true witness, the beginning of the creation of God" (Revelation 1:5; 3:14).

"The truth" to which Jesus bore witness certainly includes the fact of his kingship: but it was comprehensive of much more. The truth of God covers all His purposes, and in the fullest of senses Jesus was bearing witness to it in the laying down of his life. Jesus added, "Every one that is of the truth heareth my voice". This was a clear challenge that his death would not end his work. He was the head and leader of many yet to come who would witness as he did, and hold aloft the truth. The testimony to the purpose of God would go on, even though it meant that individual witnesses were silenced.

It must have sounded an absurd claim to Pilate. It appeared to belong to the world of thought and philosophy and not of fact and action. Many adjectives have been used to describe Pilate's attitude as he rejoined "What is truth?"

Did he mock? or jest? Or may we not see the half-pitying, impatient reaction of a practical man of affairs who has been induced to conduct a trial which, contrary to his expectations, is not proving to be a simple ratification of a decision the Jews had reached.

He does not wait for an answer—probably was not wanting one. But the absurdity of the action of the Jews is evident, and he goes out and makes the first of three statements pronouncing the innocence of Jesus, and offering his release according to the custom at the Feast. His contempt is not disguised: "Shall I release to you the King of the Jews?"

The crowd repeats a previous demand for Barabbas (verse 40). "Now Barabbas was a robber", says John. He was a man of violence. They demanded the release of a man guilty of the very charge they had made against Jesus.

When Pilate announced "No crime in him" (John 18:38, RV) it should have closed the trial and Jesus should have been discharged. It was a sentence of acquittal. Luke, however, records that the words of Pilate provoked a fierce storm among the rulers, who boldly charged Jesus with stirring up the people from Galilee to Judea. The mention of Galilee seemed to provide a way of escape for the harassed governor. He would send Jesus to Herod.

This decision was fatal. He should have held to his decision, instead of which he faltered, and what should have been the end of the trial really proved for Pilate to be, in the words of Innes,

"The first step in that downward course of weakness the world knows so well: a course which, beginning with indecision and complaisance, passed through all the phases of alternate bluster and subserviency; persuasion, evasion, protest, and compromise; superstitious dread, conscientious reluctance, cautious duplicity, and sheer moral cowardice at last; until this Roman remains photographed for ever as the perfect feature of the unjust judge, deciding 'against his better knowledge, not deceived'".

The offer that Jesus should be released according to the custom at the feast, and the demand of the crowd for Barabbas, occurred after Jesus returned from Herod, and marks a further downward step for Pilate.

Luke again adds a detail which explains John. Pilate, after telling the Jews that both he and Herod had found no fault in Jesus, adds, "I will therefore chastise him and release him" (23:16). He was "now willing to mangle an innocent man with the savage Roman scourge". It was part of a capital punishment, and it would seem to have been imposed by Pilate in the hope that it would suffice as a compromise.

The scourging led to the mockery of the soldiers, while Jesus was in their hands. They crowned him with thorns, robed him in purple, rendered him mock obeisance, and in place of the gift they gave a blow—"mocking thus the Saviour's claim".

After this, Pilate led Jesus out to the people, making an appeal to their sympathy and humanity; "Behold the man", he cries (verses 4,5). Here in this poor figure there was no disputant of Caesar's throne or royal office. But the softer feeling shown by Pilate found no response in the accusers. Their only answer was a further demand that Jesus should be crucified. The answer goaded Pilate into a response which was at once unworthy of his office and yet an avowal that if Jesus were to be crucified it would be by them and not by him. They could not do it themselves—it was thus in part a taunt: "Take him yourselves, and crucify him, for I find no fault in him". It was a further effort to be rid of the responsibility. The taunt was **met** by a challenge. Pilate might treat the charge of sedition lightly; he might mock them in their subjection; but he must regard the law of a subject nation. That law they state: "We have a law, and by our law he ought to die, because he made himself the Son of God". Had the claim of Jesus been untrue, the law of blasphemy (Leviticus 24:16) here invoked, would have stood: but when were claims based wholly on truth blasphemy? The rulers' charge that Jesus claimed to be God's Son, was true; but so also was the claim of Jesus. For a true claim they demanded his death.

The effect upon Pilate was unexpected. The demeanour of the prisoner, his words, and the strange dream of his wife, and now the charge that the prisoner claimed to be the Son of God, unnerved Pilate. Fearfully he went into the judgment hall, and asked Jesus, "Whence art thou?" (verse 9). From the moment when Pilate began to vacillate Jesus had given no answer. Now he kept silence.

Says Innes:

"Pilate, accordingly, at the very time when he is described as inwardly 'more afraid', flashes out in that insolent tone which less discriminating secular historians regard as the only one characteristic of him, 'Speakest thou not unto me? Knowest thou not that I have power to crucify thee, and have power to release thee?' Jesus breaks the silence by a final word of answer which is of high importance for our subject: 'Thou wouldest have no power against me, except it were given thee from above: therefore he that delivered me unto thee hath greater sin'. Some writers who hold that Pilate alone had jurisdiction in this case, and that the proceedings of the Sanhedrin were usurpation, have appealed to this text, as containing in its first clause an acknowledgment of the exclusive right of the Roman tribunal, and in its last a denunciation of the illegality, as well as treachery, of Caiaphas. This is unwarranted, and in the circumstances grotesque. Yet, while we notice here first of all the extreme consideration and almost tenderness with which the sufferer judges his judge, we must confess that the words, 'Thy power is given thee from above', do relate themselves to the previous acknowledgment of a 'kingdom of this world', a *kosmos* in which men are to give to Caesar the things that are Caesar's; while they add to that former acknowledgment the explicit idea (afterwards enforced by the apostles) that this earthly kingdom with its earthly aims is also from above. The powers that be are ordained of God: Pilate, who knew this not, was abusing a great and legitimate office partly through a heathen's ignorance; and in so far he was less guilty than the false accusers who sat in Moses' seat. It was not strange that words so noble should have prompted one last effort on the judge's part to save himself from his weakness. But it was too late."

The answer of Jesus so impressed Pilate that he made repeated efforts to secure his release. But Pilate had already failed when he continued the trial after proclaiming the innocence of Jesus. The Jews had the measure of the man, and now used their last argument: "If thou let this man go, thou art not Caesar's friend: whosoever maketh himself a king speaketh against Caesar". If Pilate was actuated by personal feeling and not by justice in his effort to secure the release of Jesus, then a stronger personal feeling was now invoked by the Jews to secure their ends. Pilate feared for his own position, and a charge that he protected one accused of treason would have made him liable to the same indictment; and his position was not sufficiently well held to meet such a charge.

Pilate at that cry gave way. He sat in the judgment seat to give sentence in public as was required. John notes the place, The Pavement; the day, Friday, which was currently called The Preparation; the time, 6 a.m., when judicial proceedings began.

With the bitter irony of a thwarted man, Pilate says, "Behold your king"; to which they answer, "Away with him, crucify him". Again the taunt: "Shall I crucify your king?" With a fatefulness not perceived the rulers answer, "We have no king but Caesar". They had appealed to friendship of Caesar as a motive; implicit therein was their interest in Caesar; thus they perjured themselves, and degraded the royal priestly status of their nation. As a result they are led to accept his kingship, as by their words and their act in rejecting Jesus they repudiated the kingship of their God.

"Therefore he delivered him unto them to be crucified."

THE CRUCIFIXION (19:17–22)

WHEN Pilate yielded to the clamour of the multitude "he delivered Jesus unto them". The Jews accepted this decision and action, as John notes. Pilate delivered and "they took" or "received Jesus". This word "received" is significant in this place. John used it in 1:11: "He came unto his own (things),

but his own (people) received him not". The careful reader
who observes the touch of irony that occurs in the fourth
gospel will not miss it here. The people received not the one
who was the manifestation of the Father, except to crucify
him.

John also finds a significance in the details of the trans-
action. Jesus "went forth" as the sin offering was taken
"without the gate" (Hebrews 13:12). He bore "the cross for
himself" (RV), doing in literal fact what he had urged as a
spiritual necessity for all who would follow him; and in its
full significance he bore it for himself, that others might then
enter the fellowship of his sufferings that they might partake
of the exaltation which is his because of obedience unto
death. And the shape of the hillock where he was crucified
had the ominous name—"place of a skull". The mockery of his
claims was maintained to the last; they put him in the place
of honour, "in the midst". Seditious men were crucified with
him, as though his kingship was over such. He who had
resisted the offer of the kingdoms of the world and their glory,
who had refused the popular appeal that he should be king,
was now lifted up as though enthroned over those who would
have striven to make Israel free. As a crowning irony Pilate
wrote a title, placed over the head of Jesus:

> JESUS OF NAZARETH,
> THE KING OF THE JEWS

The title was meant to insult the Jews; it was Pilate's reply
to their successful forcing of his hands in condemning Jesus.
In a grim way it declared *their* guilt: for John says the
place was "nigh to the city". There could be no question
whose guilt it was: "it was nigh to the city" of Jerusalem. The
law required when one was smitten outside a city, that the
city nearest by measurement should offer sacrifices and
their elders say, "Our hands have not shed this blood"
(Deuteronomy 21:1–9). Jerusalem, which had killed the
prophets and stoned them whom God had sent, had already
accepted the guilt of this deed when they said, "His blood be
on us".

The title was in Hebrew, Greek and Latin. All could read
it. The three great languages of the day all bore the message.
Jesus was placarded before men indeed. The languages of the
three races which had prepared the way for the gospel to be
preached to all, are used to proclaim the kingship of Jesus.

Rankling from the insult, the Jews requested that the title be changed so that the statement became a claim of Jesus. Unconsciously they were witnessing to his teaching that he was their Messiah. But Pilate had recovered from his fears of the earlier hours. What he had written remained; and he curtly dismissed them.

FOUR SOLDIERS AND FOUR WOMEN (19:23–27)

FOUR soldiers, the usual number of a guard, were left to keep watch at the Cross. The garments of a crucified man fell to them as perquisites, and they proceeded to divide the clothes. The coat, however, was seamless. Usually it was in two pieces, but the garment worn by a high priest was of one piece. Is there in this a hint that the King on the cross was a priest too? The soldiers cared little about any possible significance. They saw that to divide would spoil it, and agreed to dice for it. In so doing they added another detail in the wonderful series of prophecies in Psalm 22, fulfilled in the crucifixion of Jesus.

In contrast to the four soldiers in one group taking possession of what had been the prisoner's, stands another group of four women, who had continually been with Jesus and had ministered to him. Three bore the name of Mary, and the fourth being a sister of the Lord's mother, was probably John's own mother. Jesus shows a son's care for a widowed mother to the end, committing her to the care of John. The beloved disciple accepts the trust and at once gives effect to it, taking away the stricken mother from witnessing the final agony of her son. The sword had already pierced her soul.

"I THIRST": "IT IS FINISHED" (19:28–30)

TWO Psalms in particular describe in detail the final sufferings of the Son of God (22 and 69). Unconsciously the Jewish leaders and the soldiers had fulfilled some of the things that were written. Jesus, however, knew what was written: "Thus it is written" was the rule of his life. Now, as the end is near, the same rule governs his thought. He knew the end was near; he knew the scripture yet unfulfilled. He therefore said, "I thirst". Responding to the cry, the soldiers performed another act in fulfilment of Psalm 69: "They gave him vinegar to drink".

223

There are many things recorded in Scripture which involve the inspiration of the writer. John here records the knowledge of Jesus concerning the fulfilment of the scriptures as the reason for the words of Jesus. How did John know this? The explanation that alone fully meets the case is that John was guided into all truth by the Spirit of Truth. The innermost thoughts of Jesus are therefore revealed.

After he had received the vinegar, Jesus said: "It is finished". The work for which he had been sent had been performed, and he could now lay down his life. It is significant that none of the gospels merely say "he died". Matthew says "he yielded up his spirit". Mark and Luke record that "he expired". John says "he gave up his spirit". It was a voluntary surrender of his life, and he could say, "Father, into thy hands I commend my spirit" (Luke 23:46), in the assurance that after his flesh had rested for a short while in the grave, the life would be taken up again. He had said: "No man taketh it from me, but I lay it down of myself. I have power to lay it down, and I have power to take it again" (John 10:18). The records of his death are in keeping with this saying.

Two Petitions (19:31–37)

THE day of the crucifixion is called "'Preparation'" (verse 31), or more fully in verse 14, "Preparation of the Passover". This means the Friday of the Passover week; for, as McClellan says:

"'Preparation' was (as now) the Greek name for Friday, and for no other day".

To this may be added the words of Sir Robert Anderson:

"'The preparation' was a term in common use among the Jews to describe the day before the weekly sabbath. It is so used by each of the Evangelists ... Every Friday was 'the preparation'; this particular Friday was 'the Passover preparation'".

The sabbath following is described by John as "a high day". On which Anderson comments:

"True; for not only was it, as being the sabbath of Passover week, one of the greatest sabbaths of the year, but further, as being the second day of the Feast it was kept by the Jews as 'the day of the Firstfruits'—one of the 'red-letter days' in the calendar."

The Roman custom was to leave the bodies of the crucified hanging on the cross to putrefy. But the law of Moses required the removal of a corpse before nightfall. The law in Deuteronomy 21:22,23 seems to have been provided with a view to the work of Christ, for the reason given for the removal of the bodies of any hanged on a tree—"for he that is hanged is accursed of God"—is used by Paul to explain how the curse of the law fell on Jesus in the mode of his death, and was at the same time removed by his death (Galatians 3:13). To the requirements of the law, the fact that the sabbath was a high day was also urged as a special reason why death should be hastened and the bodies buried. The Jews may also have been moved by a willingness to inflict the maximum pain and suffering on Jesus, when they went to Pilate to ask that the legs of the crucified should be broken. The request was granted and the soldiers proceeded, probably two of them dealing with the criminals on the right and left of Jesus at the same time. They thus came to Jesus together, but found him already dead. It was a critical moment, when prophecy was never so near being falsified: for it was written, "A bone of him shall not be broken". The ordinance of the Passover appropriately contains the prediction: "In one house shall it be eaten; thou shalt not carry forth aught of the flesh abroad out of the house; neither shall ye break a bone thereof" (Exodus 12:46). The injunction is repeated in Numbers 9:12. There is an additional reference in the Psalms, probably of general application in a figurative sense, but which acquires a precision and fulness of literal meaning when applied to Jesus. David is speaking of the poor man who cries to God, Who saves him out of all his troubles. The angel of the Lord encampeth around such; and God "keepeth all his bones: not one of them is broken" (Psalm 34:20).

The Word of God never fails. The soldiers must have felt that the prisoner in the centre of the scene was different from any other they had had to deal with. Some sense of awe must have struck them as it did the centurion in charge. They glanced at Jesus: they observed he was dead; it was therefore not necessary that his legs should be broken. Had the order been given a few minutes earlier, how different the result!

Moved by some strange impulse, however, one of the soldiers thrust his spear in the side of Jesus, and the stay of action that allowed the fulfilment of one prophecy led to the fulfilment of another.

In David's prophecy of the one who will rule over men in justice and fear of God, he speaks of certain sons of Belial to

225

be burned as thorns, adding the remarkable statement that the man to do this "must be filled with iron and the staff of a spear" (2 Samuel 23:7). It must have been a perplexing note in the prophecy of a victorious and righteous ruler, until it was remembered that the King was the Saviour, and therefore one who would die for men's sins. How it would be accomplished must have been a matter of speculation.

Another prediction, Zechariah 12:10, revealing the manner of God's deliverance of Israel in the day when Jerusalem is besieged, when all nations have burdened themselves with the problems of the Holy Land, shows that with the destruction of the nations that have come against Jerusalem there will be a dramatic revelation of the deliverer.

God will pour upon Israel the spirit of grace and of supplication: they will realize with thankfulness that their deliverance has been of God. They will look at the one who in an unexpected way has intervened: who is he? from where has he come? "They shall look upon me whom they have pierced, and shall mourn for him", says God.

The change in pronouns is an indication, particularly when combined with hints in other chapters in the same prophecy (as, for example, 11:13), that the deliverer is one who is a manifestation of God: one in whom the God of Israel is revealed. The effect of seeing the deliverer, contrary to the joy one would expect under such circumstances, is an outburst of grief and mourning such as that in Egypt at the first Passover, when every house in Egypt mourned for its firstborn.

Such an unexpected result of a wonderful deliverance can only be adequately explained by the fact that Israel then recognizes that the Deliverer is none other than the crucified One whom the nation has reviled for centuries as a blasphemer. No incident can be imagined more charged with dramatic power than that which brings such a recognition. The mourning is an inevitable consequence.

The thirteenth chapter adds the details. The innocent enquiry, "What are these wounds in thine hands?" elicits the answer, "Those with which I was wounded in the house of my friends" (verse 6). This is explained in the next verse by the prophecy interpolated in the record of deliverance, calling on the sword to awake against the man who is God's fellow, and to smite the shepherd.

The piercing of the side of Jesus led to an efflux of blood and water. It is generally recognized that the spear entered the body in the region of the heart, and the flow of blood and serum has by many been taken as evidence that Jesus died of a broken heart. "Reproach hath broken my heart" occurs in the context of the statement that God "keepeth all his bones".

In contrast to the petition of the Jewish authorities that the legs of Jesus be broken, thereby mutilating his body, John tells of two rulers who were anxious about the body for very different purposes. The soldiers had fulfilled the Scriptures in their treatment of the body; now another scripture had to be fulfilled. Isaiah had long before said that the "Arm of the Lord" would make "his grave with the wicked, and with the rich in his death". The first half of this had come to pass: the second would not fail. Pilate who gave the order that Jesus should be crucified with malefactors also ordered that the body should be given into the custody of a rich man for burial.

Joseph of Arimathea was a secret disciple of Jesus. He was rich, a member of the Sanhedrin, a good and just man who had not consented to the Council's crime in condemning Jesus, and he also waited for the Kingdom of God. He was joined by Nicodemus, another secret disciple, and a fellow-member of the Sanhedrin. He also had opposed the Council in its attitude to Jesus, pleading for fairness and justice. His visit to Jesus as a representative of the Pharisees bore fruit, although it left those he represented unconvinced.

God always has ready the men for His work. Joseph little knew, when he prepared the tomb, the honourable use to which it would be put: and even less would Nicodemus think of this night errand when he first "came to Jesus by night". While Joseph was interviewing Pilate, Nicodemus was buying the myrrh and aloes for the burial. The quantities bought were large; it was a royal burial. The spices were wrapped with the linen around the body. The burial conformed naturally to Jewish procedure, although John comments that the method employed was "the manner of the Jews to bury". Egyptian methods would have mutilated the body for embalming; but nothing was done beyond carefully rolling the body in the linen with the spices. The tomb was new: no corruption had unfitted it for the reception of the body that had to see no corruption. And it was in a garden: as in the beginning the man began his life in a garden, so the new man wakened to life again in a garden. Between the two was the long history of sin and sorrow, and the sweat of the garden of Gethsemane. But the two men busy with their task had no thought for this. Haste was necessary: the sabbath was at hand: and therefore they hurriedly performed their self-appointed duty, and with a pathos lost in the AV John ends his record of the burial with the words, "There ... laid they Jesus".

SECTION 7

THE RESURRECTION
THE EMPTY TOMB (20:1–10)

THE day appointed for the offering of the wave-sheaf—the first-fruits of the harvest—dawned. By a singular misreading of the law after the exile the Jews had made this offering on the sabbath instead of the following day. While Jesus lay in the tomb they performed the most important of the types which pointed forward to the resurrection of the Lord "on the third day". They blunderingly destroyed the type and then refused to accept the antitype.

Yet the Jews had taken very keen notice of the references to the third day in the Lord's statements concerning the destruction of the temple and raising it in three days. This fact comes out in the trial, and also in the precautions that they took to have the stone sealed and a guard set. But John does not mention these things.

All the gospels record that it was on the first day of the week that Jesus arose. The details of all that happened on that day are not told by any one of the gospels; but facts are mentioned in John which presuppose a knowledge of what was already written in the earlier gospels. He tells only of the visit of Mary Magdalene to the grave, whereas we learn from Matthew and Mark of two other Marys being present as well. The presence of others besides the Magdalene is however indicated by her words to Peter and John when she hurried to them after finding the stone rolled away from the sepulchre. "They have taken away the Lord out of the sepulchre, and *we* know not where they have laid him". By that "we" the presence of others is revealed.

It was a natural inference that the body had been removed. They did not think of the resurrection; were not in fact expecting it. As in the case of Peter and John, who hurried to the tomb on receiving the message, it was evidence of fact which produced the conviction that Jesus was risen. At one time the sceptic endeavoured to undermine the evidence for the resurrection by saying that the disciples were the victims of hallucination. But this would have required that they were expecting the resurrection. The fact is all the other

229

way: they were not looking for it, and they accepted the truth
as the result of what they saw. The empty tomb was the first
fact that led the apostles to believe that Jesus was risen.

The removal of the body by either enemy or friend so early
in the morning would have left the tomb in a different state
from that in which Peter and John found it. There were no
signs of haste, but of calm and orderly action. The clothes in
which the body had been rolled were folded, and the head
covering was by itself.

The light broke on John first. When he "saw" inside the
tomb "he believed". And as if to anticipate the critical doubts,
John adds that as yet they knew not the Scripture that he
must rise from the dead. The event illumined the prophecy in
their case, and fact and Scripture prediction together then
wrought so strong a conviction that they went forth and
preached the resurrection to a hostile and mocking world,
laying down their lives for the gospel's sake in the certain
hope that the risen Jesus would raise them up when he
returned.

JESUS APPEARS TO MARY (20:11–18)

WHILE Peter and John had gone to their home, Mary
remained by the sepulchre. Probably she had not kept pace
with them as they ran to the sepulchre, and they had left
with their new-born understanding before she again reached
the tomb. They had reached conviction on the evidence
supplied by the empty tomb. To Mary was granted the first
meeting with the risen Lord, and the first positive evidence
that Jesus was alive.

She stooped and looked into the tomb. Two angels in white
were sitting there, one at the head and the other at the foot
of where the body had lain. The presence of angels is
mentioned by all four gospels; ministers on this occasion to
the Heir of Salvation. Angels had ministered to him before, in
the wilderness, and in Gethsemane. It was beautifully fitting
that angelic hands should do whatever was needful when the
Son of God awoke to life again. They had been witnesses to
the long history of human woe. They had communicated to
the prophets the message concerning the manifestation of
God in a Son. They had heralded his birth; now they attend
to the needs of him who is so exalted that angels are subject
unto him.

Mary does not appear to have been dismayed by what she saw. The intensity of her grief seems to rule out every other emotion. To the angel's enquiry why she was weeping so, she answered that the body of her Lord had been removed and she knew not where he had been laid. There was no thought in her mind of any other explanation of the empty tomb than that the body had been removed elsewhere.

After answering the angel she turns, perhaps aware that another has approached the tomb. Jesus was standing there, but, blinded with tears, she recognized him not. Jesus repeats the question of the angels, and so absorbed is Mary in her own loss that she does not even name Jesus when she answers the questioner, supposing him to be the gardener, "Sir, if thou have borne him hence, tell me where thou hast laid him, and I will take him away". The answer is true to life—there is no thought of human weakness and the practical impossibility of a woman removing the body as in her love for Jesus she offers to find another burial place. But the conversation has by this quieted her a little, and Jesus speaks her name. The stranger's personal knowledge causes her to turn, and speaking in Hebrew she says "My Master", and clings to him.

The answer of Jesus has occasioned much speculation. "Touch me not", he said; and then added as a reason: "for I am not yet ascended unto the Father; but go unto my brethren, and say to them, I ascend unto my Father and your Father, and to my God and your God."

"Take not hold on me" is the RV marginal rendering; "Do not cling to me" that of Weymouth, and the footnote of Rotherham. This seems to be the idea; it is not that Mary had not to touch him at all, as though some defilement might follow the touch, but that she was holding him when he spoke and he wanted her to release her grasp.

The reason which he gave, that he was to ascend to the Father, cannot be referred to the ascent from the Mount of Olives some forty days later. It was hardly necessary to send a message concerning *that* when he would be with them so many times before he went to the Father. Dr. Thomas is doubtless right in referring the words of Jesus to the change of nature which was about to take place "in the twinkling of an eye". Jesus was to become the antitype of the wavesheaf, with its accompanying meal offering made by the fire, the one waved before the Lord in the holy place, signifying an approach to the presence of the Father, and the other ascending for a sweet savour.

Some have thought that a literal ascent took place. In view of the universal presence of the Father by the spirit, such would not be necessary. The language based in part on the types, and also on the fact that Jesus was about to assume higher nature, is fully met by transformation from a body of weakness to a body of glory about to take place.

"Go tell my *brethren*" is a gracious indication that he is not only Lord and Master but brother. "I will declare thy name unto my brethren" was written in Psalm 22 as a sequel to his sufferings. It is not yet fulfilled, but Jesus hints at it, when he declares the relationship immediately after his resurrection. Paul says that "he that sanctifieth and they who are sanctified are all of one (Father), for which cause he is not ashamed to call them brethren". How fitting that at the moment when his sanctification is about to be accomplished he expresses this relationship in his message!

But while he calls them brethren there is a difference which is brought out in the next words, although not reproduced in translation. It is noticeable he does not say, "*Our* Father, and *our* God". Yet in the relationship expressed by the word God there is no difference: "My God, and your God". God is the God of Jesus (Ephesians 1:3; 2 Corinthians 11:31; 1 Peter 1:3) as well as the God of all who are sanctified. But when he relates himself and them to The Father, he distinguishes between them. "The Father of me, and your Father" may seem to indicate no difference to the English reader, yet he does not say "the God of me, and your God" but "my God, and your God". In the words of Pearson, written nearly three hundred years ago:

"'I ascend unto my Father, and your Father', saith our Saviour; the same of both, but in a different manner, denoted by the article prefixed before the one, and not the other: which distinction in the original we may preserve by this translation, 'I ascend unto the Father of me, and Father of you'; first of *me*, and then *of you*: not therefore his, because ours; but therefore ours, because his."

A second time Mary seeks the apostles, but with how different a message. "I have seen the Lord"; and he had spoken these words to her.

THE FIRST MANIFESTATION (20:19–23)

JOHN records three appearances of Jesus to his disciples. The last occasion is noted as the third (21:14). Twice he met them in Jerusalem, and once by the sea of Galilee.

The first manifestation was on the day of the resurrection. John says it was in the evening—but it must have been late evening since the two disciples who had been to Emmaus had returned to Jerusalem and met the other disciples, and they had pleaded that Jesus should stay as it was nigh evening, when they were in Emmaus.

The disciples feared "the Jews"—that is the rulers whom John so describes—and had taken the precaution of fastening doors. They would naturally expect that the hatred shown to Jesus would be now vented on themselves. While thus assembled Jesus suddenly appeared in their midst. It might be the subject of speculation what exactly happened, but we are not told, and therefore any explanation is only speculation. We do not know the powers and capabilities of the spirit body—it is like a fourth dimension, outside our present experience.

There are some things of which we are sure, which are revealed. The body of Jesus was restored to life, and at the second manifestation he invited Thomas to thrust his finger into wound-prints of hands and side. Thomas would think, in saying he required this, that he was imposing a very rigorous test that Jesus was raised. That he did not apply the test, but was satisfied with different, but still conclusive evidence, does not affect the fact that the test was capable of application. The evidence of wounded hands will yet be the startling means of bringing conviction to unbelieving Israel in the day of Christ's appearing.

The body of Jesus is, however, now energized by the spirit of God, and his life is not dependent upon the conditions of present human life. With God is the fountain of life, and when the immortality of God is bestowed the present means of sustaining life will be unnecessary. The ascent of Jesus to the Father illustrates the freedom from the conditions which beset us now. Man cannot ascend very high before he needs to apply artificially the oxygen which becomes rarer as he ascends, and without which he soon loses consciousness, and then life. "The body of his glory" is the description of Paul of the body of Jesus now.

Jesus is the heir to David's throne, and the heirship is based upon physical descent from David. In his case, as the heir, identity with the line of David is essential. That identity is based upon the body of flesh born of Mary: and to maintain the title there must be continuity of body, though changed in nature, in the past and present states of Jesus. The theory once put forward by C. T. Russell, the founder of the society now known as "Jehovah's Witnesses", that Jesus has a spiritual body in no way connected with "the body of his flesh", which God may have preserved as a memorial of God's work in him, or which may have dissolved into gases, destroys the very link upon which the title of Jesus to be heir to the throne of David is based.

The future work of Jesus upon earth as king will reveal a man, substantial and real as present monarchs, but possessed of powers and royal dignity never known by mortal ruler. Jesus will be visibly, actually, present. "Thine eyes shall see the king in his beauty" is written of him in that day.

The bodies of those who are found faithful at his judgment seat, whether they are dead or living at his appearing, will be fashioned like unto the body of his glory by the working of that energy whereby he will be able to subdue all things to himself.

He will change these mortal bodies: this mortal must put on immortality. The suffering and the trial of the present are real enough: but when the saints "receive in body according to that they have done", those who have striven to enter the Kingdom will know in body the greater realities of an energy drawn from the source of all power. "They shall run and not be weary; walk and not faint", because they are one in nature with Him who faints not, neither is weary. The place of trial will be the place of reward. The twelve will be with Jesus, known of the twelve tribes as David and Solomon were known in the past. The saints over five or over ten cities will be no less real than the mayors and lord mayors of to-day.

Jesus greeted them with the word "Peace". It had been his last word to them when he was about to suffer: "In the world ye shall have tribulation ... these things have I spoken that in me ye may have peace" (16:33). As the first taste of that tribulation they were met in fear of the Jews: and he is with them speaking peace. With him it was no casual salutation, nor even only a fervent wish: it was a benediction and a promise: "Peace I leave with you; my peace I give unto you". It was in his power to leave peace with them: as he lived and continued with them, so his peace remained ever present.

As he thus calmed their fears he added conviction of his restoration to life by showing them his hands and his side.

234

The evidential value of this in connection with the risen Lord is seen from John's epistle, where, speaking of *the Word of life*, he says: "We have seen with our eyes, and our hands have handled" (1 John 1:1). Seeing him brought gladness and fuller realization that he was the Lord.

That John is thinking of this conviction of the Lordship of Jesus seems clear from the way he describes the further invocation of peace by Jesus. "Jesus therefore said to them again, Peace be unto you: as the Father hath sent me, even so send I you." The repetition of "peace" had a deeper significance with the added recognition of the status of the speaker. They were then prepared for the fuller import of his word, and also for the reference to the work now to be placed in their hands. John uses two words represented by the one English word "send". The first is from the same root as apostle: the second denotes merely the mission. There is not thus a parallel indicated between his mission and theirs; as he was the risen Lord this could hardly be. But in his apostolic authority he sends them.

Closely connected with this view of his words is the next act of Jesus. He breathed on them, and said: "Receive ye the Holy Spirit: whosesoever sins ye forgive, they are forgiven unto them; and whosesoever sins ye retain, they are retained." On this it may be noticed that the action of Jesus is described by the same word as that used in the Septuagint of God *breathing* into man the breath of life. As God gave life to the body by that act, was Jesus giving life to the Body he had been forming during his ministry? He was giving it power too—the power of God. "Take the Holy Spirit" he said, and as the word denotes receptivity on their part, there is option implied; and with that there is a call for co-operation by their taking and using. It was at this point an anticipation of the fuller bestowal of Pentecost.

The conferring of power to remit and retain sin must be understood in the light of certain fundamental facts. It is only in God's power to forgive sins, and He does so, in fact can only do so, when certain conditions obtain. There must be repentance and faith before God forgives. And in this we have the key to the saying. The message of the apostles was an announcement of the grace of God in Jesus, offering forgiveness when men turned from sin with faith in God. Such an announcement, startling were it not familiar, required authoritative proclamation. The Spirit gave that authoritativeness to the declaration of the apostles that in the name of Christ is forgiveness. To conclude otherwise, that there was given to men a power that a corrupt priestcraft has presumed to possess, is to violate the moral essentials of the problem of forgiveness. Sin is against God: no man forgives what is only in the power of God to remit.

THE SECOND MANIFESTATION (20:24–29)

AT the first manifestation of Jesus, Thomas called Didymus was not with the apostles. When they met him they told him of their experience and their new-found conviction that Jesus was living: "We have seen the Lord". Thomas appears to have been of a very practical turn of mind. Men sometimes see what they wish to see or what they think they see: sight is not the convincing proof to some that it is to others. Thomas required to add touch to sight, and the evidence of touch which he demanded was of an exacting character. He expressed his view in no uncertain terms. As Bullinger has pointed out, he uses an emphatic negative: "Unless", he said, "I see the wounds, and put my finger into the wounds, I will *never, never* believe" And, as Bullinger also points out, in every case where man has been so assertive, using that emphatic form of speech, he has not kept his word. Peter said he would never, never, deny: but he did. Thomas said he would in nowise believe unless he had the evidence he demanded: but he believed without it. Yet the evidence which made him a believer was very convincing to him.

A week after the first manifestation the disciples were gathered together; the eight days mentioned by John having an inclusive reckoning. Thus early we may trace the practice of meeting on the first day of the week. The same conditions existed as the week before; and Jesus stood in their midst and gave them the salutation he had used before—"Peace be unto you".

Then, turning to Thomas, he said: "Reach hither thy finger, and behold my hands; and reach hither thy hand, and thrust it into my side: and be not faithless but believing". The language of Jesus was the same as that Thomas had used. Jesus invited him to make the very test he had demanded.

It revealed a knowledge on the part of Jesus of what Thomas had said. Such knowledge had been a distinguishing feature of the power of Jesus all through his ministry. "He knew what was in man", as John records; and this was in a particular as well as a general way. He knew the thoughts of

Nathanael, and his statement revealing the knowledge wrought conviction in Nathanael.

A similar evidence of a supernatural knowledge brought conviction to Thomas. The demand of Jesus that he should become a believer met at once a hearty response. For the manifestation of this power meant even more to Thomas than it had to Nathanael. Thomas recognized in it the same thing he had known in Jesus: and the man before him offering hands and side for him to touch was showing by his invitation those marks of power that Thomas recognized belonged to Jesus. The man was Jesus; features and words were compared by this known characteristic.

The spontaneous answer of Thomas was, "My Lord and my God". This has presented difficulty to some, but the difficulty fades away if we take Scripture usage for our guide. None find a difficulty in the title "Lord" being used of Jesus as well as of God. Thomas can call Jesus "my Lord" and he can use the word of God, without confusion. But when he calls Jesus "my God" then stumbling occurs. Yet "God" is used of the rulers of Israel by Moses (Exodus 22:28), and several prophecies use it of Jesus. Two may be cited, both from the Psalms. In Psalm 45 where David writes of "the King", he says:

"Thy throne, O God, is for ever and ever: the sceptre of thy kingdom is a right sceptre. Thou lovest righteousness and hatest wickedness: therefore God, thy God, hath anointed thee with the oil of gladness above thy fellows."

(verses 6,7)

The king is "God". Yet he is at once distinguished from the Eternal, who is called "God, thy God". The king has fellows: and should the Trinitarian find the "fellows" in the other members of the Trinity, his difficulty is great every way. For the action of one of three upon another member of the group leaves only one, and therefore "fellows" is inapplicable numerically. The incongruity of one co-equal anointing another above a third co-equal destroys sense. The application to Jesus is beyond dispute; for Paul says: "To the Son he says, Thy throne, O God". The Son is "O God", and we must learn how the language can be used of him without confusing the Father and the Son.

The other Psalm is a prophecy of the contentions of Jesus in the days of his ministry. "God standeth in the congregation of the mighty; he judgeth among the gods" (82:1). The judging "God" is the Lord Jesus, and the rulers of Israel are the "gods" whom he judged.

237

With such Old Testament usage the disciple would find no difficulty in speaking of Jesus as "My God"; the difficulty arises from reading back into such words the theological ideas of later times.

Apart from the Old Testament language, which of course was the source of much of the language of the apostles, the current speech of the day included a free use of both lord and god, applied to a supposed higher order of beings and to men. There were, as Paul says, gods many and lords many, including angels and a host of other celestials, and also men like the emperor to whom divine honour was paid.

If by this explanation we only change the form of the difficulty, we must ask exactly what Thomas meant; and we may find an answer in the basis upon which in the Old Testament the rulers were called gods. These rulers in the theocratic state of Israel were God's representatives, and probably have therefore the divine name given to them. So also the angels are gods: for the LXX render by "angels" the "elohim" of Psalm 97:7: "Worship him, all ye gods". This is one of the places referred to by Paul, when, showing the superiority of Jesus to the angels, he recalls that at the second appearing of the Son God calls upon the angels to worship him (Hebrews 1:6). In the phrase "sons of God" in the book of Job (38:7), used of the angels at creation, "sons of" may not denote "descent from" so much as "company of", as the "sons of the prophets" are not the children of the prophets but the guild of prophets.

The angelic "gods" are the messengers of the Eternal, as Israel's rulers were His representatives.

Without doubt Thomas was ascribing to Jesus divine authority and majesty, but he could do that without in any way thinking of Jesus as the Creator.

Jesus said to Thomas: "Because thou hast seen me, thou hast believed: blessed are they that have not seen, yet have believed".

Jesus knew that a work would continue, first through the oral testimony of the apostles and then by that same testimony preserved in their writings. Thomas believed because he saw the Lord: but so did the other disciples, and upon the testimony of those who saw all believe. The contrast then which is indicated by Jesus cannot be between seeing and not seeing, as a natural process. There appears to be a deeper meaning. Thomas believed in the resurrection because he had come into physical contact with Jesus. Others both at the time and since have not had that experience: but they have believed because they have known the broad purpose of God which necessitates the resurrection of Jesus: and faith has had a broader basis than visual evidence.

PURPOSE OF THE GOSPEL (20:30,31)

JOHN adds a note about the reason for writing his gospel, which connects with the statement of Jesus about not seeing, yet believing. Jesus gave many signs, by which John refers to the inner significance of the miracles which Jesus did. John however gives eight only: but these eight are chosen to illustrate three particular aspects of Jesus: his Messiahship, his Sonship, and his work as the Lifebringer. These represent the broad objects God had in view in sending His Son. Rightly grasped, they lead to faith, and by induction into his name, to life.

THE GOSPEL OF JOHN

SECTION 8

THE EPILOGUE
THE EIGHTH SIGN (21:1–14)

IT is clear from the closing words of chapter 20 that at that point we reach the close of the narrative. The last chapter is in the nature of an epilogue. There is no doubt that it is by the same writer as the chapters preceding; and there is no textual evidence in support of the suggestion that the gospel was in its earliest form without the last chapter. All MSS contain it, and there is no evidence that a shorter version of the gospel was ever in circulation. The epilogue balances the prologue.

The occasion when the eighth sign of this gospel was performed is called the third manifestation (verse 14). The place is in Galilee. John says nothing about any command that they should return there, but Matthew and Mark record that Jesus had commanded them to go to Galilee, where he would see them (Matthew 28:10; Mark 16:7). Two gospels record the instruction, but John tells us that they went.

Seven were present; and it is a reasonable suggestion that they belonged to the neighbourhood. It was a natural thing that they should return to their fishing while waiting for further instructions. Their needs would by that means be met. Neither faith nor the want of it enters into the question. It was Peter who took the lead: " I go afishing", he said, and the others at once joined him.

It was night time, when men usually ply their craft on the sea; but on this occasion the labour was in vain. This can only be regarded as exceptional; over-ruled, without doubt, to prepare the necessary setting for the miracle about to be performed.

As the dawn was breaking they saw a man on the shore about a hundred yards away. They did not recognize him— perhaps the light was not yet sufficiently clear; perhaps also it was necessary for the lesson to be enforced, that they should not know him. The stranger calls to them: "Children, have ye any meat?" as though he would purchase some of their catch. They answered, "No"; whereupon they were told to cast their net on the right side of the ship and they would find. At once the net was so full of fishes that they could not draw it.

John was the first to discern that the stranger was Jesus. Peter was the first to act when John said that it was the Lord. He was only partially clothed; he seized his outer garment, girt it about him and swam to the shore. The other disciples dragged the net to the shore.

As on the previous "manifestations" there was something about the stranger in their midst that led to identification of the Lord with the crucified leader, and which wrought conviction that Jesus was risen, so in this miracle. The earlier miraculous catch of fishes would be recalled by John, with his greater sensitiveness to the Lord's work; and in the provision of needed food all would recognize the same friendly care for them that Jesus had always shown. When he took bread and gave to them, the characteristic courtesy and love of the Master shone forth.

A meal was prepared, but was supplemented by their own catch. To do this Peter gives a hand in dragging the net to land. They see with practised eye the exceptional character of the haul. The catch was a large one, all the fishes were big ones, and numbered one hundred and fifty-three.

They become the guests of the Lord, who invites them to break their fast; he takes bread and fish and gives to them.

The incident is full of instruction. The fruitlessness of their labour until they receive the command of the Lord indicates that they must wait the time when he commands them to become fishers of men. Then blessing crowns their labour.

The labour was theirs, but it was a divine work: the miraculous entered into the results of their efforts apart from the miracles and wonders they performed. The inclusion in the gospel net is an act of God. "Of his own will he begat us", as James declares. It was a work in which they held the tenderest of relationships to the risen Lord. He had called them "brethren" not long before; now they are "children". It is a friendly term, but in the circumstances in which it was used might be pressed to a more literal significance. Paul puts "brethren" and "children" side by side, when he speaks of those for whom Christ died (Hebrews 2). "I and the *children* the Father hath given me", and, " I will declare thy name unto my *brethren*", are both prophetic utterances of the Christ-spirit, one by the prophet Isaiah and the other by the Psalmist, and the Christ himself uses both terms of those the Father has given him.

The disciples are fishers. At an early stage in his ministry Jesus had used fishing as an object lesson. He had himself then pointed to its significance: "From henceforth thou shalt catch men". In view of this application it cannot be fanciful to see a similar lesson in the commission to cast their net; then the wonderful catch of "great fishes", counted and all secure in the net, points to the numbered men and women of whom none are lost who will be gathered in by the labours of the apostles when the Lord is again manifested. That too will be the morning, when the toils of the night have passed.

The previous miracle, which included good and bad fishes, represents the present ingathering of those who are called to sharing the Kingdom.

The meal bespeaks fellowship with the Lord of Glory. He is host and provides part, but they must contribute a part. It recalls the ascent of the seventy elders who ate before the God of Israel after the old covenant had been confirmed (Exodus 24).

The eighth sign, one beyond the seven, is after the Lord's resurrection: and in its significance seals the evidence that the risen man is the Son of God, the Messiah, and the Life giver.

PETER'S COMMISSION (21:15–19)

THE meal with the Risen Lord was finished, and Jesus turned to Peter with a question. "Simon, son of Jonas", he said, "lovest thou me more than these?" It was a question that requires the record in the other gospels for its understanding. We can dismiss the idea that Jesus meant, Did Peter love him more than he loved the fishes? or, in other words, Did he love Jesus more than his fisherman's calling? The comparison is with the other apostles, and recalls the confident assertion of Peter that although all men should stumble at Jesus, he would not. It was a vain boast, as we know. Peter denied his Lord, thus marking out his defection above the others. The others forsook Jesus and fled; but Peter rallied and ventured into the courtyard of the high priest with John, whose constancy alone did not fail, and then thrice denied his Lord. Now Jesus tries the once assertive but repentant disciple before he restores him.

"He appeared unto Cephas", says Paul in his enumeration of those who were seen by Jesus after his resurrection. This meeting took place early on the day Jesus rose, and what occurred is not recorded. There must have been some reference to the failure of Peter; we cannot imagine a meeting of Jesus and Peter without its being mentioned and the stain removed. It may seem strange that Jesus should revive the subject even by allusion. We must however remember the public character of Peter's confident assertion of loyalty, and his position among the Twelve called for a public restoration.

It is generally known that two different Greek words are used in this conversation. The first, used by Jesus in his question, indicates a love based upon intellectual preference, esteem, choice. It is more exalted than the word Peter uses in his reply, which denotes personal, emotional, feeling. Do you regard, esteem, me more than these other disciples? Jesus had said. Peter does not venture such an assertion now, but he feels he can speak of his personal affection: "Yea, Lord, thou knowest that I love thee". "Feed my lambs", responded Jesus.

Again Jesus asked Peter, "Regardest thou me?" In his first answer Peter had made no comparison with the others, contenting himself with the simple assertion of personal love. Jesus also now omits "more than these" from his question. It is a simple question of fact. Again Peter answers by reaffirming his personal love for Jesus. Jesus responds, "Tend my sheep".

On the third time that Jesus puts the question, he changes the word he had twice used to the word used by Peter. "Do you love me indeed with that warm personal love that you say?" This "grieved" Peter; at least he felt sure of the warmth of his own feeling, and that the Lord should seem to question that hurt him. "Lord, thou knowest all things; thou perceivest that I love thee." "Jesus saith unto him, Feed my sheep."

The threefold denial is balanced by this threefold affirmation of his love and the threefold injunction to tend the flock of Christ. In this injunction there is a slight progress of thought. In "Feed my lambs", food is the chief thought; in "Shepherd my sheep" guidance is indicated as well as the provision of food; "Feed my sheep" covers the duty of looking after all the flock, sheep and lambs.

In this restoration of Peter there is nothing that lends the least support to any pre-eminence of Peter which is essential for the stupendous assertions that have been put forward by the Popes who claim to be Peter's successors. Peter's own words in his epistles, which are clearly reminiscent of this incident, are a final disproof.

Addressing fellow elders, he exhorts them:

"Feed the flock of God which is among you, taking the oversight thereof, not by constraint, but willingly; not for filthy lucre, but of a ready mind; neither as being lords over God's heritage, but being ensamples to the flock. And when the chief Shepherd shall appear, ye shall receive a crown of glory that fadeth not away."   (1 Peter 5:1–4)

When Peter wrote these words he was an old man, and the day was drawing nearer for the fulfilment of the saying of Jesus which he spake after giving to Peter his commission as a shepherd of the flock. "Verily, verily, I say unto thee, When thou wast young, thou girdedst thyself, and walkedst whither thou wouldest: but when thou shalt be old, thou shalt stretch forth thy hands, and another shall gird thee, and carry thee whither thou wouldest not."

The ultimate significance of this is given by John. Jesus was thinking of the manner of death by which Peter should glorify God. And that death, yielded to as his Lord had yielded to it, and by the same mode of crucifixion, suggests an underlying metaphorical meaning. This impulsive and headstrong apostle would learn life's discipline and render obedience and service to others.

Having thus spoken, Jesus called upon Peter and John to follow him. It was at once a call to turn aside with him for further private conversation, and also a call to follow in that way where the steps of the Master had marked the road.

Peter observed John following, and enquired of his end. The decision for that rested with John's Lord, even if it involved John's survival unto the second advent. John did tarry much longer than Peter, probably for a quarter of a century. Perhaps this fact led to the circulation of the story that John would remain until Christ came. This story John corrects by repeating what Jesus had said.

CONCLUDING NOTES (21:24,25)

"THIS is the disciple that beareth witness of these things, and wrote these things: and we know that his witness is true." By this note the writer identifies himself with the apostle John; and in his use of the word "witness" as a description of his work he joins himself with the divine testimony of which he has made record. John the Baptist was a witness (1:7,15). God bore witness to Jesus in the works Jesus did, and by the testimony of Scripture (5:31–39; 8:18;

10:25). Jesus told the apostles that the Spirit which should be given them would "bear witness" of him; and "ye also shall bear witness, because ye have been with me from the beginning" (15:26,27). In personal fulfilment of this John "bore witness".

But immediately there are conjoined others: "We know that his witness is true". Who are comprehended in this "we"? John uses "we" in more than one sense, of himself, of the twelve, of the whole body of believers. Are we to regard the latter half of verse 24 as an added testimony to that of John, from the Ephesian eldership, who thereby gave a prophetic endorsement to his writing?

When John says (1:14) "we beheld his glory", it would appear that he has the apostles in mind. So also the pronoun "we" in the opening of his first epistle points to the apostles:

"That which was from the beginning, which we have heard, which we have seen with our eyes, which we have looked upon, and our hands have handled, of the Word of life; for the life was manifested, and *we have seen it, and bear witness* ... that which we have seen and heard declare we unto you, that ye also may have fellowship with us: and truly our fellowship is with the Father, and with his Son Jesus Christ."   (1 John 1:1–3)

Here is the "apostles' doctrine and fellowship" in which the first believers rejoiced (Acts 2:42); it was through apostolic testimony believers were enfolded in the fellowship, as the changes from "we" to "you" in the above quotation indicate. But the "we" in later references embraces the men who had believed through the apostles; for example, when he writes, "we know that we are of the truth" (1 John 3:19), and "if we love one another, God dwelleth in us" (4:12), it is clear that the "we" includes all who believe.

When John changes from his own witness to the "we know", in keeping with John's style we must conclude that the "we" indicates that what he has said in his gospel is also supported by the witness of the apostles in general. If others are comprehended, it is because they have in measure partaken of apostolic authority by that witness of the spirit-gifts received by the laying on of the apostle's hand. This view does not exclude the Ephesian eldership, but it makes the phrase "we know that his testimony is true" a part of John's own writing: and it includes John in the "we", since the "we" is the corporate body of witnesses, based upon the apostles of Jesus Christ.

With this view the first person comes naturally in the next and last verse when John says that he supposes if all that Jesus did were written the world could not contain the books.

So ends the record in which Jesus is set forth as the Son of God—a record of so great depth that its full significance may not be exhausted, but which brings the earnest reader to the conviction that Jesus "is the Messiah, the Son of God".

THE GOSPEL OF JOHN

SCRIPTURE INDEX

The references from John's Gospel covered in the Contents
(pages v-x) are not included below.

249

Other works by the same author: